Modern Android 13 Development Cookbook

Over 70 recipes to solve Android development issues and create better apps with Kotlin and Jetpack Compose

Madona S. Wambua

BIRMINGHAM—MUMBAI

Modern Android 13 Development Cookbook

Group Product Manager: Rohit Rajkumar
Publishing Product Manager: Vaideeshwari Muralikrishnan
Content Development Editor: Abhishek Jadhav
Technical Editor: Simran Ali
Copy Editor: Safis Editing
Project Coordinator: Aishwarya Mohan
Proofreader: Safis Editing
Indexer: Sejal Dsilva
Production Designer: Aparna Bhagat
Marketing Coordinator: Nivedita Pandey

First published: July 2023

Production reference: 1080623

Published by Packt Publishing Ltd.
Livery Place
35 Livery Street
Birmingham
B3 2PB, UK.

ISBN 978-1-80323-557-8

www.packtpub.com

To my mother, Joyce Wanza, and father, Jackson Wambua, and my entire family, thank you very much for cheering me on and supporting me through this process, and giving me the encouragement to keep pushing and believing in myself. I appreciate you all.

To my sons, Muthoka and Kisomo, for constantly cheerleading for me, showing me love, and telling me what a cool mom I am; your support and inspiration mean a lot.

To my reviewers, Sierra, Carlos, and Kanthi, thank you all for your outstanding work; I could not have done this without your feedback and support.

Contributors

About the author

Madona S. Wambua is a Google Developer Expert in the Android category, an Android engineer programming in Kotlin, and the founder of Budgeting Buddy, a free budgeting tool. She is also a Women Techmakers Ambassador and Women Who Code Mobile Global Lead. She has over seven years of experience in the field and has worked on both consumer-facing applications and building software development kits for developers. She also worked on the famous Google Glass during her tenure at a start-up and got an opportunity to work on interactive AR videos to transform lives through machine learning and computer vision. Madona continues to broaden her development skills while working remotely as an Android engineer as she continues her education at the Samuel Ginn College of Engineering.

About the reviewers

Sierra OBryan is a software engineer focused on native Android. She loves building beautiful and accessible Android apps, sharing knowledge with the community, and mentoring aspiring mobile developers. She is a Google Developer Expert for Android and serves as director of Women Who Code Cincinnati, director of technology for getWITit (Women in Tech), and a Women Techmakers Global Ambassador. She is also a former Global Leadership Fellow for Women Who Code Mobile.

Carlos Mota is an Android GDE and can usually be spotted either working on Android applications written in Kotlin or developing them along with Kotlin Multiplatform. He's enthusiastic about new technology and constantly trying to reach that last 20% of all of his side projects that seems to be really far away. He loves to share his knowledge with others by giving talks, teaching, or writing along with enjoying a cold beer in the nearest pub. A GDG Coimbra organizer and Kotlin evangelist, he also has a giant passion for travel, photography, space, and the occasional run.

Kanthi Nalamati is an experienced Android application developer with deep expertise in the Android platform, APIs, frameworks, and libraries. He is an expert in building user interfaces, implementing architecture patterns, and utilizing Android's navigation framework, ensuring the creation of intuitive and easy-to-use app interfaces. Kanthi has developed a wide range of mobile apps for clients across different industries, from simple utilities to complex enterprise solutions. With expertise in Java and Kotlin, he creates robust, efficient apps with exceptional user experiences.

Table of Contents

2

Creating Screens Using a Declarative UI and Exploring Compose Principles 29

3

Handling the UI State in Jetpack Compose and Using Hilt 59

4

Navigation in Modern Android Development 89

5

Using DataStore to Store Data and Testing 111

6

Using the Room Database and Testing 135

7

Getting Started with WorkManager 159

8

Getting Started with Paging 179

9

Building for Large Screens 203

10

Implementing Your First Wear OS Using Jetpack Compose 225

11

GUI Alerts – What's New in Menus, Dialog, Toast, Snackbars, and More in Modern Android Development 251

12

Android Studio Tips and Tricks to Help You during Development 271

Preface

Modern Android 13 Development Cookbook serves as a comprehensive guide for developers seeking to build cutting-edge Android applications using the latest advancements in technology. Android is the most widely used mobile operating system worldwide, powering billions of devices.

Android 13, the latest major release of the Android platform, introduces several exciting features and enhancements, designed to enhance user experiences, improve performance, and enable developers to create robust and innovative applications. This cookbook focuses on leveraging these new capabilities to build modern, feature-rich Android apps that meet the demands of today's users.

With the rapid evolution of the Android ecosystem, developers face the challenge of staying up to date with the latest tools, libraries, and best practices. *Modern Android 13 Development Cookbook* addresses this challenge by providing practical recipes and step-by-step instructions to solve everyday development tasks and implement modern Android app architecture patterns.

As you progress through the recipes in this cookbook, you'll build new short projects that will expose you to more patterns and components, helping you acquire valuable insights into building modern Android applications. I opted for this approach since this is a cookbook, and building one project for all chapters would have become redundant, so get ready to build. Whether you're a beginner starting your Android development journey or an experienced developer seeking to level up your skills, *Modern Android 13 Development Cookbook* is your go-to resource to master the latest techniques and best practices in Android app development.

Who this book is for

This book is designed to cater to Android developers with one to four years of experience in the field. Whether you're a junior developer looking to expand your knowledge or a mid-level developer seeking to refine your skills, *Modern Android 13 Development Cookbook* provides valuable insights and practical solutions to enhance your Android development expertise.

By assuming a foundational understanding of Android development concepts and familiarity with the Android ecosystem, this book delves into more advanced topics and modern development techniques. It serves as a comprehensive resource to help you stay up to date with the latest advancements in Android 13 and learn how to leverage them effectively in your projects.

The cookbook format offers a practical approach, presenting a series of recipes that address everyday development tasks and challenges faced by Android developers. Each recipe provides clear, step-by-step instructions and relevant code examples, allowing you to implement the solutions directly in your projects.

With *Modern Android 13 Development Cookbook* as your guide, you'll have the knowledge and skills to tackle Android projects as you advance your skills.

What this book covers

Chapter 1, Getting Started with Modern Android Development Skills, provides an introduction to Modern Android Development and begins by introducing the basics of Android development, including the Android Studio IDE and the Kotlin programming language. It then goes on to discuss the different components of an Android app, such as creating your first button in Compose, the Android project structure, and utilizing the Gradlew command to run your Android project.

Chapter 2, Creating Screens Using a Declarative UI and Exploring Compose Principles, introduces the concept of a declarative UI and how it can be used to create screens in Android apps. Declarative UI is a way of describing the UI of an app in terms of what it should look like, rather than how it should be implemented. This makes it easier to create complex UIs that are both visually appealing and easy to maintain. The chapter then goes on to explore the fundamental principles of Jetpack Compose, the declarative UI framework for Android, with simple-to-follow projects.

Chapter 3, Handling the UI State in Jetpack Compose and Using Hilt, dives into the essential concepts of handling the UI state and using Hilt in Jetpack Compose, providing you with practical recipes to manage the state and ensure the robustness of your app effectively. By the end of this chapter, you'll have a solid understanding of ViewModel concepts, Dependency Injection with Hilt, integrating Compose into existing projects, and writing comprehensive tests for both Compose views and ViewModels.

Chapter 4, Navigation in Modern Android Development, delves into the topic of navigation in Compose, exploring various recipes that will equip you with the skills needed to implement efficient and seamless navigation experiences in your Android app. By the end of this chapter, you'll have a comprehensive understanding of navigation concepts and techniques in Compose, empowering you to build intuitive and interactive user experiences that seamlessly guide users through your app.

Chapter 5, Using Datastore to Store Data and Testing, dives into the essential aspects of implementing and managing DataStore in Android applications. We will cover a range of topics and provide practical recipes to help you become proficient in handling data within your Android projects. By the end of this chapter, you'll have a comprehensive understanding of implementing DataStore, employing Dependency Injection, choosing between Android Proto DataStore and DataStore, managing data migration, and writing practice tests for your DataStore implementation.

Chapter 6, Using the Room Database and Testing, explores the powerful features of the Room database library and dives into testing strategies to ensure the integrity and functionality of your database-driven Android applications. By the end of this chapter, you'll have a solid grasp of using the Room database library and testing strategies to ensure the quality and reliability of your database-driven Android applications.

Chapter 7, Getting Started with WorkManager, provides an overview of WorkManager, a powerful Jetpack library that enables efficient and flexible background processing in Android applications. We will cover the fundamental concepts and features of WorkManager, empowering you to incorporate background tasks seamlessly into your projects. By the end of this chapter, you'll have a solid foundation in using WorkManager, enabling you to integrate efficient and reliable background processing capabilities into your Android applications.

Chapter 8, Getting Started with Paging, provides an introduction to Paging, a powerful Jetpack library that facilitates efficient and seamless data loading in Android applications. We cover the essential concepts and features of Paging, empowering you to implement data pagination and optimize the performance of your app. By the end of this chapter, you'll have a solid understanding of Paging and its capabilities, enabling you to implement efficient data pagination in your Android applications.

Chapter 9, Building for Large Screens, explores the principles and techniques to design and build Android applications that deliver engaging experiences on foldable and other large screens, such as tablets. We will cover various aspects of adapting your app's user interface, optimizing layouts, and leveraging the additional screen of real estate effectively as we utilize Material 3. By the end of this chapter, you'll have a solid understanding of the principles and techniques to design and build Android applications that deliver engaging experiences on large screens.

Chapter 10, Implementing Your First Wear OS Using Jetpack Compose, provides guidance on the process of implementing your first Wear OS app using Jetpack Compose, a modern UI toolkit to build Android applications. We will cover the essential steps and concepts to create engaging and intuitive wearable experiences. By the end of this chapter, you'll have a grasp of how components are created in Wear OS and be able to run Wear OS on your virtual device.

Chapter 11, GUI Alerts – What's New in Menus, Dialog, Toast, Snackbars, and More in Modern Android Development, explores the latest enhancements and features in GUI alerts, menus, dialogs, toasts, snackbars, and other user interface components in Modern Android Development. We will cover the advancements that enable developers to create more interactive and engaging user experiences.

Chapter 12, Android Studio Tips and Tricks to Help You during Development, shares a collection of valuable tips and tricks to help you maximize your productivity and efficiency while using Android Studio for Android app development. We will cover the various features, shortcuts, and hidden gems that can streamline your workflow and enhance your development experience.

To get the most out of this book

You will need to have Java installed on your laptop and Android Studio, which is the IDE we use. We assume that you have knowledge of Java installation and Git source control, since you will need to be able to get most of the code from the *Technical requirement* section to code along.

Software/hardware covered in the book	Operating system requirements
Android Studio	Windows, macOS, or Linux
Java Version 11	
Android Studio Version	Android Studio Flamingo | 2022.2.1 Patch 1

If you are using the digital version of this book, we advise you to type the code yourself or access the code from the book's GitHub repository (a link is available in the next section). Doing so will help you avoid any potential errors related to the copying and pasting of code.

Download the example code files

You can download the example code files for this book from GitHub at `https://github.com/PacktPublishing/Modern-Android-13-Development-Cookbook`. If there's an update to the code, it will be updated in the GitHub repository.

We also have other code bundles from our rich catalog of books and videos available at `https://github.com/PacktPublishing/`. Check them out!

Download the color images

We also provide a PDF file that has color images of the screenshots and diagrams used in this book. You can download it here: `https://packt.link/HlgRf`.

Conventions used

There are a number of text conventions used throughout this book.

`Code in text`: Indicates code words in text, database table names, folder names, filenames, file extensions, pathnames, dummy URLs, user input, and Twitter handles. Here is an example: "In our second example, we have two functions, `main()` and `reverseString()`. `main()` takes nothing in its input."

A block of code is set as follows:

```
fun main() {
    val stringToBeReversed = "Community"
    println(reverseString(stringToBeReversed))
}
fun reverseString(stringToReverse: String): String {
    return stringToReverse.reversed()
}
```

When we wish to draw your attention to a particular part of a code block, the relevant lines or items are set in bold:

```
data class City(
    val id: Int,
    @StringRes val nameResourceId: Int,
    @DrawableRes val imageResourceId: Int
)
```

Any command-line input or output is written as follows:

```
$ git clone git@github.com:PacktPublishing/Modern-Android-13-
Development-Cookbook.git
```

Bold: Indicates a new term, an important word, or words that you see on screen. For instance, words in menus or dialog boxes appear in **bold**. Here is an example: "Click **Finish** and wait for Gradle to sync."

> **Tips or important notes**
> Appear like this.

Get in touch

Feedback from our readers is always welcome.

General feedback: If you have questions about any aspect of this book, email us at `customercare@packtpub.com` and mention the book title in the subject of your message.

Errata: Although we have taken every care to ensure the accuracy of our content, mistakes do happen. If you have found a mistake in this book, we would be grateful if you would report this to us. Please visit `www.packtpub.com/support/errata` and fill in the form.

Piracy: If you come across any illegal copies of our works in any form on the internet, we would be grateful if you would provide us with the location address or website name. Please contact us at `copyright@packt.com` with a link to the material.

If you are interested in becoming an author: If there is a topic that you have expertise in and you are interested in either writing or contributing to a book, please visit `authors.packtpub.com`.

Share Your Thoughts

Once you've read *Modern Android 13 Development Cookbook*, we'd love to hear your thoughts! Scan the QR code below to go straight to the Amazon review page for this book and share your feedback.

https://www.amazon.in/review/create-review/?asin=1803235578

Your review is important to us and the tech community and will help us make sure we're delivering excellent quality content.

Download a free PDF copy of this book

Thanks for purchasing this book!

Do you like to read on the go but are unable to carry your print books everywhere? Is your eBook purchase not compatible with the device of your choice?

Don't worry, now with every Packt book you get a DRM-free PDF version of that book at no cost.

Read anywhere, any place, on any device. Search, copy, and paste code from your favorite technical books directly into your application.

The perks don't stop there, you can get exclusive access to discounts, newsletters, and great free content in your inbox daily

Follow these simple steps to get the benefits:

1. Scan the QR code or visit the link below

`https://packt.link/free-ebook/9781803235578`

2. Submit your proof of purchase
3. That's it! We'll send your free PDF and other benefits to your email directly

1

Getting Started with Modern Android Development Skills

The Android **Operating System** (**OS**) is one of the most favored platforms for mobile devices, with many users worldwide. The OS is used in cars and wearables such as smart watches, TVs, and phones, which makes the market quite wide for Android developers. Hence, there is a need for new developers to learn how to build Android applications utilizing new **Modern Android Development** (**MAD**) skills.

Android has come a long way since being launched in 2008 and used in the first **Integrated Development Environments** (**IDEs**), Eclipse and NetBeans. Today, Android Studio is the recommended IDE for Android development and, unlike before, when Java was the preferred language, Kotlin is now the language of choice.

Android Studio includes support for Kotlin, Java, C++, and other programming languages, making this IDE suitable for developers with different skill sets.

Hence, by the end of this chapter, following the recipes, you will have Android Studio installed, have built your first Android application using Jetpack Compose, and have learned some Kotlin syntax, utilizing the preferred language for Android development. In addition, this introduction will prepare the base for you to understand advanced material that will be crucial for MAD.

In this chapter, we'll be covering the following recipes:

- Writing your first program in Kotlin using variables and idioms
- Creating a Hello, Android Community app using Android Studio
- Setting up your emulator in Android Studio
- Creating a button in Jetpack Compose
- Utilizing `gradlew` commands to clean and run your project in Android Studio
- Understanding the Android project structure
- Debugging and logging in Android Studio

Technical requirements

Running the Android IDE and an emulator successfully can be daunting for your computer. You may have heard the joke about how machines running Android Studio can be used as heaters in winter. Well, there is some truth in that, so your computer should have the following specifications to ensure your system can cope with the IDE's demands:

- 64-bit Microsoft Windows, macOS, or Linux installed along with a stable internet connection. Recipes in this book have been developed within macOS. You can also use a Windows or Linux laptop, as there is no difference between using either.
- For Windows and Linux users, you can follow this link to install Android Studio: `https://developer.android.com/studio/install`.
- Minimum of 8 GB of RAM or more.
- Minimum of 8 GB of available disk space for Android Studio, the Android **Software Development Kit** (**SDK**), and the Android Emulator.
- A minimum screen resolution of 1280 x 800 is preferred.
- You can download Android Studio at `https://developer.android.com/studio`.

The complete source code for this chapter is available on GitHub at: `https://github.com/PacktPublishing/Modern-Android-13-Development-Cookbook/tree/main/chapter_one`

Writing your first program in Kotlin using variables and idioms

Kotlin is the recommended language for Android development; you can still use Java as your language of choice, as many legacy applications still heavily rely on Java. However, in this book, we will use Kotlin, and if this is the first time you are building Android applications using the Kotlin language, the Kotlin organization has excellent resources to help you get started with free practice exercises and self-paced assessments called **Kotlin Koans** (`https://play.kotlinlang.org/koans/overview`).

In addition, you can use the Kotlin language for multiplatform development using **Kotlin Multiplatform Mobile** (**KMM**), in which you can share standard code between iOS and Android apps and write platform-specific code only where necessary. KMM is currently in Alpha.

Getting ready

In this recipe, you can either use the online Kotlin playground (`https://play.kotlinlang.org/`) to run your code or run the code in your Android Studio IDE. Alternatively, you can download and use the IntelliJ IDEA IDE if you plan on doing more Kotlin practice questions with Koans.

How to do it...

In this recipe, we will explore and modify a simple program that we will write in Kotlin; you can think of a program as instructions we give a computer or mobile devices to perform actions that we give them. For instance, we will create a greeting in our program and later write a different program.

For this recipe, you can choose either Android Studio or the free online IDE since we will touch on some Kotlin functionalities:

1. If you opt to use the Kotlin online playground for the first time, you will see something like the following screenshot, with a `println` statement that says `Hello, world`, but for our example, we will change that greeting to *Hello, Android Community*, and run the code.

```
/**
 * You can edit, run, and share this code.
 * play.kotlinlang.org
 */

fun main() {
    println("Hello, Android Community")
}
```

```
Hello, Android Community
```

Figure 1.1 – The online Kotlin editor

2. Let's look at another example; a popular algorithm problem used in interviews – reversing a string. For example, you have a string, `Community`, and we want to reverse the string so that the output will be `ytinummoC`. There are several ways to solve this problem, but we will solve it using the Kotlin idiomatic way.

3. Input the following code in the playground of your IDE or the Kotlin playground:

```
fun main() {
    val stringToBeReversed = "Community"
    println(reverseString(stringToBeReversed))
}
fun reverseString(stringToReverse: String): String {
    return stringToReverse.reversed()
}
```

How it works...

It is essential to mention in Kotlin, that there are unique ways to keep your code cleaner, more precise, and simpler by taking advantage of the default parameter value and only setting the parameters you need to alter.

`fun` is a word in Kotlin programming language that stands for *function*, and a function in Kotlin is a section of a program that performs a specific task. The name of the function in our first example is `main()`, and in our `main()` function, we do not have any inputs. Functions, in general, have names so that we are able to distinguish them from each other if our code base is complex.

In addition, in Java, a function is similar to a method. The function name has two parentheses and curly braces, and `println`, which tells the system to print a line of text.

If you have used Java, you might notice that the Kotlin programming language is very similar to Java. However, developers now talk about how great Kotlin language is for developers because it provides more expressive syntax and sophisticated type systems and handles the Null pointer problem that Java had for many years. To take full advantage of the Kotlin language power and write more concise code, knowing about Kotlin idioms can be beneficial. Kotlin idioms are frequently used collections that help to manipulate data and make Android developers' experience more effortless.

In our second example, we have two functions, `main()` and `reverseString().main()` takes nothing in its input, but `reverseString()` does take in a String input. You will also notice we use `val`, which is a unique word used by Kotlin to refer to an immutable value that can only be set to one value, as compared to `var`, which is a mutable variable, meaning it can be resigned.

We create a `val stringToBeReversed` which is a String and call it `"Community"`, then call `println` inside the `main()` function, and pass in the text we want to print in our `reverseString()` function. Furthermore, in this example, our `reverseString` function takes in a `string` argument from the String object and then returns a string type.

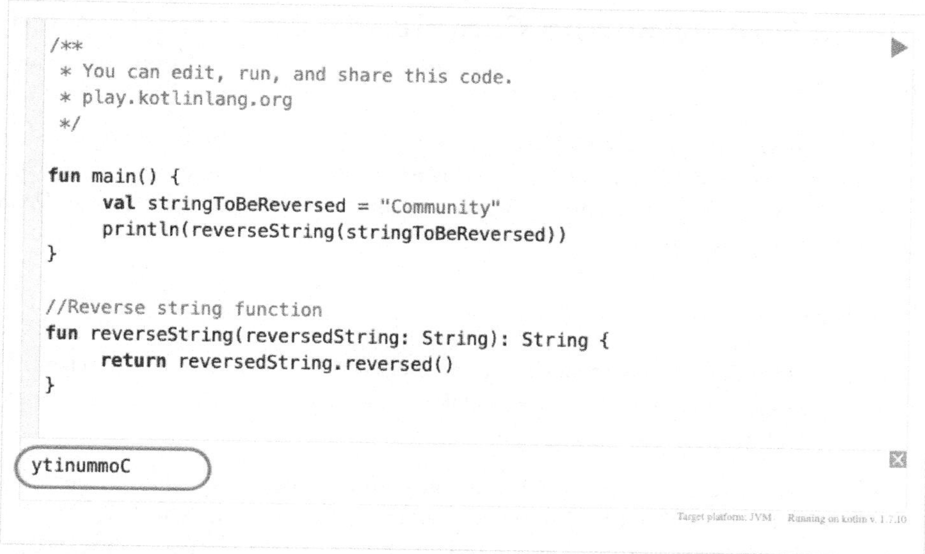

```
/**
 * You can edit, run, and share this code.
 * play.kotlinlang.org
 */

fun main() {
     val stringToBeReversed = "Community"
     println(reverseString(stringToBeReversed))
}

//Reverse string function
fun reverseString(reversedString: String): String {
     return reversedString.reversed()
}
```

```
ytinummoC
```

Target platform: JVM   Running on kotlin v. 1.7.10

Figure 1.2 – The reversed string on the Kotlin playground

There is more to learn, and it is fair to acknowledge that what we have covered in this recipe is just a tiny part of what you can do with Kotlin idioms. This recipe aimed to introduce concepts that we might touch on or use in later chapters, not in depth, however, since we will explore more of Kotlin in later chapters. Hence, it's good to know what Kotlin idioms are and why they are essential for now.

See also

A better understanding of the Kotlin syntax and popular use cases will be vital for your day-to-day work, so look at the following resources:

- The JetBrains Academy has a great free Kotlin Basics course here: `https://hyperskill.org/tracks/18`.
- The Kotlin documentation is also a great resource to keep handy: `https://kotlinlang.org/docs/home.html`.

Creating a Hello, Android Community app using Android Studio

We will create our first Android application now that we have installed Android Studio. In addition, we will use Compose – just to mention in advance, in this recipe, we will not go in depth about Compose, as we have a dedicated chapter on Compose, which is *Chapter 2, Creating Screens Using a Declarative UI and Exploring Compose Principles*.

Getting ready

Before you begin, it's helpful to know where your Android projects are for consistency. By default, Android Studio creates a package in your home directory, and the package name is `AndroidStudioProjects`; here, you will find all the projects you create.

You can also decide where the folder should be if you want to change it. In addition, ensure you are using the latest version of Android Studio to utilize all the great features. To find out what the latest Android version is, you can use the following link: `https://developer.android.com/studio/releases`.

How to do it...

In the Android Studio IDE, a project template is an Android app that has all the necessary parts to create an application and helps you get started and set up.

So, step by step, we will make our first Android application and launch it on the emulator:

1. Start Android Studio by clicking on the Android Studio icon in your dock or wherever you have stored Android Studio.
2. You will see a welcome Android Studio window open up, and you can click on **New Project**. Alternatively, you can go to **File** and click **New Project**.
3. Select **Empty Compose Activity** and click on **Next**.

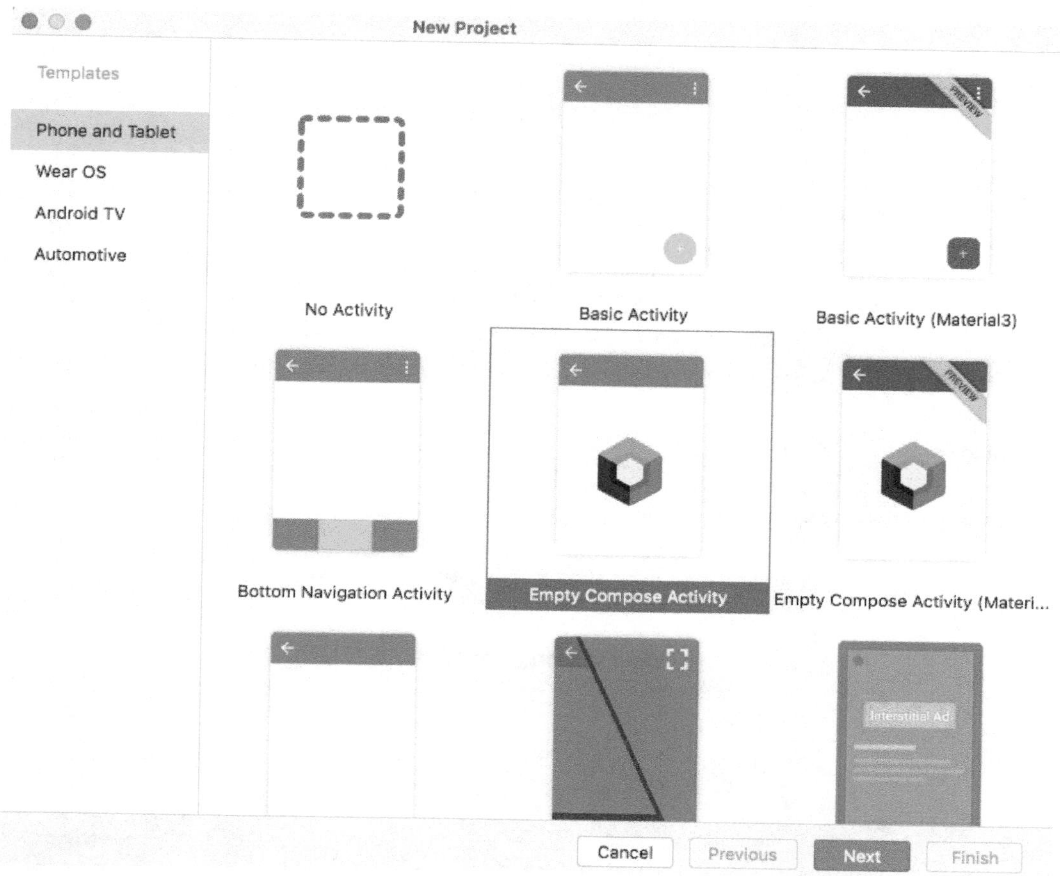

Figure 1.3 – Creating an empty Compose activity

4. Once the empty Compose activity screen loads (*Figure 1.4*), you will see fields including **Name**, **Package name**, **Save Location**, **Language**, and **Minimum SDK**. For this chapter, you can name the project `Android Community` and leave the other settings as is. You will also notice that the language is **Kotlin** by default.

   As for **Minimum SDK**, our target is **API 21: Android 5.0 (Lollipop)**, which indicates the minimum version of Android that your app can run, which, in our case, is approximately 98.8% of devices. You can also click on the dropdown and learn more about the minimum SDK.

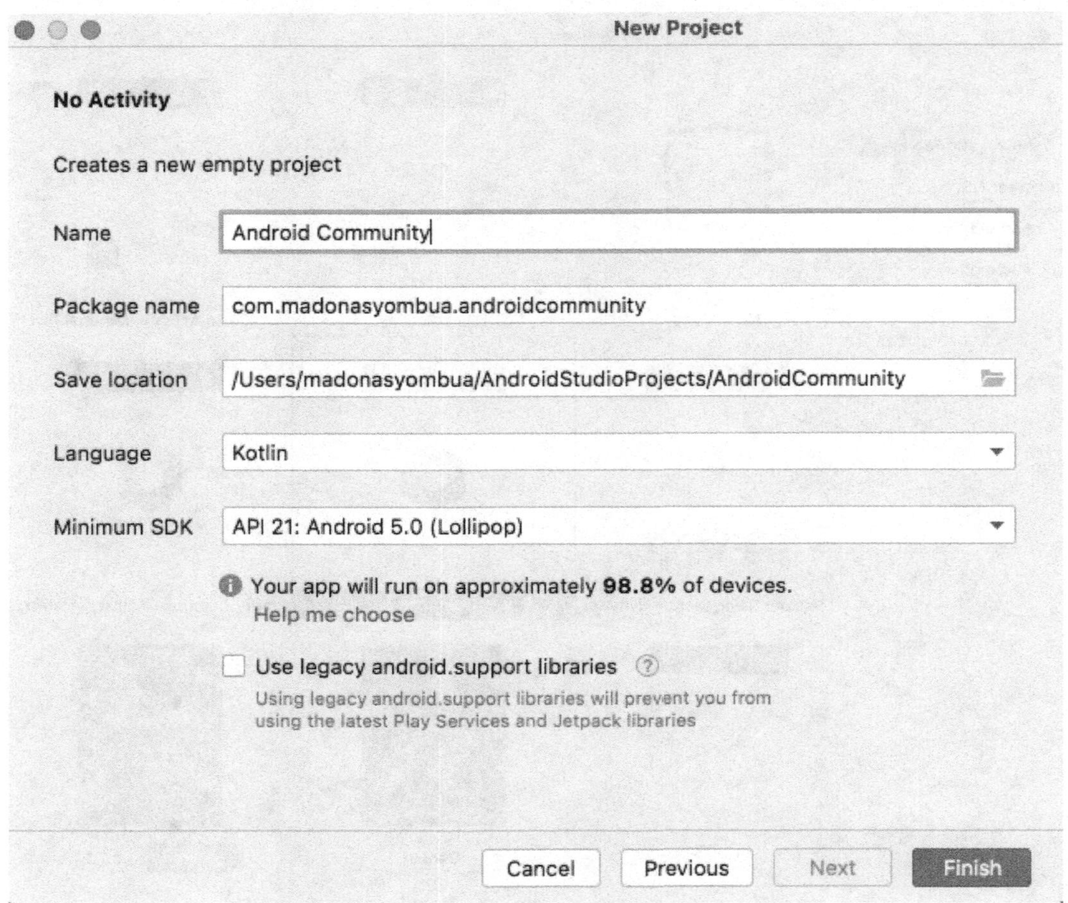

Figure 1.4 – Naming your empty Compose activity

Click **Finish** and wait for Gradle to sync.

5. Go ahead and play around with the packages, and you will notice a `MainActivity` class that extends a `ComponentActivity()` which extends `Activity()`; inside, we have a `fun onCreate`, which is an override from the `ComponentActivity`. You will also see a `setContent{}`, which is a function used to set the content of a Composable function. The `setContent{}` function takes a lambda expression that contains the UI elements that should be displayed, and in our case it holds the theme of our application. In the `Greeting()` function, we will change what is provided and add our own greeting which is `"Hello, Android Community"` and run, and we will have created our first `Greeting`:

```
class MainActivity : ComponentActivity() {
    override fun onCreate(savedInstanceState: Bundle?)
    {
```

```
            super.onCreate(savedInstanceState)
            setContent {
                AndroidCommunityTheme {

                    Surface(
                        modifier = Modifier.fillMaxSize(),
                        color =
                        MaterialTheme.colors.background
                    ) {
                        Greeting("Hello, Android
                                  Community")
                    }
                }
            }
        }
    }
```

6. Let's go ahead and modify the `Greeting()` function and assign the `name` argument to the text:

```
@Composable
fun Greeting(name: String) {
    Text(
        text = name
    )
}
```

In addition, you can also just pass `"Hello, Android Community"` into the default implementation, and this will produce the same UI.

7. Like in an XML view, you can easily view the UI you are building without running the app in an emulator using `@Preview(showBackground = true)`, so let's go ahead and add this to our code if it is not available. By default, the project comes with a template that has a `Preview()`:

```
@Preview(showBackground = true)
@Composable
fun DefaultPreview() {

}
```

8. Finally, when you run the application, you should have a screen like in *Figure 1.5*. In the following recipe, we will look at how you can set up your emulator step by step, so do not worry about that yet.

Figure 1.5 – Screen displaying Hello, Android Community

How it works...

The key benefits of using Jetpack Compose for creating your view are that it speeds up the development time since you use the same language to write your entire code base (Kotlin) and it is easier to test. You can also create reusable components that you can customize to your needs.

Therefore, ensuring lower chances of errors and having to write views with XML because it is tedious and cumbersome. The `onCreate()` function is considered the entry point to the application in Android. Furthermore, we use `modifier` functions to add behavior and decorate the composable. We'll talk more about what `modifier` and `Surface` functions can do in the next chapter.

Setting up your emulator in Android Studio

Android Studio is a reliable and mature IDE. As a result, Android Studio has been the favored IDE for developing Android applications since 2014. Of course, you can still use other IDEs, but the advantage of Android Studio is that you do not need to install the Android SDK separately.

Getting ready

You need to have done the previous recipe to be able to follow along with this recipe since we will be setting up our emulator in order to run the project we just created.

How to do it...

This chapter seeks to be friendly to beginners and also move you smoothly toward more advanced Android as you work through the recipes.

Let's follow these steps to see how you can set up your emulator and run your project in the *Creating a Hello, Android Community App using Android Studio* recipe:

1. Navigate to **Tools | Device Manager**. Once the device manager is ready, you have two options: **Virtual** or **Physical**. **Virtual** means you will be using an emulator, and **Physical** means you will be enabling your Android phone to debug Android applications. For our purposes, we will choose **Virtual**.
2. Click on **Create device**, and the **Virtual Device Configuration** screen will pop up.
3. Pick **Phone**. You will notice Android Studio has other categories, such as **TV**, **Wear OS**, **Tablet**, and **Automotive**. Let's use **Phone** for now, and in a future chapter, we will try using **Wear OS**. Click on **Next**.

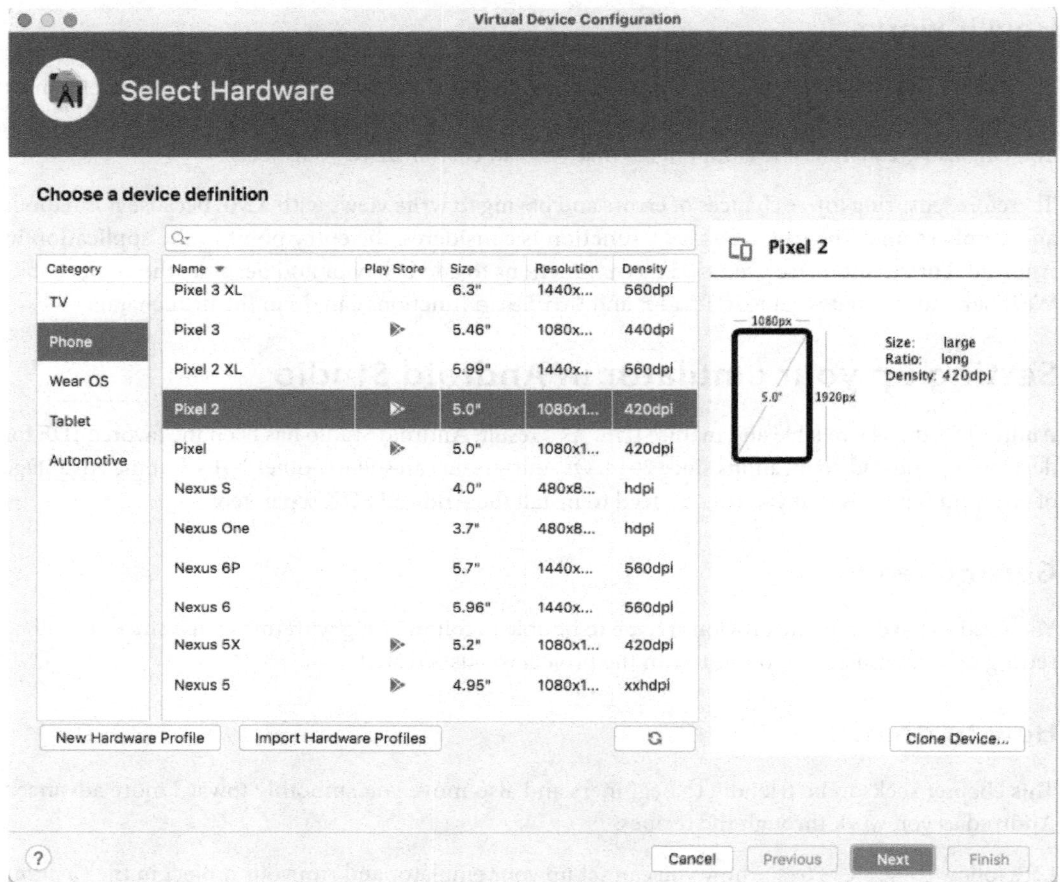

Figure 1.6 – Selecting a virtual device

4. In *Figure 1.7*, you will see a list of **Recommended system images**. You can choose any or use the default one, which is **S** in our case for Android 12, although you might want to use the latest API, **33**, and then click **Next**.

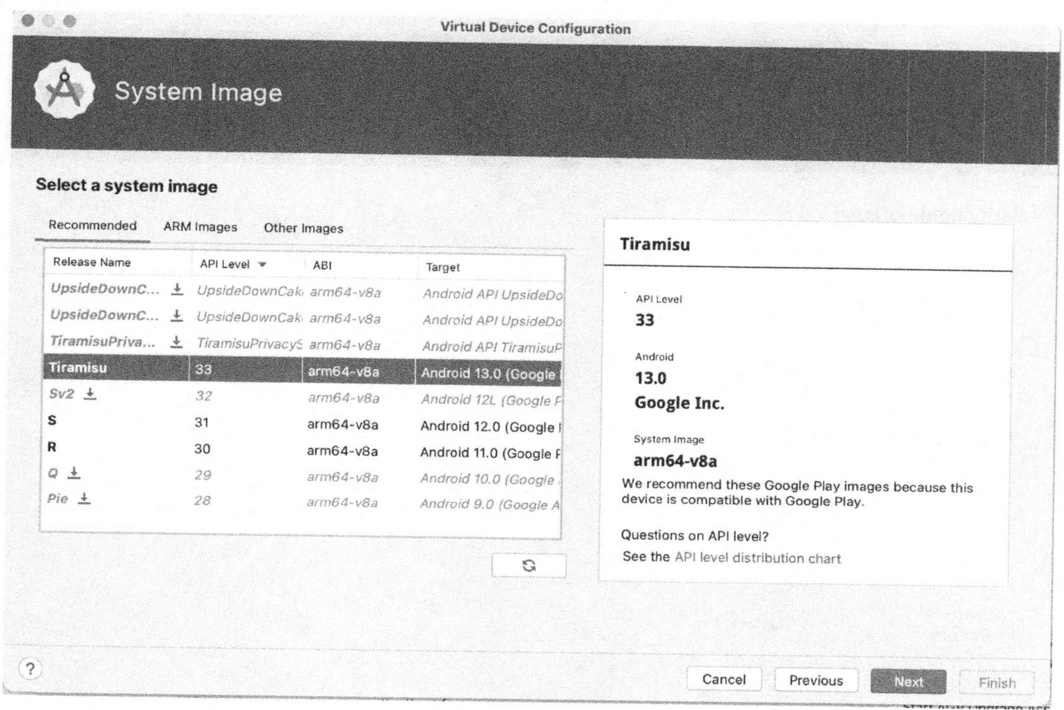

Figure 1.7 – Selecting a system image

5. You will now arrive at the **Android Virtual Device** (**AVD**) screen, where you can name your virtual device. You can enter a name or just leave the default, **Pixel 2 API 31**, and then hit **Finish**.

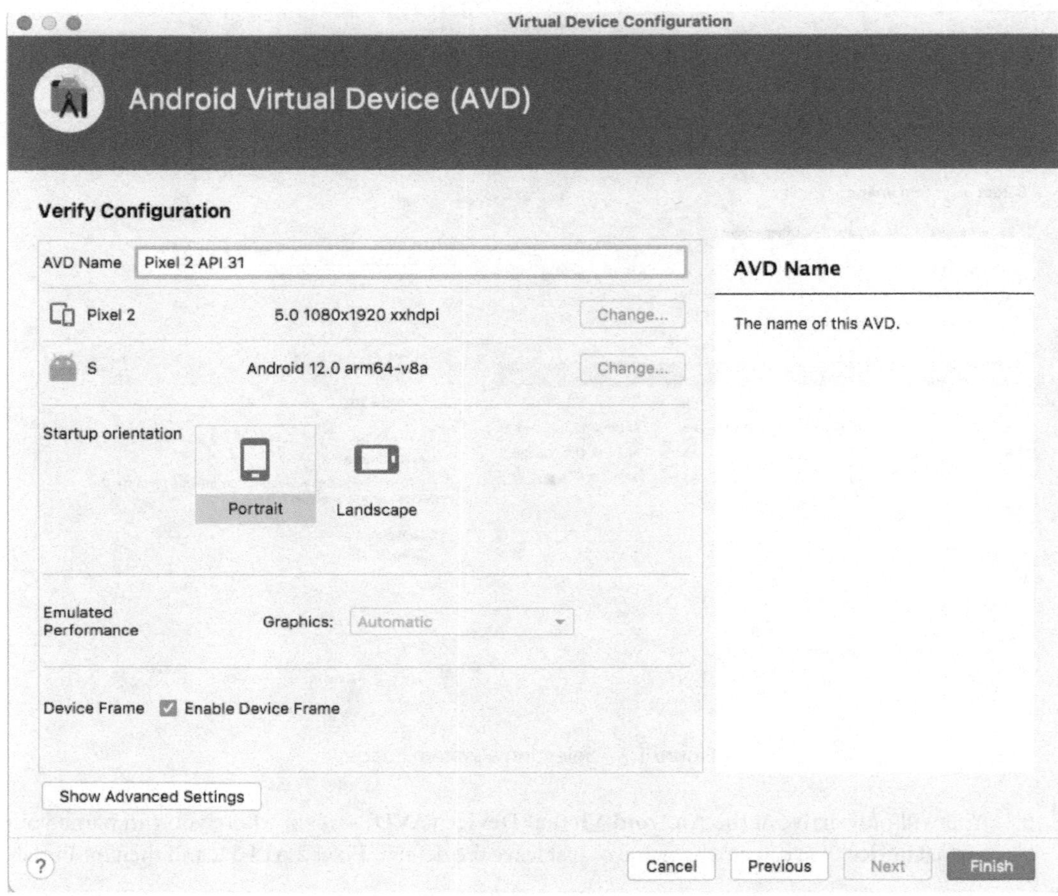

Figure 1.8 – Final steps of setting up the AVD

6. Test your virtual device by running it and ensure it works as expected. You should see something similar to *Figure 1.9* once you run your application on the emulator.

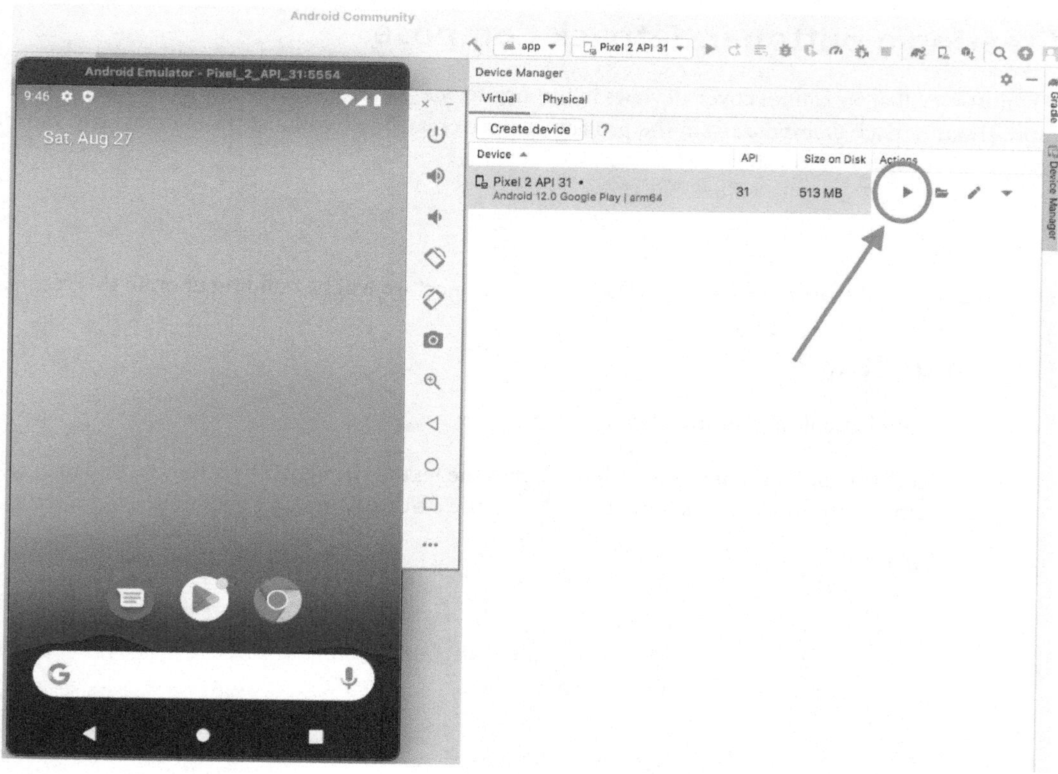

Figure 1.9 – The Device Manager section to run the emulator

> **Important note**
>
> To create a physical testing device, you must go to **Settings** on your Android phone and select **About phone | Software information | Build number** and hold down the button as you release until you see **You are now four steps away from being a developer**. Once the count is complete, you will see a notification saying **Developer options successfully enabled**. All you need now is to use a **Universal Serial Bus (USB)** and toggle USB debugging. Finally, you will see that your physical phone is ready for testing.

How it works...

Testing and ensuring your applications display the expected outcome is very important. That is why Android Studio uses the emulator to help developers ensure their application functions as it would on standard devices. Furthermore, Android phones come with a developer's option ready for developers to use, which makes it even easier for the different number of devices that Android supports and also for helping reproduce bugs that are hard to find in emulators.

Creating a button in Jetpack Compose

We must note that we cannot cover all views in just one recipe; we have a chapter dedicated to learning more about Jetpack Compose, so in the project we have created, we will just try to create two more additional views for our project.

Getting ready

Open the **Android Community** project, as that is the project we will be building upon in this recipe.

How to do it...

Let's start by implementing a simple button in Compose:

1. Let's go ahead and organize our code and align the text to the center by adding a `Column()` to organize our views. This should be added to the `setContent{}` function:

```
Column(
    modifier = Modifier
        .fillMaxSize()
        .wrapContentSize(Alignment.Center),
    horizontalAlignment = Alignment.CenterHorizontally
) {
    Greeting("Hello, Android Community")
  }
}
```

2. Now, create a function and call it `SampleButton`; we will pass nothing in this example. However, we will have a `RowScope{}`, which defines the `modifier` functions applicable to our button in this case, and we will give our button a name: `click me`.
3. In Compose, when you create a button, you can set its shape, icon, and elevation, check whether it is enabled or not, check its content, and more. You can check how to customize your button by command-clicking on the `Button()` component:

```
@Composable
fun SampleButton() {
    Button(
        onClick = { /*TODO*/ },
        modifier = Modifier
            .fillMaxWidth()
            .padding(24.dp),
        shape = RoundedCornerShape(20.dp),
```

```
            border = BorderStroke(2.dp, Color.Blue),
            colors = ButtonDefaults.buttonColors(
                contentColor = Color.Gray,
                backgroundColor = Color.White
            )
        ) {
            Text(
                text = stringResource(id =
                           R.string.click_me),
                fontSize = 14.sp,
                modifier = Modifier.padding(horizontal =
                               30.dp, vertical = 6.dp)
            )

        }
    }
```

In our SampleButton, onClick does not do anything; our button has a modifier of the maximum fill width, padding of 24 **density-independent pixels** (**dp**), and round corners with a radius of 20 dp.

We have also set the button's color and added click me as text. We set our font size to 14 **scale-independent pixels** (**sp**), as this helps in ensuring that the text will adjust well for both the screen and users' preferences.

4. Also, click **Split** in the top right to preview your screen elements, or you can click on the **Design** section to view the entire screen without the code.

Figure 1.10 – View both the code and design in Android Studio

5. Finally, let's call our SampleButton function, where the Greeting function is, and run the app:

```
Column(
    modifier = Modifier
        .fillMaxSize()
        .wrapContentSize(Alignment.Center),
    horizontalAlignment = Alignment.CenterHorizontally
) {
    Greeting("Hello, Android Community")
```

```
        SampleButton()
    }
```

6. Compile and run the program; your app should look similar to *Figure 1.11*.

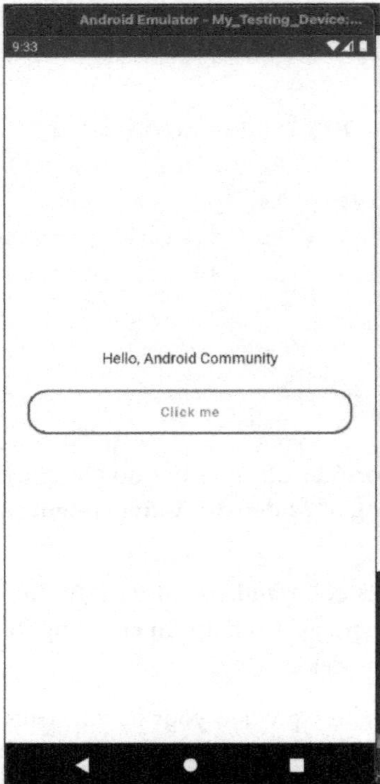

Figure 1.11 – A screenshot showing the text and a button

How it works...

A Composable app comprises several composable functions, just normal functions annotated with `@Composable`. As Google documentation explains, the annotation tells the Compose to add exceptional support to the procedure for updating and maintaining your UI over time. Compose also lets you structure your code into small maintainable chunks that you can adjust and reuse at any given point.

There's more...

Since it's hard to cover all views in a single recipe, we will work on more views in *Chapter 2, Creating Screens Using a Declarative UI and Exploring Compose Principles*, explore the best practices, and test our composable views.

Utilizing gradlew commands to clean and run your project in Android Studio

The `gradlew` command is a robust Gradle wrapper that has excellent usage. In Android Studio, however, you do not need to install it because it is a script that comes packaged within the project.

Getting ready

For now, however, we will not look into all the Gradle commands but instead use the most popular ones to clean, build, provide info, debug, and scan our project to find any issues when we run our application. You can run the commands in your laptop's terminal as long as you are in the correct directory or use the terminal provided by Android Studio.

How to do it...

Follow these steps to check and confirm whether Gradle works as anticipated:

1. You can check the version by simply running `./gradlew`.

```
Terminal: Local × + ∨
madonasyombua@Madonas-MacBook-Pro AndroidCommunity % ./gradlew
Starting a Gradle Daemon, 1 incompatible and 1 stopped Daemons could not be reused, use --status for details

> Task :help

Welcome to Gradle 7.3.3.

To run a build, run gradlew <task> ...

To see a list of available tasks, run gradlew tasks

To see more detail about a task, run gradlew help --task <task>

To see a list of command-line options, run gradlew --help

For more detail on using Gradle, see https://docs.gradle.org/7.3.3/userguide/command_line_interface.html

For troubleshooting, visit https://help.gradle.org

BUILD SUCCESSFUL in 12s
1 actionable task: 1 executed
madonasyombua@Madonas-MacBook-Pro AndroidCommunity %
```

Figure 1.12 – gradlew version

2. To build and clean your project, you can run the `./gradlew clean` and `./gradlew build` commands. If anything is wrong with your project, the build will fail, and you can investigate the error. In addition, in Android, you can always run your project without using the Gradle commands, and just utilize the IDE run and clean options. We will discuss this topic in depth in *Chapter 12, Android Studio Tips and Tricks to Help You during Development*.

3. The following are a few more useful `gradlew` commands; for example, when your build fails and you want to know what went wrong, use the commands to investigate or click on the error message (see *Figure 1.13*):

   - Run with the `--stacktrace` option to get the stack trace
   - Run with the `--info` or `--debug` option to get more log output
   - Run with `--scan` to get full insights

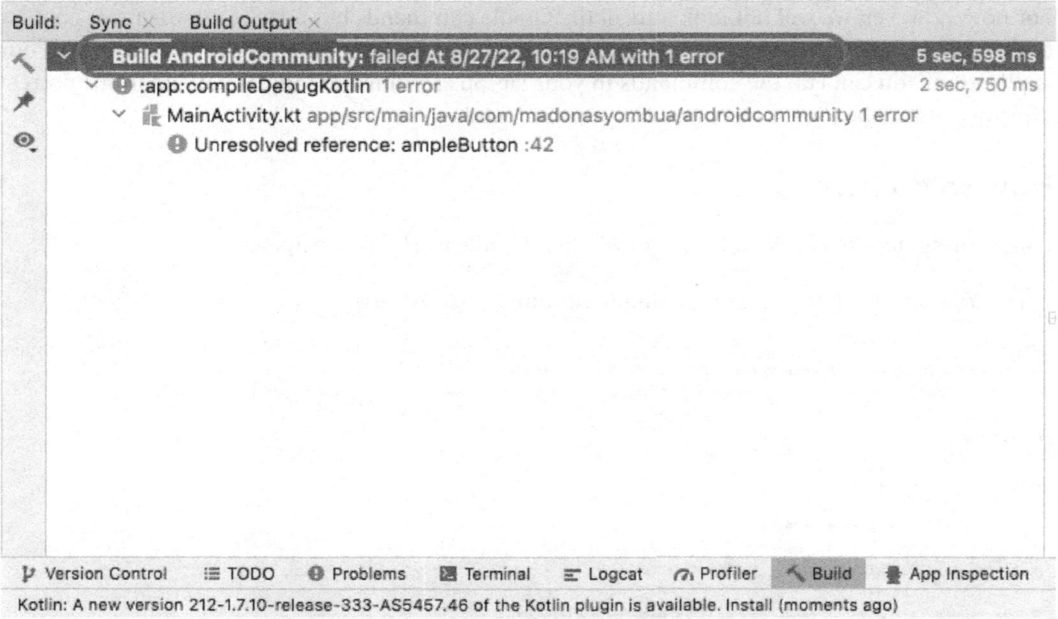

Figure 1.13 – Build error output

How it works

Gradle is a general-purpose build tool that proves to be very powerful in Android development. In addition, you can create and publish your custom plugins to encapsulate your conventions and build functionality. Advantages of Gradle include incremental build works for test execution, compilation, and any other task that happens in your build system.

See also

More about Gradle and what it does can be found here: `https://gradle.org/`.

Understanding the Android project structure

If this is your first time looking at the Android project folder, you might wonder where to add your code and what the packages mean. This recipe will walk through what each folder holds and what code goes where.

Getting ready

If you open your project, you will notice many folders. The main folders in your Android project are listed here:

- The `manifest` folder
- The `java` folder (`test/androidTest`)
- The `Res Resource` folder
- `Gradle Scripts`

How to do it...

Let's navigate through each folder as we learn what is stored, where, and why:

1. In *Figure 1.14*, you can see the **Packages** dropdown; click on that, and a window with **Project**, **Packages**, **Project Files**, and more will pop up.
2. You can opt to view your project using the Android logo, via **Project**, or the `Project` highlighted section next to the drop-down menu. The Project view is best when you have many modules in your application and want to add specific code. Feel free to click on the sections and see what they hold.

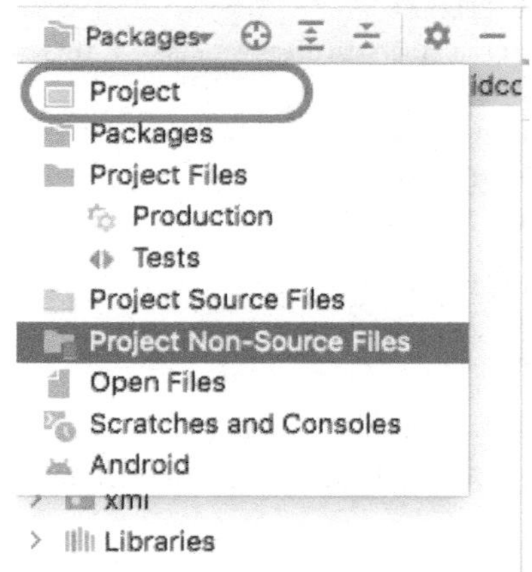

Figure 1.14 – Android Studio project structure

3. The `manifest` folder is the source of truth for the Android application; it contains `AndroidManifest.xml`. Click inside the file, and you will notice you have an intent launcher that launches the Android application on your emulator.
4. In addition, the version number is typically set in Gradle and then merged into `manifest` and in the manifest is where we add all needed permissions. You will also notice the package name, metadata, data extraction rules, theme, and icon; if you have a unique icon, you can add one here.

```xml
<?xml version="1.0" encoding="utf-8"?>
<manifest xmlns:android="http://schemas.android.com/apk/res/android"
    xmlns:tools="http://schemas.android.com/tools"
    package="com.madonasyombua.androidcommunity">

    <application
        android:allowBackup="true"
        android:dataExtractionRules="@xml/data_extraction_rules"
        android:fullBackupContent="@xml/backup_rules"
        android:icon="@mipmap/ic_launcher"
        android:label="AndroidCommunity"
        android:roundIcon="@mipmap/ic_launcher_round"
        android:supportsRtl="true"
        android:theme="@style/Theme.AndroidCommunity"
        tools:targetApi="31">
        <activity
            android:name=".MainActivity"
            android:exported="true"
            android:label="AndroidCommunity"
            android:theme="@style/Theme.AndroidCommunity">
            <intent-filter>
                <action android:name="android.intent.action.MAIN" />

                <category android:name="android.intent.category.LAUNCHER" />
            </intent-filter>
        </activity>
    </application>

</manifest>
```

Figure 1.15 – Android Studio project structure manifest file

> **Important note**
>
> Making your icon adaptive is the new favored way to add icons to your applications. Adaptive icons display differently depending on individual user theming in MAD. See `https://developer.android.com/develop/ui/views/launch/icon_design_adaptive`.

5. The `java` folder contains all the Kotlin (`.kt`) and Java (`.java`) files we create as we build our Android applications. For example, in *Figure 1.16*, we have a package with **(androidTest)** and **(test)**, and this is where we add our tests. Go ahead and click on all the folders and see what they contain.

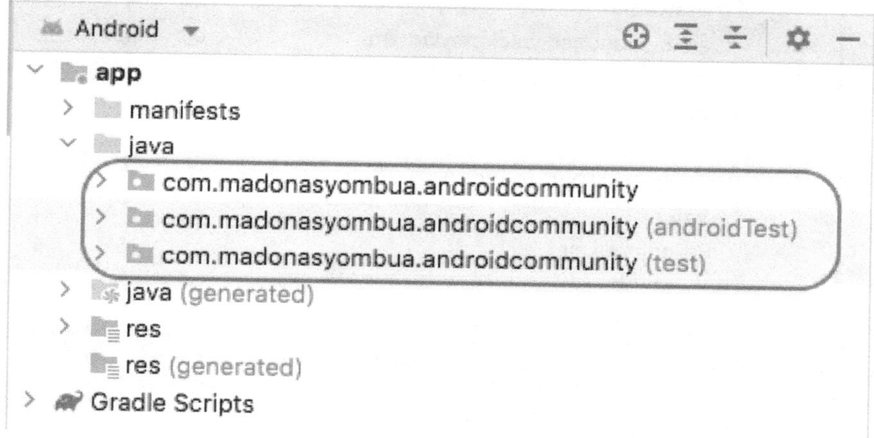

Figure 1.16 – Android Studio project structure Java folders

6. In the `androidTest` folder, we write our UI tests to test the UI functionalities, and in the test folder, we write our unit test. Unit testing tests small pieces of our code to ensure the required behavior is as anticipated. **Test-Driven Development** (**TDD**) is excellent and valuable during app development. Some companies follow this rule, but some do not enforce it. However, it is a great skill to have, as it is good practice to always test your code.

   The `res` folder contains XML layouts, UI strings, drawable images, and Mipmap icons. On the other hand, the `values` folder contains many useful XML files such as `dimensions`, `colors`, and `themes`. Go ahead and click on the `res` folder to get familiar with what is there, as we will use it in the next chapter.

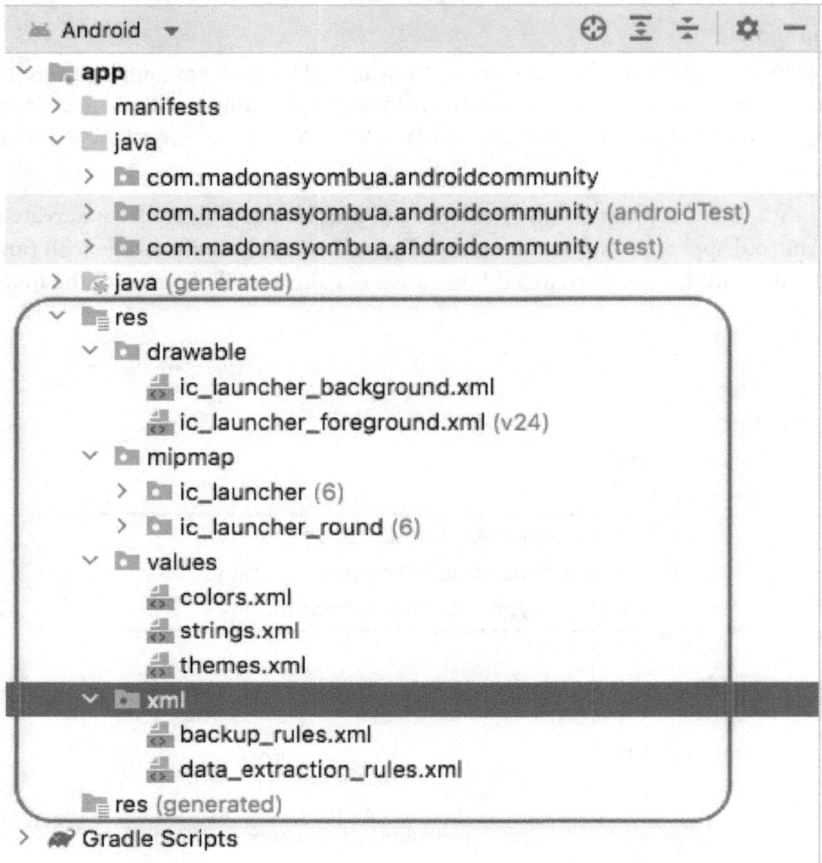

Figure 1.17 – Android Studio project structure res folder

> **Important note**
>
> Unless you are building a new project from scratch, many applications still use XML layouts, and developers opt to develop new screens with Jetpack Compose as an advancement now. Therefore, you might have to maintain or know how to write views in XML.

7. Finally, in `Gradle Scripts`, you will see the files that define the build configuration we can apply in our modules. For example, in `build.gradle(Project: AndroidCommunity)`, you will see a top-level file where you can add configuration options common to all your sub-project modules.

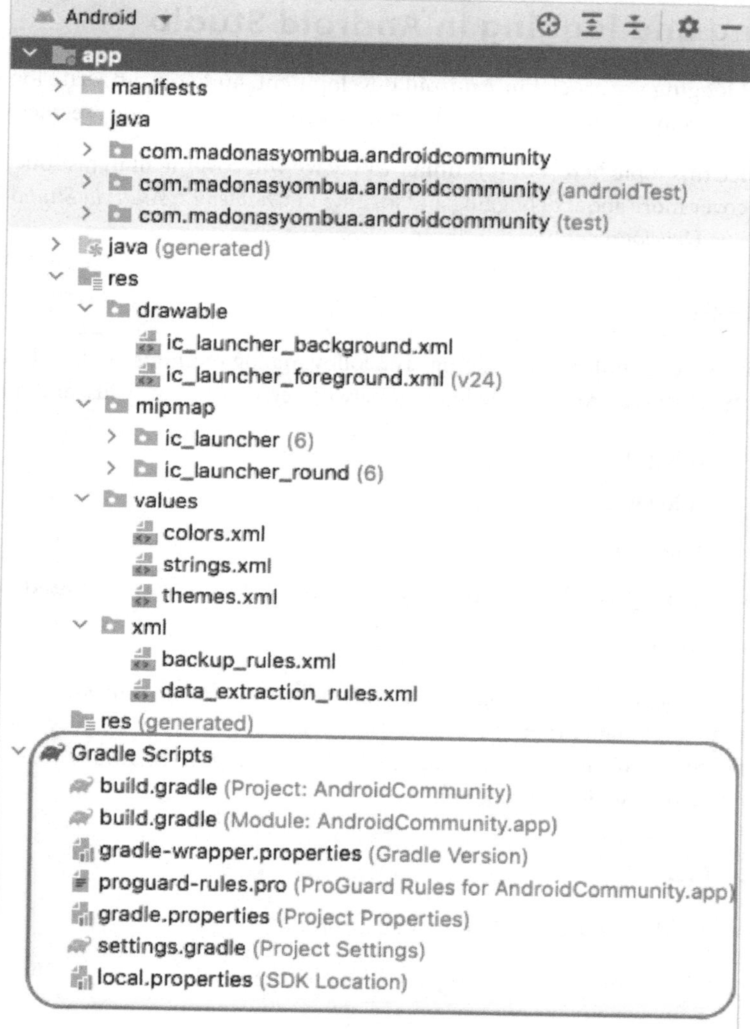

Figure 1.18 – Gradle scripts in the Android Studio project structure

How it works...

In Android Studio, it can be overwhelming for first-time users not to know where files go and what is essential. Hence, having a step-by-step guide on where to add your tests or code and understanding the Android project structure is vital. In addition, in complex projects, you might find different modules; hence, understanding the project structure is helpful. A module in Android Studio is a collection of source files and build settings that allow you to divide your project into distinct entities with specific purposes.

Debugging and logging in Android Studio

Debugging and logging are crucial in Android development, and you can write log messages that appear in Logcat to help you find issues in your code or verify a piece of code executes when it should.

We will introduce this topic here, but it is unfair to say we will cover it all in just one recipe; for that reason, we will cover more about debugging and logging in *Chapter 12, Android Studio Tips and Tricks to Help You during Development*.

Getting ready

Let us use an example to understand logging. The following log methods are listed from the highest to lowest priority. They are proper when logging network errors, success calls, and other errors:

- `Log.e()`: A log error
- `Log.w()`: A log warning
- `Log.i()`: Log information
- `Log.d()`: Debugging shows critical messages to developers, the most used log
- `Log.v()`: Verbose

A good practice is associating every log with a `TAG` to identify the error message in Logcat quickly. A "`TAG"` refers to a text label that can be assigned to a View or other UI element in an Android application. The primary purpose of using **tags** in Android is to provide a way to associate additional information or metadata with a UI element.

How to do it...

Let's go ahead and add a log message to our small project:

1. We will go ahead and create a debug log, then run the application:

   ```
   Log.d(TAG, "asdf Testing call")
   ```

   In the **Logcat** section, in the search box, enter `asdf` and see whether you can find the message.

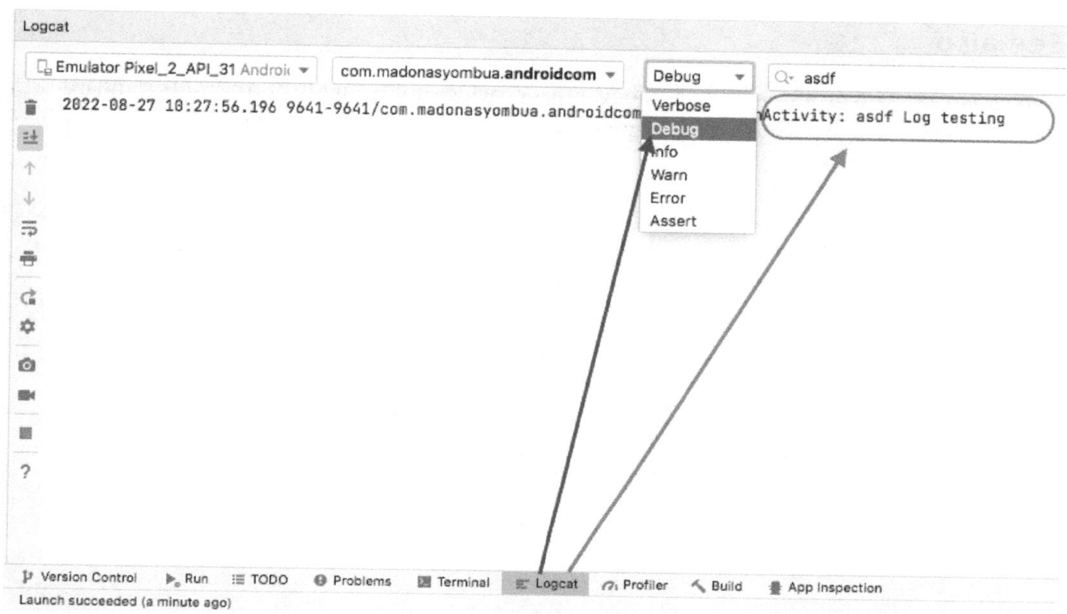

Figure 1.19 – Android Logcat

You will notice that the log has a class name, our `TAG` (`MainActivity`), and the log message displayed; see the right arrow in *Figure 1.19*.

2. The left arrow shows the mentioned log types and using the dropdown, you can quickly view your message based on the specification.

How it works...

Debugging is when you put breakpoints in your classes, slow down your emulator, and try to find issues in your code. Debugging is very powerful if, for instance, you encounter a race condition in your code or if your code works on some devices and does not work on others.

In addition, to take advantage of debugging, you need first to attach a debugger to the emulator, and then run in **Debug** mode. **Logging**, on the other hand, helps you log information that might be helpful to you when you encounter issues. Sometimes, debugging can be challenging, but placing logs where needed in your code might be very helpful.

A practical case is when you are loading data from an API; you might want to log it when there is a network error to inform you what happens if the network call fails. Hence, debugging using breakpoints might help slow down the process as you evaluate the values, and since we did not build a lot in this chapter, we can revisit this topic in a different recipe in later chapters.

See also

Timber is a logger with a small, extensible API that provides utility on top of Android's standard `Log` class, and many developers use it for logging. For more information about Timber, see `https://github.com/JakeWharton/timber`.

2

Creating Screens Using a Declarative UI and Exploring Compose Principles

Mobile applications require a **User Interface** (**UI**) for user interactions. For instance, the old way of creating the UI was imperative in Android. This meant having a separate prototype of the application's UI using unique **Extensible Markup Language** (**XML**) layouts and not the same language used to build your logic.

However, with Modern Android Development, there is a push to stop using imperative programming and start using a declarative way of making the UI, which means developers design the UI based on the data received. This design paradigm uses one programming language to create an entire application.

It is fair to acknowledge it may seem difficult for new developers to decide what to learn when building a UI: the old way of creating views or opting for the new Jetpack Compose. However, suppose you've built an Android application before the Jetpack Compose era.

In such a case, you may already know using XML is a bit tedious, especially if your code base is complex. However, utilizing Jetpack Compose as your first choice makes work easier. In addition, it simplifies UI development by ensuring developers use less code, as they take advantage of the intuitive Kotlin APIs. Hence, there is a logical push by new developers when creating views to use Jetpack Compose instead of XML.

However, knowing both can be beneficial since many applications still use XML layouts, and you might have to maintain the view but build new ones using Jetpack Compose. In this chapter, we will look at Jetpack Compose basics by trying to implement small examples using columns, rows, boxes, lazy columns, and more.

In this chapter, we'll be covering the following recipes:

- Implementing Android views in Jetpack Compose
- Implementing a scrollable list in Jetpack Compose
- Implementing your first tab layout with a view pager using Jetpack Compose
- Implementing animations in Compose
- Implementing accessibility in Jetpack Compose
- Implementing declarative graphics using Jetpack Compose

Technical requirements

The complete source code for this chapter can be found at `https://github.com/PacktPublishing/Modern-Android-13-Development-Cookbook/tree/main/chapter-two`. To be able to view all the recipes, you will need to run all the preview functions separately. Hence, look for the `@Preview` composable function to view the UI created.

Implementing Android views in Jetpack Compose

In every Android application, having a UI element is very crucial. A view in Android is a simple building block for a UI. A view ensures users can interact with your application through a tap or other motion. This recipe will look at different Compose UI elements and see how we can build them.

Getting ready

In this recipe, we will create one project that we will re-use for the entire chapter, so let's go ahead and follow the steps in *Chapter 1, Getting Started with Modern Android Development Skills*, on how to create your first Android project.

Create a project and call it `Compose Basics`. In addition, we will mostly use the **Preview** section to view the UI element we create.

How to do it...

Once you have created the project, follow these steps to build several Compose UI elements:

1. Inside our project, let us go ahead and create a new package and call it components. This is where we will add all the components we create.
2. Create a Kotlin file and call it `UIComponents.kt`; inside `UIComponent`, go ahead and create a composable function, call it `EditTextExample()`, and call the `OutlinedTextField()`

function; this will prompt you to import the required import, which is `androidx.Compose.material.OutlinedTextField`:

```
@Composable
fun EditTextExample() {
    OutlinedTextField()
}
```

3. When you look deep into `OutlineTextField` (see *Figure 2.1*), you will notice the function accepts several inputs, and this is very useful when you need to customize your own composable functions.

```
@Composable
public fun OutlinedTextField(
    value: String,
    onValueChange: (String) -> Unit,
    modifier: Modifier,
    enabled: Boolean,
    readOnly: Boolean,
    textStyle: TextStyle,
    label: @Composable() (() -> Unit)?,
    placeholder: @Composable() (() -> Unit)?,
    leadingIcon: @Composable() (() -> Unit)?,
    trailingIcon: @Composable() (() -> Unit)?,
    isError: Boolean,
    visualTransformation: VisualTransformation,
    keyboardOptions: KeyboardOptions,
    keyboardActions: KeyboardActions,
    singleLine: Boolean,
    maxLines: Int,
    interactionSource: MutableInteractionSource,
    shape: Shape,
    colors: TextFieldColors
): Unit
```

Material Design outlined text field.
Outlined text fields have less visual emphasis than filled text fields. When they appear in places like forms, where many text fields are placed together, their reduced emphasis helps simplify the layout.

Figure 2.1 – The OutlinedTextField input

4. For our example, we will not do much with the UI we create and will rather just look at how we create them.

5. Now, to fully create our `OutlinedTextField()` based on the types of input we see it accepts, we can give it a text and color and we can decorate it using a `Modifier()`; that is, by giving it specific instructions such as `fillMaxWidth()`, which sets the max width. When we say fill, we are simply specifying it should be fully filled. We set `.padding(top)` to `16.dp`, which applies additional space along each edge of the content in dp. It also has a value, which is the value to be entered in the `OutlinedTextField`, and an `onValueChange` lambda that listens to the input change.

6. We also give our `OutlinedText` some border colors when focused and when not focused to reflect the different states. Hence, if you start entering input, the box will change color to blue, as specified in the code:

```
@Composable
fun EditTextExample() {
    OutlinedTextField(
        value = "",
        onValueChange = {},
        label = { Text(stringResource(id =
        R.string.sample)) },
        modifier = Modifier
            .fillMaxWidth()
            .padding(top = 16.dp),
        colors =
            TextFieldDefaults.outlinedTextFieldColors(
                focusedBorderColor = Color.Blue,
                unfocusedBorderColor = Color.Black
            )
    )
}
```

7. We also have another type of `TextField`, which is not outlined, and if you compare what `OutlinedTextField` takes in as input, you will notice they are fairly similar:

```
@Composable
fun NotOutlinedEditTextExample() {
    TextField(
        value = "",
        onValueChange = {},
        label = { Text(stringResource(id =
        R.string.sample)) },
        modifier = Modifier
            .fillMaxWidth()
            .padding(top = 8.dp, bottom = 16.dp),
        colors =
            TextFieldDefaults.outlinedTextFieldColors(
                focusedBorderColor = Color.Blue,
                unfocusedBorderColor = Color.Black
            )
    )
}
```

8. You can run the application by adding the Compose functions inside the `@Preview` composable function. In our example, we can create `UIElementPreview()`, which is a preview function for displaying our UI. In *Figure 2.2*, the top view is `OutlinedTextField`, whereas the second one is a normal `TextField`.

Figure 2.2 – OutlinedTextField and TextField

9. Now, let's go ahead and look at button examples. We will look at different ways to create buttons with different shapes. If you hover over the `Button()` composable function, you will see what it accepts as input, as shown in *Figure 2.3*.

```
@Composable
public fun Button(
    onClick: () -> Unit,
    modifier: Modifier,
    enabled: Boolean,
    interactionSource: MutableInteractionSource,
    elevation: ButtonElevation?,
    shape: Shape,
    border: BorderStroke?,
    colors: ButtonColors,
    contentPadding: PaddingValues,
    content: @Composable() (RowScope.() -> Unit)
): Unit
```

Material Design contained button.

Contained buttons are high-emphasis, distinguished by their use of elevation and fill. They contain actions that are primary to your app.

!Contained button image ↗

The default text style for internal `Text` components will be set to `Typography.button`.

Params: `onClick` - Will be called when the user clicks the button
`modifier` - Modifier to be applied to the button
`enabled` - Controls the enabled state of the button. When `false`, this button will not be clickable
`interactionSource` - the `MutableInteractionSource` representing the stream of `Interactions` for this Button. You can create and pass in your own remembered

Figure 2.3 – Button input

In our second example, we will try to create a button with an icon on it. In addition, we will add text, which is crucial when creating buttons since we need to specify to users what action or what the button will be doing once it is clicked on.

10. So, go ahead and create a Compose function in the same Kotlin file and call it `ButtonWithIcon()`, and then import the `Button()` composable function.
11. Inside it, you will need to import an `Icon()` with `painterResource` input, a content description, `Modifier`, and `tint`. We will also need `Text()`, which will give our button a name. For our example, we will not use `tint`:

```
@Composable
fun ButtonWithIcon() {
    Button(onClick = {}) {
        Icon(
            painterResource(id =
                R.drawable.ic_baseline_shopping_
bag_24                 ),
            contentDescription = stringResource(
                id = R.string.shop),
```

```
            modifier = Modifier.size(20.dp)
        )

        Text(text = stringResource(id = R.string.buy),
            Modifier.padding(start = 10.dp))
    }
}
```

12. Let us also go ahead and create a new composable function and call it `CornerCutShapeButton()`; in this example, we will try to create a button with cut corners:

```
@Composable
fun CornerCutShapeButton() {
    Button(onClick = {}, shape = CutCornerShape(10)) {
        Text(text = stringResource(
            id = R.string.cornerButton))  }}}}
```

13. Let us also go ahead and create a new composable function and call it `RoundCornerShapeButton()`; in this example, we will try to create a button with round corners:

```
@Composable
fun RoundCornerShapeButton() {
    Button(onClick = {}, shape =
    RoundedCornerShape(10.dp)) {
        Text(text = stringResource(
            id = R.string.rounded))
    }
}
```

14. Let us also go ahead and create a new composable function and call it `ElevatedButtonExample()`; in this example, we will try to create a button with elevation:

```
@Composable
fun ElevatedButtonExample() {
    Button(
        onClick = {},
        elevation = ButtonDefaults.elevation(
            defaultElevation = 8.dp,
            pressedElevation = 10.dp,
            disabledElevation = 0.dp
        )
    ) {
```

```
            Text(text = stringResource(
                id = R.string.elevated))
        }
    }
```

15. When you run the application, you should have an image similar to *Figure 2.4*; the first button after `TextField` is `ButtonWithIcon()`, the second one is `CornerCutShapeButton()`, the third is `RoundCornerShapeButton()`, and, lastly, we have `ElevatedButtonExample()`.

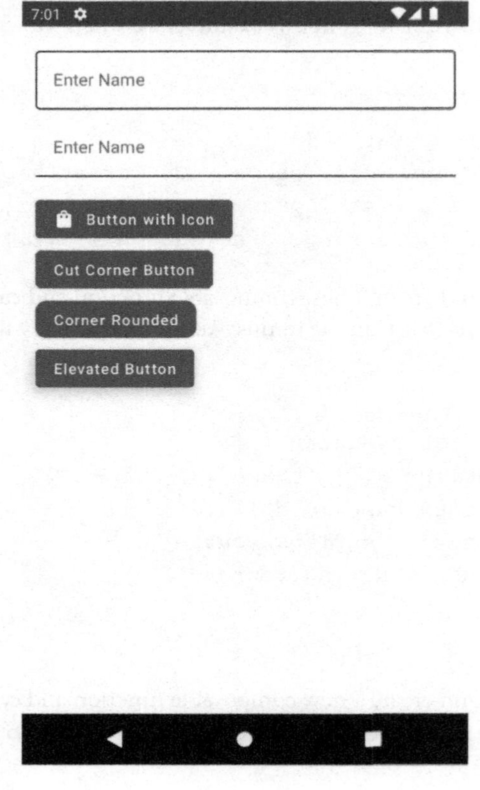

Figure 2.4 – The different button types and other UI elements

16. Now, let us look at one last example since we will be using different views and styles throughout the book and will learn more in the process. Now, let us look at an image view; the `Image()` composable function takes in several inputs, as shown in *Figure 2.5*.

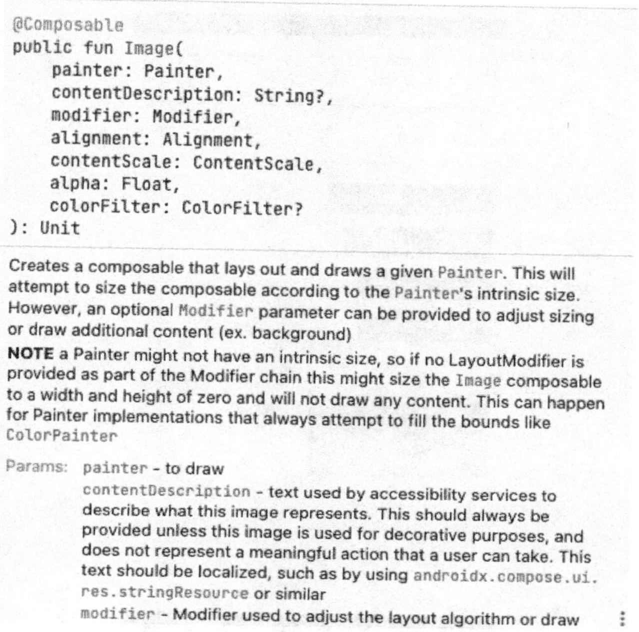

```
@Composable
public fun Image(
    painter: Painter,
    contentDescription: String?,
    modifier: Modifier,
    alignment: Alignment,
    contentScale: ContentScale,
    alpha: Float,
    colorFilter: ColorFilter?
): Unit
```

Creates a composable that lays out and draws a given `Painter`. This will attempt to size the composable according to the `Painter`'s intrinsic size. However, an optional `Modifier` parameter can be provided to adjust sizing or draw additional content (ex. background)

NOTE a Painter might not have an intrinsic size, so if no LayoutModifier is provided as part of the Modifier chain this might size the `Image` composable to a width and height of zero and will not draw any content. This can happen for Painter implementations that always attempt to fill the bounds like `ColorPainter`

Params: `painter` - to draw
`contentDescription` - text used by accessibility services to describe what this image represents. This should always be provided unless this image is used for decorative purposes, and does not represent a meaningful action that a user can take. This text should be localized, such as by using `androidx.compose.ui.res.stringResource` or similar
`modifier` - Modifier used to adjust the layout algorithm or draw

Figure 2.5 – Different ImageView input types

17. In our example, `Image()` will only have a painter, which is not nullable, meaning you need to provide an image for this composable function, a content description for accessibility, and a modifier:

```
@Composable
fun ImageViewExample() {
    Image(
        painterResource(id = R.drawable.android),
        contentDescription = stringResource(
           id = R.string.image),
        modifier = Modifier.size(200.dp)
    )
}
```

18. You can also try to play around with others things, such as adding `RadioButton()` and `CheckBox()` elements and customizing them. When you run your application, you should have something similar to *Figure 2.6*.

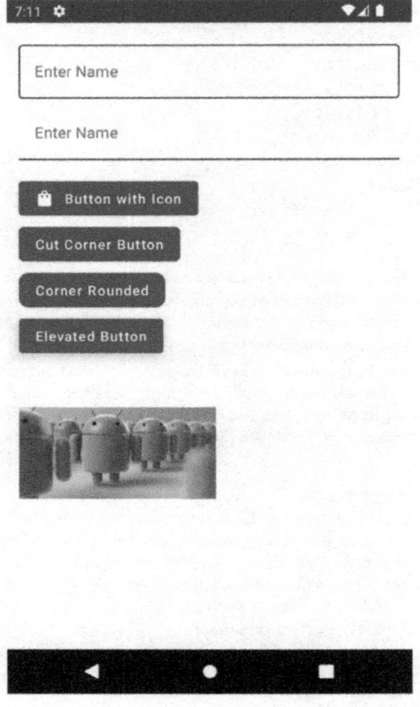

Figure 2.6 – Several UI components

How it works...

Every composable function is annotated with the `@Composable` annotation. This annotation tells the Compose compiler that the provided compiler is intended to convert the provided data into a UI. It is also important to note each composable function name needs to be a noun and not a verb or an adjective, and Google provides these guidelines. Any composable function you create can accept parameters that enable the app logic to describe or modify your UI.

We mention the Compose compiler, which means that a compiler is any special program that takes the code we wrote, examines it, and translates it into something the computer can understand – or machine language.

In `Icon()`, `painterResouce` specifies the icon we will be adding to the button, the content description helps with accessibility, and the modifier is used to decorate our icon.

We can preview the UI elements we build by adding the `@Preview` annotation and adding `showBackground = true`:

```
@Preview(showBackground = true)
```

`@Preview` is powerful, and we will look at how you can utilize it better in future chapters.

Implementing a scrollable list in Jetpack Compose

When building Android applications, one thing that we can all agree on is you must know how to build a `RecyclerView` to display your data. With our new, modern way of building Android applications, if we need to use `RecyclerView`, we can use `LazyColumn`, which is similar. In this recipe, we will look at rows, columns, and `LazyColumn`, and build a scrollable list using our dummy data.

In addition, we will be learning some Kotlin in the process.

Getting ready

We will continue using the `Compose Basics` project to build a scrollable list; hence, to get started, you need to have done the previous recipe.

How to do it...

Follow these steps to build your first scrollable list:

1. Let us go ahead and build our first scrollable list, but first, we need to create our dummy data, and this is the item we want to be displayed on our list. Hence, create a package called `favoritecity` where our scrollable example will live.
2. Inside the `favoritecity` package, create a new data class and call it `City`; this will be our dummy data source – `data class City ()`.
3. Let us model our `City` data class. Make sure you add the necessary imports once you have added the annotated values:

```
data class City(
    val id: Int,
    @StringRes val nameResourceId: Int,
    @DrawableRes val imageResourceId: Int
)
```

4. Now, in our dummy data, we need to create a Kotlin class and call this class `CityDataSource`. In this class, we will create a function called `loadCities()`, which will return our list of `List<City>`, which we will display in our scrollable list. Check the *Technical requirements* section for all the required imports to get all the code and images:

```
class CityDataSource {
    fun loadCities(): List<City> {
        return listOf<City>(
            City(1, R.string.spain, R.drawable.spain),
            City(2, R.string.new_york,
                R.drawable.newyork),
```

```
                City(3, R.string.tokyo, R.drawable.tokyo),
                City(4, R.string.switzerland,
                    R.drawable.switzerland),
                City(5, R.string.singapore,
                    R.drawable.singapore),
                City(6, R.string.paris, R.drawable.paris),
            )
        }
    }
```

5. Now, we have our dummy data, and it is time to display this on our scrollable list. Let's create a new Kotlin file in our `components` package and call it `CityComponents`. In `CityComponents`, we will create our `@Preview` function:

```
@Preview(showBackground = true)
@Composable
private fun CityCardPreview() {
    CityApp()
}
```

6. Inside our `@Preview` function, we have another composable function, `CityApp()`; inside this function, we will call our `CityList` composable function, which has the list as a parameter. In addition, in this composable function, we will call `LazyColumn`, and `items` will be `CityCard(cities)`. See the *How it works* section for further explanation about `LazyColumn` and `items`:

```
@Composable
fun CityList(cityList: List<City>) {
    LazyColumn {
        items(cityList) { cities ->
            CityCard(cities)
        }
    }
}
```

7. Finally, let us construct our `CityCard(city)` composable function:

```
@Composable
fun CityCard(city: City) {
    Card(modifier = Modifier.padding(10.dp),
    elevation = 4.dp) {
        Column {
            Image(
                painter = painterResource(
```

```
                    city.imageResourceId),
                contentDescription = stringResource(
                    city.nameResourceId),
                modifier = Modifier
                    .fillMaxWidth()
                    .height(154.dp),
                contentScale = ContentScale.Crop
            )
            Text(
                text = LocalContext.current.getString(
                    city.nameResourceId),
                modifier = Modifier.padding(16.dp),
                style = MaterialTheme.typography.h5
            )
        }
    }
}
```

8. When you run the `CityCardPreview` composable function, you should have a scrollable list, as seen in *Figure 2.6*.

Figure 2.7 – A scrollable list of cities

How it works...

In Kotlin, a list has two types, **immutable** and **mutable**. Immutable lists are items that cannot be modified, whereas mutable lists are items in the list that can be modified. To define a list, we can say a list is a generic ordered collection of elements, and these elements can be in the form of integers, strings, images, and so on, which is mostly informed by the type of data we want our lists to contain. For instance, in our example, we have a string and image helping identify our favorite cities by name and image.

In our `City` data class, we use `@StringRes`, and `@DrawableRes` in order to just pull this directly from the `res` folders for `Drawable` and `String` easily, and they also represent the ID for the images and string.

We created `CityList` and annotated it with the composable function and declared the list of city objects as our parameter in the function. A scrollable list in Jetpack Compose is made using `LazyColumn`. The main difference between `LazyColumn` and `Column` is that when using `Column`, you can only display small items, as Compose loads all items at once.

In addition, a column can only hold fixed composable functions, whereas `LazyColumn`, as the name suggests, loads the content as required on demand, making it good for loading more items when needed. In addition, `LazyColumn` comes with a scrolling ability inbuilt, which makes work easier for developers.

We also created a composable function, `CityCard`, where we import the `Card()` element from Compose. A card contains content and actions about a single object; in our example, for instance, our card has an image and the name of the city. A `Card()` element in Compose has the following inputs in its parameter:

```
@Composable
fun Card(
    modifier: Modifier = Modifier,
    shape: Shape = MaterialTheme.shapes.medium,
    backgroundColor: Color = MaterialTheme.colors.surface,
    contentColor: Color = contentColorFor(backgroundColor),
    border: BorderStroke? = null,
    elevation: Dp = 1.dp,
    content: @Composable () -> Unit
),
```

This means you can easily model your card to the best fitting; our card has padding and elevation, and the scope has a column. In this column, we have an image and text, which helps describe the image for more context.

See also

There is more to learn about lists and grids in Compose; you can use this link to learn more: `https://developer.android.com/jetpack/compose/lists`.

Implementing your first tab layout with a view pager using Jetpack Compose

In Android development, having a slide between pages is very common, with a significant use case being onboarding or even when you are trying to display specific data in a tabbed, carousel way. In this recipe, we will build a simple horizontal pager in Compose and see how we can utilize the new knowledge to build better and more modern Android apps.

Getting ready

In this example, we will build a horizontal pager that changes colors when selected to show the state is selected. We will look into states in *Chapter 3, Handling the UI State in Jetpack Compose and Using Hilt*, for better understanding. Open the `Compose Basics` project to get started.

How to do it...

Follow these steps to build your tab carousel:

1. Add the following pager dependencies to `build.gradle(Module:app)`:

```
implementation "com.google.accompanist:accompanist-pager:0.x.x"
implementation "com.google.accompanist:accompanist-pager-
indicators:0.x.x"
implementation 'androidx.Compose.material:material:1.x.x'
```

   Jetpack Compose offers **Accompanist**, a group of libraries that aims to support it with commonly required features by developers – for instance, in our case, the pager.

2. In the same project from previous recipes, let's create a package and call it `pagerexample`; inside it, create a Kotlin file and call it `CityTabExample`; inside this file, create a composable function and call it `CityTabCarousel`:

```
@Composable
fun CityTabCarousel(){}
```

3. Now, let us go ahead and build our `CityTabCarousel`; for our example, we will create a dummy list of pages with our cities from the previous project:

```
@Composable
fun CityTabCarousel(
    pages: MutableList<String> = arrayListOf(
        "Spain",
        "New York",
        "Tokyo",
        "Switzerland",
```

```
        "Singapore",
        "Paris" )) {. . .}
```

4. We will need to change the color of the button based on the state, and to do this; we need to use `LocalContext`, which provides the context we can use. We will also need to create a `var pagerState = rememberPagerState()`, which will remember our pager state, and finally, when clicked, we will need to move to the next city in our pager, which will be very helpful. Hence, go ahead and add the following to the `CityTabCarousel` composable function:

```
val context = LocalContext.current
var pagerState = rememberPagerState()
val coroutineScope = rememberCoroutineScope()
```

5. Now, let's create the `Column` element and add our `ScrollableTabRow()` composable function:

```
Column {
    ScrollableTabRow(
        selectedTabIndex = pagerState.currentPage,
        indicator = { tabPositions ->
            TabRowDefaults.Indicator(...)
        },
        edgePadding = 0.dp,
        backgroundColor = Color(
            context.resources.getColor(R.color.white,
                null)),
    ) {
        pages.forEachIndexed { index, title ->
            val isSelected =
                pagerState.currentPage == index
            TabHeader(
                title,
                isSelected,
                onClick = { coroutineScope.launch {
                pagerState.animateScrollToPage(index)
                } },
            )
        }
    }
```

6. Add `Text()` and `TabHeader()` for `HorizontalPager`:

```
    HorizontalPager(
        count = pages.size,
        state = pagerState,
```

```
        modifier = Modifier
            .fillMaxWidth()
            .fillMaxHeight()
            .background(Color.White)

    ) { page ->
        Text(
            text = "Display City Name:
                ${pages[page]}",
            modifier = Modifier.fillMaxWidth(),
            style = TextStyle(
                textAlign = TextAlign.Center
            )
        )
    }
```

7. Please download the entire code for this recipe by following the link provided in the *Technical requirements* section to add all the required code. Finally, run the `@Preview` function, and your app should look like *Figure 2.8*.

Figure 2.8 – Tabs with cities

How it works...

Accompanist comes with some significant libraries – for example, System UI Controller, AppCompact Compose Theme Adapter, Material Theme Adapter, Pager, Drawable Painter, and Flow Layouts, just to mention a few.

The `ScrollableTabRow()` that we use inside `Column` in the `CityTabCarousel` function contains a row of tabs and helps display an indicator underneath the currently focused or selected tab. In addition, as the name suggests, it enables scrolling and you do not have to implement further scrolling tooling. It also places its tab offsets at the starting edge, and you can quickly scroll tabs that are off-screen, as you will see when you run the `@Preview` function and play around with it.

When we invoke `remember()`, in Compose, this means we keep any value consistent across recomposition. Compose provides this function to help us store single objects in memory. When we trigger our application to run, `remember()` stores the initial value. As the word means, it simply retains the value and returns the stored value so that the composable function can use it.

Furthermore, whenever the stored value changes, you can update it, and the `remember()` function will keep it. The next time we trigger another run in our app and recomposition occurs, the `remember()` function will provide the latest stored value.

You will also notice our `MutableList<String>` is indexed at each position, and we do this to check which is selected. It is within this Lambda that we call `TabHeader` and showcase the selected tab pages. `forEachIndexed` performs the given action on each element, providing a sequential index of elements. We also ensure when a user clicks on a specific tab, we are on the right page:

```
onClick = { coroutineScope.launch { pagerState.
animateScrollToPage(index) } }
```

`HorizontalPager` is a horizontally scrolling layout that allows our users to flip between items from left to right. It takes in several inputs, but we supply it with the count, state, and modifier to decorate it in our use case. In the Lambda, we display text – in our example, showing which page we are on, which helps when navigating, as shown in *Figure 2.9*:

```
@ExperimentalPagerApi
@Composable
@ComposableInferredTarget
public fun HorizontalPager(
    count: Int,
    modifier: Modifier,
    state: PagerState,
    reverseLayout: Boolean,
    itemSpacing: Dp,
    contentPadding: PaddingValues,
    verticalAlignment: Alignment.Vertical,
    flingBehavior: FlingBehavior,
    key: ((Int) -> Any)?,
    userScrollEnabled: Boolean,
    content: @Composable() (PagerScope.(Int) -> Unit)
): Unit
```

Figure 2.9 – HorizontalPager

Our `TabHeader` composable function has a `Box()`; a box in Jetpack Compose will always size itself to fit the content, and this is subject to the specified constraints. In our example, we decorate our `Box` with the selectable modifier, which configures components to be selectable as part of a mutually exclusive group, allowing each item to be selected only once at any given time.

> **Important note**
>
> Ensure your target and compile SDK targets 33. In addition, you will notice that most Accompanist's libraries are experimental, which means they can change. There is debate on whether to use this in your production, so you should always consult your team on these APIs. To see the entire list of libraries supported by Accompanist, you can follow this link: `https://github.com/google/accompanist`.

Implementing animations in Compose

Animation in Android is the process of adding motion effects to views. This can be achieved using images, text, or even starting a new screen where the transition is noticeable using motion effects. Animations are vital in Modern Android Development since modern UIs are more interactive and adaptive to smoother experiences, and users like them.

Furthermore, applications these days are rated based on how great their UI and user experiences are, hence the need to ensure your application is modern and robust. In this example, we will build a collapsing toolbar, an animation that is widely used in the Android world.

Getting ready

We will continue using the `Compose Basics` project.

How to do it...

We will be building a collapsing toolbar in this recipe; there are other great animations you can now build utilizing the power of Compose. The power is in your hands:

1. We will not need to add any dependency to this recipe. We already have everything in place. So, let us go ahead and create a new package and add a Kotlin file, `collapsingtoolbar`.
2. Inside the Kotlin file, go ahead and create a new composable function, `CollapsingToolBarExample()`:

```
@Composable
fun CollapsingToolbarExample() {...}
```

3. We will have all our needed composable functions in a box; you can refer to the previous recipe to refresh your memory on that. We will also need to define the height at which we will start to collapse our view, and this can be based on preference; for our example, we can set `height` to `260.dp`:

```
private val height = 260.dp
private val titleToolbar = 50.dp
```

4. Let us go ahead and add more composable functions with dummy text data to display once we scroll our content. We can assume this app is used for reading information about the cities we display:

```
@Composable
fun CollapsingToolbarExample() {
    val scrollState: ScrollState =
        rememberScrollState(0)

    val headerHeight = with(LocalDensity.current) {
        height.toPx() }
    val toolbarHeight = with(LocalDensity.current) {
        titleToolbar.toPx() }

    Box(
        modifier = Modifier.fillMaxSize()
    ) {
        CollapsingHeader(scrollState, headerHeight)
        FactsAboutNewYork(scrollState)
```

```
            OurToolBar(scrollState, headerHeight,
                toolbarHeight)
            City()
        }
    }
```

5. In our `CollapsingHeader` function, we pass in the scroll state and the `headerHeight` a float. We decorate Box with a `Modifier.graphicLayer`, where we set a parallax effect to make it look good and presentable.
6. We also ensure we add a `Brush()` and set the colors we need, and specify where it should start:

```
Box(
    Modifier
        .fillMaxSize()
        .background(
            brush = Brush.verticalGradient(
                colors = listOf(Color.Transparent,
                Color(0xFF6D38CA)),
                startY = 1 * headerHeight / 5
            )
        )
)
...
```

7. `FactsAboutNewYork` is not a complex composable function, just dummy text; then, finally, in `ToolBar`, we utilize `AnimatedVisibility` and declare our `enter` and `exit` transition:

```
AnimatedVisibility(
    visible = showToolbar,
    enter = fadeIn(animationSpec = tween(200)),
    exit = fadeOut(animationSpec = tween(200))
) {
...
```

8. Finally, run the `@Preview` function, and you will have a collapsible toolbar, which brings a smooth experience to your UI. In addition, get the entire code in the *Technical requirements* section.

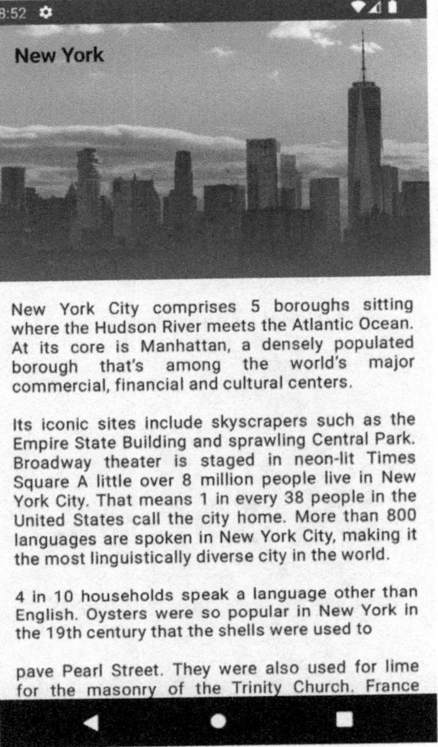

Figure 2.10 – A collapsible toolbar

How it works...

In Modern Android Development, the Jetpack Compose library has many animation APIs that are available as composable functions. For example, you might want your image or text to fade in and fade out.

Hence, if you are animating appearance and disappearance, which can be for an image, a text, a radio group, a button, and so on, you can use `AnimatedVisibility` to achieve this. Otherwise, if you are swapping content based on the state and want your content to crossfade, you can use `CrossFade`, or `AnimatedContent`.

`val headerHeight = with(LocalDensity.current) { height.toPx() }` provides density, which will be used to transform the DP and SP units, and we can use this when we provide the DP, which we will do and later convert into the body of our layout.

You can call the modifier and use `graphicsLayer` to update any of the content above it independently to minimize invalidated content. In addition, `graphicsLayer` can be used to apply effects such as scaling, rotation, opacity, shadow, or even clipping.

`translationY = -scroll.value.toFloat() / 2f` basically sets the vertical pixel offset of the layer relative to its top bound. The default value is always zero, but you can customize this to fit your needs. We also ensure the gradient is only applied to wrapping the title in `startY = 1 * headerHeight / 5`.

`EnterTransition` defines how the target content should appear; a target here can be an image, a text, or even a radio group. On the other hand, `ExitTransition` defines how the initial target content should disappear when exiting the app or navigating away.

`AnimatedContent` offers `slideIntoContainer` and `slideOutOfContainer`, and it animates its content as it changes based on the target state, which is remarkable. In addition, you can also encapsulate a transition and make it reusable by creating a class that holds all your animation values and an `Update()` function, which returns an instance of that class.

It is also fair to mention that, as with the old ways of doing animation in Android using `MotionLayout`, there are many ways to do transitions in Jetpack Compose. For instance, in *Table 2.1*, you will see the different types of transitions:

EnterTransition	**ExitTransition**
SlideIn	SlideOut
FadeIn	FadeOut
SlideInHorizontally	SlideOutHorizontally
SlideInVertically	SlideOutVertically
ScaleIn	SlaceOut
ExpandIn	ShrinkOut
ExpandHorizontally	ShinkHorizontally
ExpandVertically	ShrinkVertically

Table 2.1 – A table showing different types of transitions

In addition, you can add your own custom animation effects in Jetpack Compose beyond the already built-in enter and exit animations by simply accessing the elemental transition instance via the `transition` property inside the content lambda for `AnimatedVisibility`. You will also notice any animation states that have been added.

Implementing accessibility in Jetpack Compose

As we build Android applications, we need to always have accessibility in the back of our minds because this makes technology inclusive and ensures all people with special needs are considered as we build applications.

Accessibility should be a team effort. If well handled, the advantages include having more people using your application. An accessible application is better for everyone. You also reduce the risk of being sued.

There are different types of disabilities, such as visual, aural, and motor impairments. If you open your **Accessibility** settings, you will see the different options that people with disabilities use on their devices.

Getting ready

Like previous recipes, we will continue using our sample project from previous recipes; you do not need to install anything.

How to do it...

For this recipe, we will describe the visual elements, which are very vital:

1. By default, when we add an `Image` function, you might notice that it has two parameters, a painter for the image and a content description to visually describe the element:

```
Image(painter = , contentDescription = )
```

2. When you set the content description to `null`, you indicate to the Android framework that this element does not have an associated action or state. So, let's go ahead and update all our content descriptions:

```
Image(
    modifier = modifier
    painter = painterResource(city.imageResourceId),
    contentDescription =
        stringResource(R.string.city_images))
)
```

3. Make sure you add the string to the `string res` folder:

```
<string name="city_images">City Images</string>
```

4. So, go ahead and ensure you add a content description for every image that requires it.
5. In Compose, you can easily indicate whether a text is a heading by specifying this in the modifier and using semantics to show that that is a heading. Let's add that in our decorated text:

```
...
modifier = Modifier
      .padding(18.dp)
      .semantics { heading() }
...
```

6. Finally, we can go ahead and compile, run, and test whether our application is accessible by following this link on how to manually test using talkback or using automated testing: `https://developer.android.com/guide/topics/ui/accessibility/testing`.

How it works...

Jetpack Compose is built with accessibility in mind; that is to say, material components such as `RadioButton`, `Switch`, and so on have their size internally set, but only when these components can receive user interactions.

Furthermore, any screen element that users can click on or interact with should be large enough for reliable interaction. A standard format sets these elements to a size of at least `48dp` for `width` and `height`.

For example, `Switch` has its `onCheckChanged` parameter set to a non-null value, including width and height of at least `48dp`; we would have `CheckableSwitch()`, and `NonCheckableSwitch()`:

```
@Composable
fun CheckableSwitch(){
    var checked by remember { mutableStateOf(false) }
    Switch(checked = checked, onCheckedChange = {} )
}

@Composable
fun NonCheckableSwitch(){
    var checked by remember { mutableStateOf(false) }
    Switch(checked = checked, onCheckedChange = null )
}
```

Once you have implemented accessibility in your applications, you can easily test it by installing analysis tools from the Play Store – `uiautomatorviewer` and `lint`. You can also automate your tests using Espresso or Roboelectric to check for accessibility support.

Finally, you can manually test your application for accessibility support by going to **Settings**, then to **Accessibility**, and selecting **talkback**. This is found at the top of the screen; then press **On** or **Off** to turn the talkback functionality on or off. Then, navigate to the dialog confirmation, and click **OK** to confirm permission.

There's more...

There is more regarding accessibility that developers should consider as they build their applications, including a state with which they should be able to notify their users on whether a `Switch` button has been selected. This ensures their applications support accessibility and are up to standard.

Implementing declarative graphics using Jetpack Compose

In Android development, your application might have a different need, and this need might be building your own custom graphics for an intended purpose. This is very common in many stable and large Android code bases. The essential part of any custom view is its appearance. Furthermore, custom drawing can be a very easy or complex task based on the needs of your application. In Modern Android Development, Jetpack Compose makes it easier to work with custom graphics simply because the demand is immense. For example, many applications may need to control what happens on their screen accurately; the use case might be as simple as putting a circle on the screen or building more complex graphics to handle known use cases.

Getting ready

Open the `Compose Basics` project to get started with this recipe. You can find the entire code in the *Technical requirements* section.

How to do it...

In our project, let us create a new package and call it `circularexample`; inside this package, create a Kotlin file and call it `DrawCircleCompose`; inside the file, create a `CircleProgressIndicatorExample` composable function. You will not need to import anything for now:

1. Let us now go ahead and define our composable function. Since, in our example, we want to display a tracker in a circle, we need to float to fill in our circle. We will also define the colors to help us identify the progress:

```
@Composable
fun CircleProgressIndicatorExample(tracker: Float, progress:
Float) {
    val circleColors = listOf(
```

```
        colorResource(id = R.color.purple_700),
        colorResource(id = R.color.teal_200)
    )
```

2. Now, let's call `Canvas` to draw our arc. We give our circle the size of `200.dp` with `8.dp` padding. Where it gets interesting is in `onDraw`. `startAngle` is set at `-90`; the start angle is set in degrees to understand it better.

   The zero represents 3 o'clock, and you can also play around with your start angle to see how `-90` translates. The `useCenter` Boolean indicates whether arc is to close the center of the bounds. Hence, in our case, we set it to `false`. Then, finally, we set the `style`, which can be anything based on our preference:

```
Canvas(
    modifier = Modifier
        .size(200.dp)
        .padding(8.dp),
    onDraw = {
        this.drawIntoCanvas {
            drawArc(
                color = colorSecondary,
                startAngle = -90f,
                sweepAngle = 360f,
                useCenter = false,
                style = Stroke(width = 55f, cap =
                    StrokeCap.Butt),
                size = Size(size.width, size.height)
            )
colorResource(id = R.color.teal_200)
  . . .
```

3. We have just drawn the first part of the circle; now, we need to draw the progress with a `Brush`, which utilizes `linearGradient`:

```
drawArc(
    brush = Brush.linearGradient(colors =
        circleColors),
    startAngle = -90f,
    sweepAngle = progress(tracker, progress),
    useCenter = false,
    style = Stroke(width = 55f, cap =
        StrokeCap.Round),
```

```
        size = Size(size.width, size.height)
    ) . . .
    . . .
```

4. Finally, our `progress` function tells `sweepAngle` where our progress should be based on our tracking abilities:

```
    private fun progress(tracker: Float, progress: Float): Float {
        val totalProgress = (progress * 100) / tracker
        return ((360 * totalProgress) / 100)
    }
    . . .
```

5. Run the `preview` function, and you should see a circular progress indicator as in *Figure 2.11*.

Figure 2.11 – Showing a circular progress image

> **Important note**
>
> The `Canvas` composable function uses `Canvas` to Compose an object, which, in turn, creates and helps manage a view-base Canvas. It is also important to mention that Compose makes it easier for developers by maintaining the state and creating and freeing any necessary helper objects.

How it works...

Generally, `Canvas` allows you to specify an area on the screen where you want to draw. In the old way of building Android applications, we also utilized `Canvas`, and now in Compose, it is more powerful and valuable.

`linearGradient` create a linear gradient with the specified colors along the provided start and end coordinates. For our example, we give it simple colors that come with the project.

The drawing functions have instrumental default parameters that you can use. For instance, by default, `drawArc`, as you can see, takes in several inputs:

```
fun drawArc(
    brush: Brush,
    startAngle: Float,
    sweepAngle: Float,
    useCenter: Boolean,
    topLeft: Offset = Offset.Zero,
    size: Size = this.size.offsetSize(topLeft),
    /*@FloatRange(from = 0.0, to = 1.0)*/
    alpha: Float = 1.0f,
    style: DrawStyle = Fill,
    colorFilter: ColorFilter? = null,
    blendMode: BlendMode = DefaultBlendMode
)
```

Figure 2.12 – Showing what drawArc takes as input

`sweepAngle` in our example, which is the size of the arc in the degree that is drawn clockwise relative to `startAngle`, returns a function that calculates progress. This function can be customized to fit your needs. In our example, we pass in a tracker and progress and return a float.

Since we want to fill the circle, we create `cal totalProgress`, which checks *progress * 100* divided by the tracker, and we return *360 (circle) * our progress divided by 100*. You can customize this function to fit your needs. You can also write code to listen to where you are and make the progress move based on your input value from a listener you create.

There's more...

There is more you can do with `Canvas` and custom drawing. One amazing way to enhance your knowledge on the topic is to look into old solutions posted on Stack Overflow, such as drawing a heart or any other shape, and see whether you can do the same in Compose.

3

Handling the UI State in Jetpack Compose and Using Hilt

All Android applications display the state to users, which helps inform users on what the outcome is and when. The **state** in an Android application is any value that changes over time, and a good example is a toast that shows a message when there is an error. In this chapter, readers will learn how to handle the UI state better with the new Jetpack library.

It is fair to say with great power comes great responsibility, and managing the state of any Composable component requires a distinct approach compared to using the older way of building Android views, or as many might call it, the imperative way. This means Jetpack's library, Compose, is entirely different from XML layouts.

Handling the UI state in the XML **View System** is very straightforward. The process entails setting the properties of the views to reflect the current state – that is, showing or hiding the views accordingly. For instance, when loading data from an API, you can hide the loading view, show the content view, and populate it with the desired views.

In Compose, however, it is impossible to change a Composable component once the application has drawn it. You can, however, change the values passed to each Composable by changing the state each Composable receives. Hence, learning about managing the state better when building robust Android applications will be handy.

In this chapter, we'll be covering the following recipes:

- Implementing **Dependency Injection** (**DI**) with Jetpack Hilt
- Implementing `ViewModel` classes and understanding the state in Compose
- Implementing Compose in existing an XML layout-based project

- Understanding and handling recomposition in Jetpack Compose
- Writing UI tests for your Compose views
- Writing tests for your `ViewModel` classes

Technical requirements

The complete source code for this chapter can be found at `https://github.com/PacktPublishing/Modern-Android-13-Development-Cookbook/tree/main/chapter_three`.

Implementing DI with Jetpack Hilt

In object-oriented programming, DI is vital. Some people use it, and some prefer not to use it for their own reasons. However, DI is the practice of designing objects in a manner where they receive instances of the object from other pieces of code instead of constructing them internally.

If you know of the SOLID principles, you know their primary goal is to make software design easier to maintain, read, test, and build upon. In addition, DI helps us follow some of the SOLID principles. The dependency inversion principle allows the code base to be easily expanded and extended with new functionalities and improves reusability. In Modern Android Development, DI is essential, and we will implement it in our application in this recipe.

There are different types of libraries that you can use in Android for DI, such as Koin, Dagger, and Hilt; Hilt harnesses the power of Dagger and benefits from compile-time correctness, good runtime performance, Android studio support, and scalability. For this recipe, we will use Hilt, which provides containers for every Android class in our project and automatically manages their life cycle.

Getting ready

Just like in previous recipes, we will use the project we have used in previous recipes to add DI.

How to do it...

Hilt uses Java features; make sure your project is in the `app/build.gradle`, and you have the following compile options:

```
android {
    ...
    compileOptions {
        sourceCompatibility JavaVersion.VERSION_11
        targetCompatibility JavaVersion.VERSION_11
    }
}
```

This is already added automatically, but make sure you check that you have it just in case. Let's get started:

1. First, we must add the `Hilt-android-gradle-plugin` plugin into our project's root file, `build.gradle(Project:SampleLogin)`:

```
plugins {
    id 'com.google.dagger.Hilt.android' version '2.44'
apply false
}
```

2. Then, in our `app/build.gradle` file, add these dependencies, and sync the project. It should run without any issues:

```
plugins {
    id 'kotlin-kapt'
    id 'dagger.Hilt.android.plugin'
}
dependencies {
    implementation "com.google.dagger:Hilt-
        android:2.44"
    kapt "com.google.dagger:Hilt-compiler:2.44"
}
```

3. Now, let's go ahead and add the `Application` class. All apps that use Hilt must have an `Application` class annotated with `@HiltAndroidApp`, and we need to call the `Application` class that we create in `Manifest`:

```
@HiltAndroidApp
class LoginApp : Application()
```

4. In our `Manifest` folder, let's add `LoginApp`:

```
<application
    android:name=".LoginApp"
  ...
```

5. Now that we have the setup done, we need to start working with Hilt by adding the required annotations to our class. In `MainActivity.kt`, we need to add the `@AndroidEntryPoint` annotation:

```
@AndroidEntryPoint
class MainActivity : ComponentActivity() {
  ...
```

6. Let's go ahead and display what we did by running the `./gradlew :app:dependencies` command, and we will see something similar to *Figure 3.1*.

```
madonasyombua@Madonas-MacBook-Pro Sample Login % ./gradlew :app:dependencies
Starting a Gradle Daemon, 1 incompatible Daemon could not be reused, use --status for details

> Task :app:dependencies

------------------------------------------------------------
Project ':app'
------------------------------------------------------------

_agp_internal_javaPreCompileDebugAndroidTest_kaptClasspath
\--- com.google.dagger:hilt-compiler:2.42
     +--- com.google.dagger:dagger:2.42
     |    \--- javax.inject:javax.inject:1
     +--- com.google.dagger:dagger-compiler:2.42
     |    +--- com.google.dagger:dagger:2.42 (*)
     |    +--- com.google.dagger:dagger-producers:2.42
     |    |    +--- com.google.dagger:dagger:2.42 (*)
     |    |    +--- com.google.guava:failureaccess:1.0.1
     |    |    +--- com.google.guava:guava:31.0.1-jre
     |    |    |    +--- com.google.guava:failureaccess:1.0.1
     |    |    |    +--- com.google.guava:listenablefuture:9999.0-empty-to-avoid-conflict-with-guava
     |    |    |    +--- com.google.code.findbugs:jsr305:3.0.2
     |    |    |    +--- org.checkerframework:checker-qual:3.12.0
     |    |    |    +--- com.google.errorprone:error_prone_annotations:2.7.1
     |    |    |    \--- com.google.j2objc:j2objc-annotations:1.3
     |    |    +--- javax.inject:javax.inject:1
     |    |    \--- org.checkerframework:checker-compat-qual:2.5.5
```

Figure 3.1 – Dagger Hilt dependency tree

You can also view the dependency in Android Studio. That is by clicking on the **Gradle** tab on the right-hand side and selecting **expand:yourmodule | Tasks | android**. Then, finally, double-click on **androidDependencies** to run it.

Finally, compile and run the project; it should run successfully.

How it works...

`@HiltAndroidApp` triggers Hilt's code generation, including a base class for our application, which acts as the application-level dependency container. The `@AndroidEntryPoint` annotation adds a DI container to the Android class annotated with it. When using Hilt, the generated Hilt component is attached to the Application object's life cycle and provides its dependencies. Hilt currently supports the following Android classes:

- `ViewModel` annotated as `@HiltViewModel`
- `Application` annotated as `@HiltAndroidApp`
- `Activity`
- `Fragment`
- `View`
- `Service`
- `BroadcastReceiver`

We will use other necessary annotations in Hilt later, for instance, the `@Module` annotation, `@InstallIn`, and `@Provides`. The `@Module` annotation means the class in which you can add binding for types that cannot be injected in the constructor. `@InstallIn` indicates which Hilt-generated DI container (or singleton component) has to be available in the code module binding.

Finally, `@Provides` binds a type that cannot be constructor injected. Its return type is the binding type, it can take dependency parameters, and every time you need an instance, the function body is executed if the type is not scoped.

Implementing ViewModel classes and understanding the state in Compose

In Android, a `ViewModel` is a class responsible for consciously managing the UI-related data life cycle. There is also a lot of debate in the community about whether developers should use `ViewModel` in Compose or not. However, Manuel Vivo, a senior Android developer relations engineer at Google, says:

"I'd include them if their benefits apply to your app. No need to use them if you handle all configuration changes yourself and don't use Navigation Compose. Otherwise, use ViewModels not to reinvent the wheel."

"On the other hand, the debate as to why one should not use ViewModels is based on the argument that in pure Compose, since Compose handles configuration changes, having your Composable functions reference the ViewModel is unnecessary."

You can also refer to this tweet by Jim Sproch: `https://twitter.com/JimSproch/status/1397169679647444993`.

> **Note**
>
> You can find more info about the benefits of using the ViewModel here: `https://developer.android.com/jetpack/compose/state#viewmodels-source-of-truth`.

This means using `ViewModel` to handle the state in your application will be a question of personal choice with Jetpack Compose. The currently recommended architecture pattern in Android is **Model-View-View-Model** (**MVVM**), and many applications use it.

Jetpack Compose uses a unidirectional data flow design pattern; this means the data or state only streams down while the events stream up. Hence, a clear understanding of how we can utilize the unidirectional pattern to make our code more readable, maintainable, and testable as much as possible using the `ViewModel` class will be helpful.

In addition, `ViewModel` is suitable for providing your application with access to business logic, preparing the data for presentation on the screen, and making your code testable.

Getting ready

In this recipe, we will work with a pre-built skeleton `SampleLogin` project, which you can download from the *Technical requirements* section. We will use Hilt in this recipe since the project uses Hilt, but we will explain Hilt in a next recipe.

How to do it...

You will now create a `ViewModel` class and modify most of the code in the `LoginContent` Kotlin file:

1. To keep our classes and files well organized, let's go ahead and first create a package to hold our UI and view models. Navigate to the main `Package` folder, right-click to open a prompt, then go down to **Package**, and a dialog with a package name will appear.

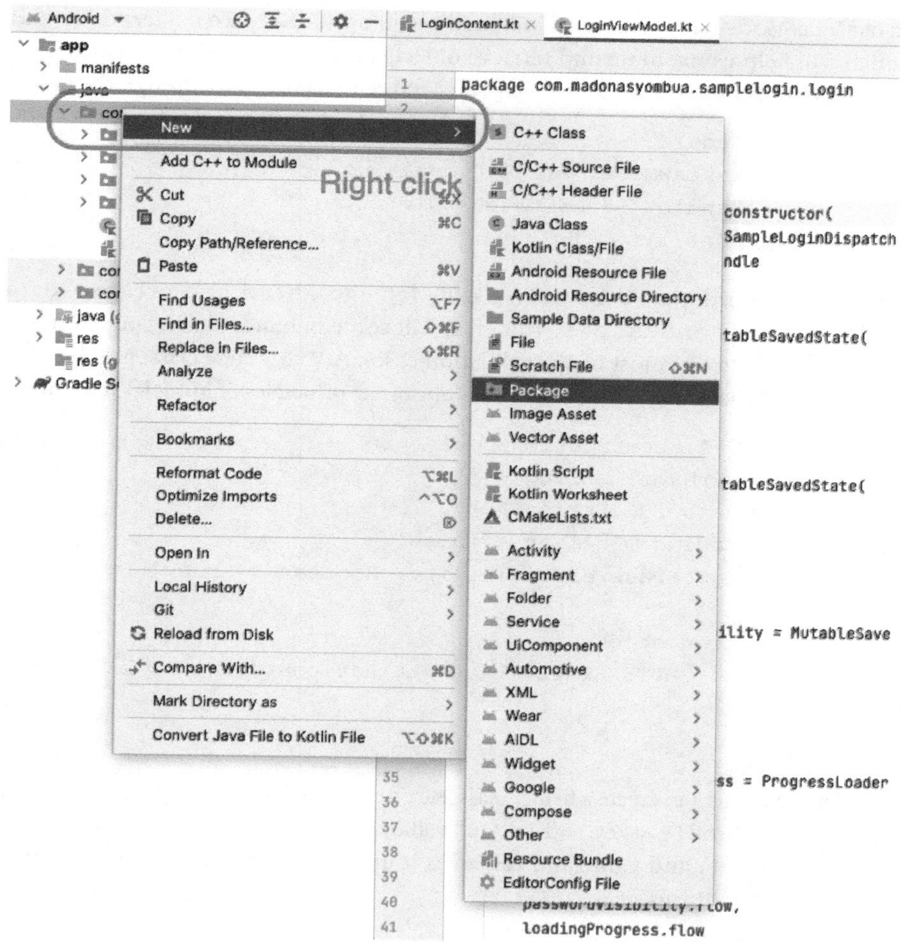

Figure 3.2 – How to create a package

2. Name the package `Login`; inside **Login**, we will move our `LoginContent` file and add the new class, `LoginViewModel`, there. Go ahead and create a `ViewModel` class:

```
class LoginViewModel {...}
```

3. Now that we have created a `LoginViewModel` class, we need to add a DI annotation of `HiltViewModel` and ensure we extend the `ViewModel` class:

```
@HiltViewModel
class LoginViewModel @Inject constructor(
): ViewModel(){. . .}
```

4. In our `ViewModel` constructor, we will need to add `stateHandle: SavedStateHandle`, which will help us maintain and retrieve objects to and from the saved state. These values persist even after the system kills the process and remain available through the same object:

```
@HiltViewModel
class LoginViewModel @Inject constructor(
    stateHandle: SavedStateHandle
) : ViewModel() {...}
```

5. Before we build our `ViewModel`, let's go ahead and create a data class, `AuthenticationState()`. This class will come in handy during our testing since we need to be able to test most of our validation cases. A `View` state class, plus having a single source of truth, has many advantages and is one of the principles of **Model-View-Intent (MVI)**:

```
data class AuthenticationState(
    val userName: String = "",
    val password: String = "",
    val loading: Boolean = false,
    var togglePasswordVisibility: Boolean = true
) {
    companion object {
        val EMPTY_STATE = AuthenticationState()
    }
}
```

6. Now, let's go ahead and create a helper class, `MutableSavedState<T>()`, which will take in `savedStateHandle`, a key, and a default value. This class acts as a `MutableStateFlow()` but saves the data and value and retrieves it upon the application's death with the help of `SavedStateHandle`:

```
class MutableSavedState<T>(
    private val savedStateHandle: SavedStateHandle,
    private val key: String,
    defValue: T,
) {
  . . .
}
```

7. Now, let's go ahead and create callbacks that will be invoked when a user enters their username and password in our `LoginViewModel`:

```
private val username = MutableSavedState(
    stateHandle,
    "UserName",
```

```
        defValue = ""
    )
    fun userNameChanged(userName: String){
        username.value = userName
    }
```

8. Go ahead and do the same for password and password toggle visibility.
9. Now, we need to create a `combineFlows` helper class. You can combine more than two flows in Kotlin; a coroutine `flow` is a type that emits multiple values sequentially, as opposed to the `suspend` function, which returns a single value. More details on how to combine flows can be found at `combine(flow1, flow2, flow3, flow4) {t1, t2, t3, t4 -> resultMapper}.stateIn(scope)`:

```
fun <T1, T2, T3, T4, T5, T6, R> combine(
    flow: Flow<T1>,
    flow2: Flow<T2>,
    flow3: Flow<T3>,
    flow4: Flow<T4>,
    flow5: Flow<T5>,
    flow6: Flow<T6>,
    transform: suspend (T1, T2, T3, T4, T5, T6) -> R
): Flow<R> = combine(
        combine(flow, flow2, flow3, ::Triple),
        combine(flow4, flow5, flow6, ::Triple)
) { t1, t2 ->
    transform(
        t1.first,
        t1.second,
        t1.third,
        t2.first,
        t2.second,
        t2.third
    )
}
```

Read more here – `https://stackoverflow.com/questions/67939183/kotlin-combine-more-than-2-flows`:

```
val state = combineFlows(
    username.flow,
    password.flow,
    passwordVisibilityToggle.flow,
    loadingProgress.flow
```

```
) { username, password, passwordToggle, isLoading ->
    AuthenticationState(
        userName = username,
        password = password,
        togglePasswordVisibility = passwordToggle,
        loading = isLoading
    )
}.stateIn(. . .)
```

10. Now, let's go ahead and create our helper class for using coroutines and call it `SampleLoginDispatchers()`; it will help us in testing our code and ensuring our code is easily readable. In addition, we use coroutine dispatchers that help determine what thread the corresponding coroutine should use for execution:

```
.stateIn(
    coroutineScope = viewModelScope + dispatchers.main,
    initialValue = AuthenticationState.EMPTY_STATE
)
```

`SharedFlow` represents a read-only state with a single updatable data value, which emits any updates to its collectors. On the other hand, a state flow is a hot flow because its active instance exists independently of the presence of collectors.

11. The `SharingStarted` coroutine flow operator in Android is used to share the execution of a flow among multiple collectors. It is commonly used to create a "hot" flow, which means that the flow starts emitting data as soon as it is created, and the data is shared among all the active collectors of the flow. These can be back-to-back emissions of the same command and have no effect:

```
fun <T> Flow<T>.stateIn(
    coroutineScope: CoroutineScope,
    initialValue: T
): StateFlow<T> = stateIn(
    scope = coroutineScope,
    started = SharingStarted.WhileSubscribed(5000),
    initialValue = initialValue
)
```

12. There are four types of dispatchers. In our example, we will only use three. In addition, you can inject a single dispatcher and achieve the same result without the class; hence, this can be preference-based. See how it works for the four types of dispatchers:

```
class SampleLoginDispatchers(
    val default: CoroutineDispatcher,
```

```
    val main: CoroutineDispatcher,
    val io: CoroutineDispatcher
) {
    companion object {
        fun createTestDispatchers(coroutineDispatcher:
        CoroutineDispatcher): SampleLoginDispatchers {
            return SampleLoginDispatchers(
                default = coroutineDispatcher,
                main = coroutineDispatcher,
                io = coroutineDispatcher
            )
        }
    }
}
```

Now that we have created our helper class, we must provide the dispatcher via DI. We have an entire recipe dedicated to Hilt, so we will look at the concepts and what the annotations mean in the Hilt recipe.

13. Create a new package and call the package `di`. In this package, create a new object and call it `AppModule`; we will provide our dispatcher to the `ViewModel` constructor via the dependency graph:

```
@Module
@InstallIn(SingletonComponent::class)
object AppModule {
    @Provides
    fun provideSlimeDispatchers():
    SampleLoginDispatchers {
        return SampleLoginDispatchers(
        default = Dispatchers.Default,
        main = Dispatchers.Main,
        io = Dispatchers.IO
        )
    }
}
```

14. We will now need to go to `LoginContent` and modify the code – that is, by adding callbacks that will correspond to our `ViewModel`, and whenever we have a view – for example, `UserNameField()` – we will use the callback. See the sample code:

```
@Composable
fun LoginContent(
    modifier: Modifier = Modifier,
```

```
    uiState: AuthenticationState,
    onUsernameUpdated: (String) -> Unit,
    onPasswordUpdated: (String) -> Unit,
    onLogin: () -> Unit,
    passwordToggleVisibility: (Boolean) -> Unit
){
. . .
UserNameField(authState = uiState, onValueChanged =
onUsernameUpdated)
PasswordInputField(
    text = stringResource(id = R.string.password),
    authState = uiState,
    onValueChanged = onPasswordUpdated,
    passwordToggleVisibility =
        passwordToggleVisibility
)
LoginButton(
    text = stringResource(id = R.string.sign_in),
    enabled = if (uiState.isValidForm()) {
        !uiState.loading
    } else {
        false
    },
    onLoginClicked = {
        onLogin.invoke()
    },
    isLoading = uiState.loading
). . .}
```

15. Now, in our `LoginContentScreen` Composable function, we will pass our `LoginViewModel`:

```
@Composable
fun LoginContentScreen(
    loginViewModel: LoginViewModel,
    onRegisterNavigateTo: () -> Unit
) {
    val viewState by
        loginViewModel.state.collectAsState()
    LoginContent(
        uiState = viewState,
        onUsernameUpdated =
```

```
            loginViewModel::userNameChanged,
        onPasswordUpdated =
            loginViewModel::passwordChanged,
        onLogin = loginViewModel::login,
        passwordToggleVisibility =
            loginViewModel::passwordVisibility,
        onRegister = onRegisterNavigateTo
    )
}
```

16. Finally, in `MainActivity`, we can now go ahead and call `LoginContentScreen`, pass in our `ViewModel`, and also specify what action we want when the user clicks `onRegister`:

```
LoginContentScreen(loginViewModel = HiltViewModel(),
onRegisterNavigateTo = {. . .}
```

17. For the entire code, please ensure you check out the link in the *Technical requirements* section.

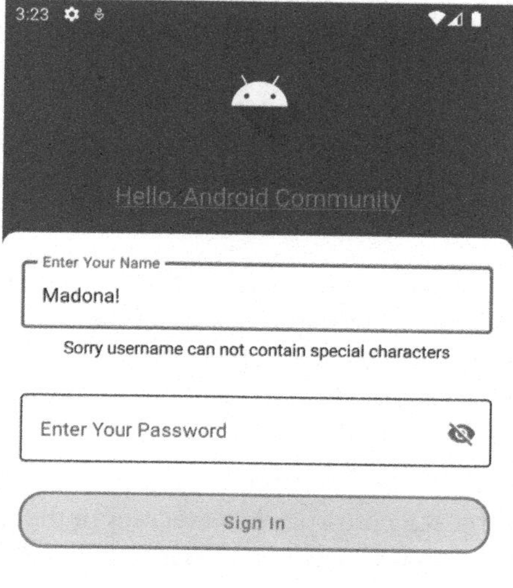

Figure 3.3 – Error state display when we enter a special character !

How it works...

Jetpack Compose uses a unidirectional data flow design pattern. This means the data or state only streams down while the events stream up, as shown in *Figure 3.4*.

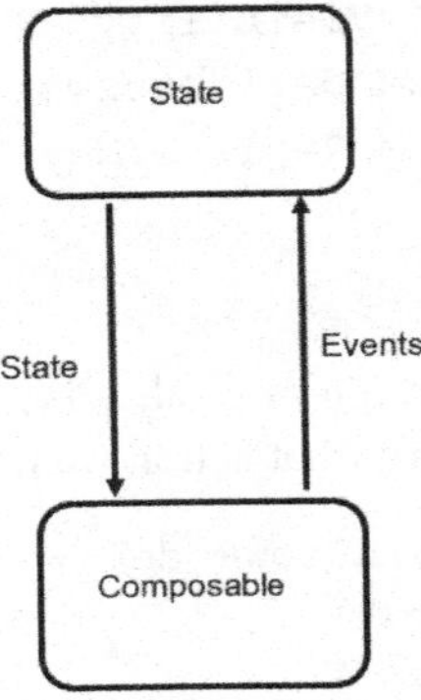

Figure 3.4 – A unidirectional data flow

That is to say, Composable functions receive the state and then display it on the screen. On the other hand, an event can cause the state to need to be updated and come from either a Composable or any other part of your application. Furthermore, whatever handles the state, in our case, `ViewModel`, receives the event and adjusts the state for us.

We also use coroutines, which are nothing but lightweight threads, and they help us handle synchronous and asynchronous programming easily. Furthermore, coroutines allow execution to be suspended and resumed later. The main advantages are that they are lightweight, have built-in cancellation support, have lower chances of memory leaks, and the Jetpack libraries provide coroutine support.

There are four types of dispatchers:

- **The Main dispatcher**: The `Main` dispatcher executes in the main thread, which is usually used when your application needs to perform some UI operations within a coroutine. This is because the UI can only be changed from the main thread. Another name for the main thread is the UI thread.
- **The IO dispatcher**: The `IO` dispatcher starts the coroutine in the I/O thread; I/O simply means input and output in programming. This is also used to perform all data work, such as networking, reading, or writing from the database. You can simply say fetching data from the I/O operation is done in the I/O thread.

- **The Default dispatcher**: The `Default` dispatcher starts in the default state. Your application can utilize this if you plan on doing complex long-running calculations, which can block the UI/main thread and make your UI freeze or cause an **Application Not Responding** (**ANR**) error. In addition, the default dispatchers are launched in `GlobalScope`, and you can use it by simply calling `GlobalScope.launch{...}`.
- **The Unconfined dispatcher**: Finally, `Unconfined`, as the name suggests, is a dispatcher not confined to any specific thread. This executes the dispatcher to perform its work in a current call frame and lets the coroutine resume whatever threads that are used by the corresponding function.

See also...

A lot was covered in this chapter, and it is fair to acknowledge that just this simple recipe cannot explain `ViewModel` in its entirety. To find out more, see the following link: `https://developer.android.com/topic/libraries/architecture/viewmodel`.

Implementing Compose in an existing XML layout-based project

Since Compose is a new UI framework, many code bases still rely heavily on XML layouts. However, many companies are opting to build new screens using Compose, and this is achievable by utilizing existing XML layouts and adding unique views using `ComposeView` XML tags. This recipe will look into adding a Compose view to an XML layout.

Getting ready

In this recipe, we can create a new project or opt to use an existing project that does not heavily rely on Compose. We will try to display `GreetingDialog` and use an XML layout to show how we can use the `ComposeView` tag in XML layouts. If you already have a project, you do not need to set this up; you can skip to *step 4* in the preceding *How to do it...* section.

How to do it...

Now let us go ahead and explore how we can utilize existing XML layouts with Compose:

1. Let's start by creating a new project or using a preexisting one; if you create a new activity that is not Compose, you can use `EmptyActivity`, and give it any name.
2. If you already have a project set up, you can skip this step. If you opt to create a new project, you will have `MainActivity`, and since this is the old way of creating views, you will notice an XML layout in the `resource` folder with a TextView that has `Hello world`. We can go ahead and remove that since we will not use it.

3. If you already have a project ready, you can launch `GreetingDialog` on any screen you want. Also, if you opt to create a button instead of a dialog, that is fine, too since the idea is to showcase how we can use XML tags in Jetpack Compose.

4. Now, let us go ahead and add an XML tag inside `activity_main.xml` and give our Compose view an `id` value. The first time you add `ComposeView`, you will see an error message if you still need to add the dependency. Go ahead and click **Add dependency on android.compose.ui:ui** and the project will sync as shown in *Figure 3.5*.

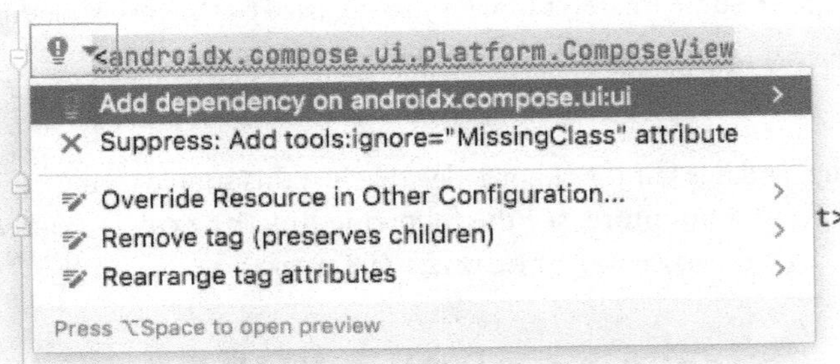

Figure 3.5 – A Compose view in XML

5. Once you have synced your project, the error will disappear, and you should be able to use this view in `MainActivity`, or where you want to use `ComposeView`:

```
<androidx.Compose.ui.platform.ComposeView
    android:id="@+id/alert_dialog"
    android:layout_width="match_parent"
    android:layout_height="match_parent"/>
```

6. Let's also add `viewBinding` to our `build.gradle(Module:app)` so that we can easily access our view in `MainActivity`. Also, if you already have `viewBinding` set up, you can skip this part:

```
buildFeatures{
    viewBinding true
}
```

7. Once we have synced the project, we can go ahead and, in `MainActivity`, access `ComposeView` through binding. Furthermore, it will have a `setContent{}` method where you can set all your Composables and wrap it into your Theme:

```
class MainActivity : AppCompatActivity() {

    private lateinit var activityBinding:
    ActivityMainBinding
```

```
    override fun onCreate(savedInstanceState: Bundle?)
    {
        super.onCreate(savedInstanceState)
        activityBinding =
           ActivityMainBinding.inflate(layoutInflater)
        setContentView(activityBinding.root)

        activityBinding.alertDialog.setContent {
            GreetingAlertDialog()
        }
    }
}
```

8. Our `GreetingAlertDialog()` will have an `AlertDialog()` Composable, a title, and text, which will provide our message as a simple text element. The title will say `Hello` since this is a greeting, and the message will be `Hello, and thank you for being part of the Android community`. You can customize this to fit your needs:

```
@Composable
fun SimpleAlertDialog() {
    AlertDialog(
        onDismissRequest = { },
        confirmButton = {
            TextButton(onClick = {})
            { Text(text = "OK") }
        },
        dismissButton = {
            TextButton(onClick = {})
            { Text(text = "OK") }
        },
        title = { Text(text = "Hello") },
        text = { Text(text = "Hello, and thank you for
        being part of the Android community") }
    )
}
```

9. To create Compose components, you will need to add the Compose Material Design dependency to your gradle app. Depending on what your application supports, you can utilize Compose Material 3 components, which is the next evolution of Material Design and comes with updated theming.

10. You can easily customize features such as dynamic color and more. We look into Material 3 in *Chapter 11, GUI Alerts – What's New in Menus, Dialog, Toast, Snackbars, and More in Modern*

Android Development. Hence, for now, since the application that I am using has not migrated to Material 3, I will use this import – `implementation "androidx.Compose.material:material:1.x.x"`. Here, you can use any import that fits your need.

11. You can also create a custom view that extends from `AbstractComposeView`:

```
class ComposeAlertDialogComponent @JvmOverloads constructor(
    context: Context,
    attrs: AttributeSet? = null,
    defStyle: Int = 0
) : AbstractComposeView(context, attrs, defStyle) {
        @Composable
    override fun Content() {
        GreetingAlertDialog()
    }
}
```

12. Finally, when you run your application, you should have a dialog that has a title and text; *Figure 3.6* shows a dialog from an already pre-existing project, so this will definitely vary based on what steps you took:

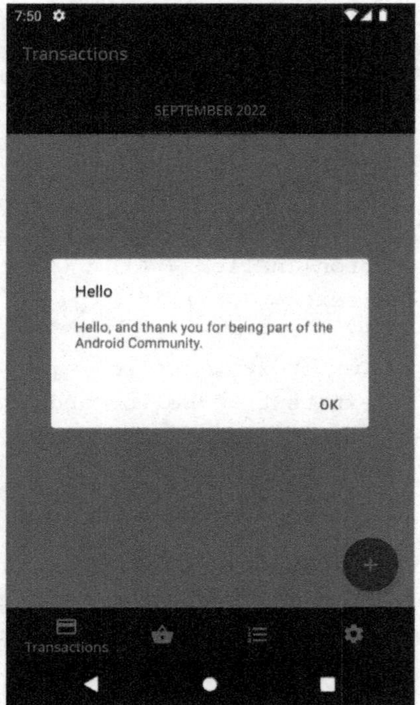

Figure 3.6 – Dialog Compose view in XML

How it works...

First, we inflate the XML layout, which we define in our layout `resource` folder. Then, using binding, we got `ComposeView` using the created XML ID, set a Compose strategy that works best for our host view, and called `setContent` to use Compose. In your activity, to be able to create any Compose-based screen, you have to ensure that you call the `setContent{}` method and pass whatever Composable function you have created.

To further explore the `setContent` method, it is written as an extension function of `ComponentActivity`, and it expects a Composable function as the last parameter. There is also a better way to demonstrate how `setContent{}` works to integrate a Composable tree into your Android application.

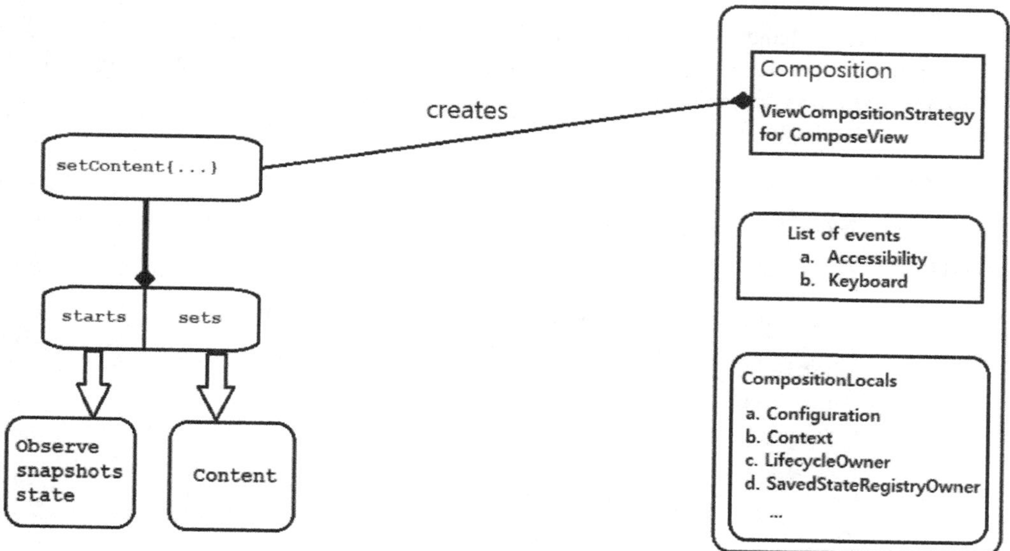

Figure 3.7 – This happens when you call setContent{}

`ViewCompositionStrategy` helps determines when to dispose of the composition; hence, Compose UI views such as `ComposeView` and the `AbstractComposeView` use `ViewCompositonStrategy`, which helps define this behavior.

You can learn more by following this link to learn more about the interoperability APIs: `https://developer.android.com/jetpack/compose/interop/interop-apis#composition-strategy`.

Understanding and handling recomposition in Jetpack Compose

Jetpack Compose is still very new, and many companies are starting to use it. Furthermore, Google has done a great job by giving developers significant documentation to help them embrace this new UI toolkit. However, despite all the documentation, one concept needs to be clarified. And that is recomposition.

Fair enough, all new software has its ups and downs, and as many people start using it, more people start giving feedback – hence, the need for more improvement. Recomposition, in Compose, involves calling your Composable again when the input changes. Or you can think of it when the composition structure and relation change.

Unless its parameters change, we want to avoid a Composable function being re-invoked in most use cases. So, in this recipe, we look into how recomposition happens and how you can debug and solve any recomposition in your application.

How to do it...

Since our view system is simple, we will be checking whether we have any recomposition in our `Login` project:

1. We can look at a simple example and how recomposition will occur:

   ```
   @Composable
   fun UserDetails(
       name: String,
       gender: String,
   ) {
       Box() {
           Text(name)
           Spacer()
           Text(gender)
       }}
   ```

   In our given example, the `Text` function will recompose when `name` changes and not when `gender` changes. In addition, the `gender:String` input value will recompose only when `gender` changes.

2. You can also launch and utilize **Layout Inspector** to debug recomposition. If it is not on your Android Studio dock, you can start it by going to **View | Tool Windows | Layout Inspector**. We will look into `LoginContent` and see whether we have any recomposition.

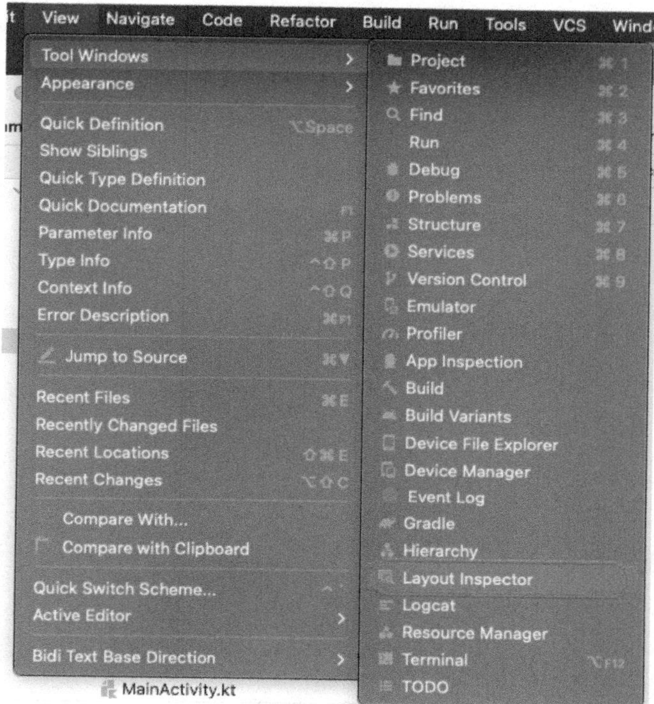

Figure 3.8 – Layout Inspector

3. Once you launch **Layout Inspector**, you need to ensure you have your emulator hooked to it.

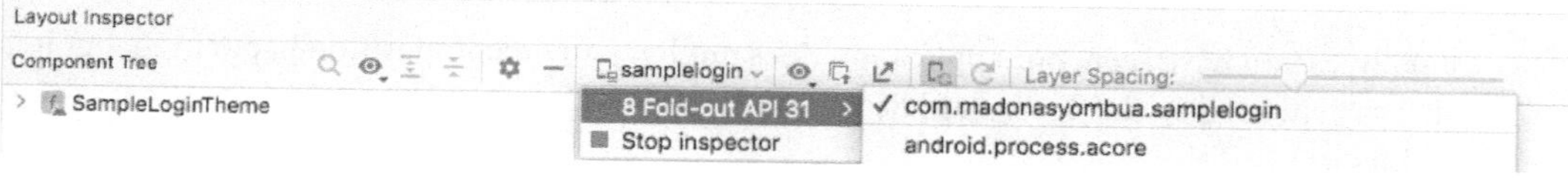

Figure 3.9 – Linking the inspector

4. Go ahead and expand the `SampleLoginTheme` entry point, and you will notice our current view system is not complex. As you can see, **Layout Inspector** does not show any recomposition counts.

   That is to say, if our application had any recomposition counts, they would show up in **Layout Inspector**.

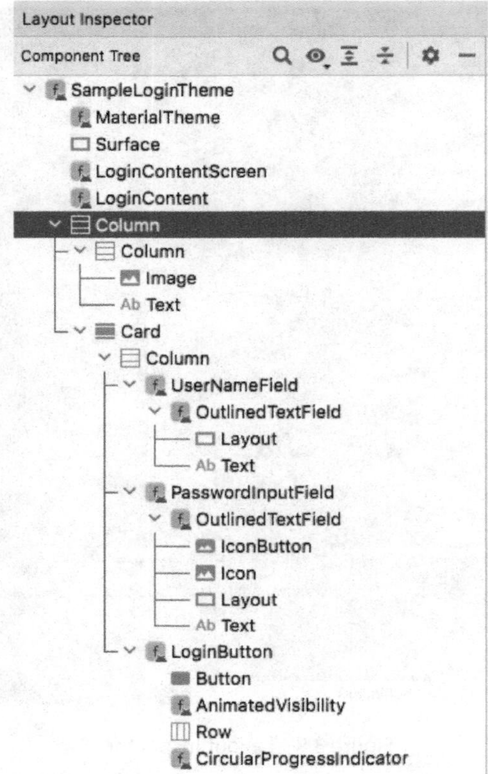

Figure 3.10 – The component tree

5. Finally, as you have seen, our application does not have any recomposition happening, but it is always beneficial to check your application to know what might be causing the recomposition and fix it.

> **Important note**
>
> Using side-effects might lead to users of your application experiencing strange and unpredictable behavior in your app. In addition, a side-effect is any change that is visible to the rest of your application. For instance, writing to a property of a shared object, updating an observable in `ViewModel`, and updating shared preferences are all dangerous side effects.

How it works...

For adaptability, Compose skips `lambda` calls or any child function that does not have any changes to its input. This better handling of resources makes sense since, in Compose, animations and other UI elements can trigger recomposition in every frame.

We can go in depth and use a diagram to showcase how the Jetpack composition life cycle works. In short, the life cycle of a Composable function is defined by three significant events:

- Being composed
- Getting recomposed or not getting recomposed
- No longer being composed

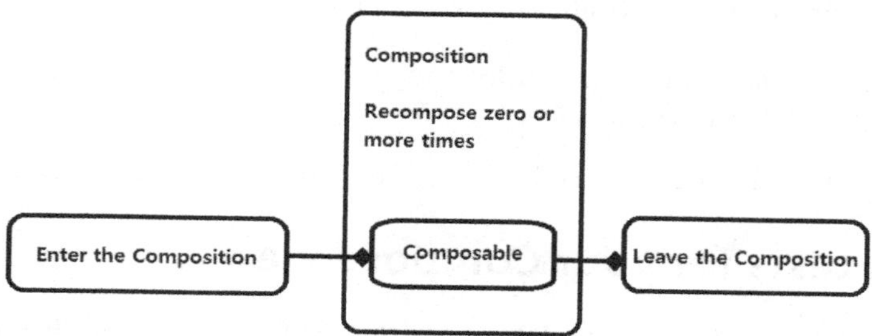

Figure 3.11 – The composition life cycle of a Composable

To fathom how Compose works, it's good to know what constitutes the Compose architectural layer. A high-level overview of the Jetpack Compose architectural layer includes **Material**, **Foundation**, **UI**, and **Runtime** aspects.

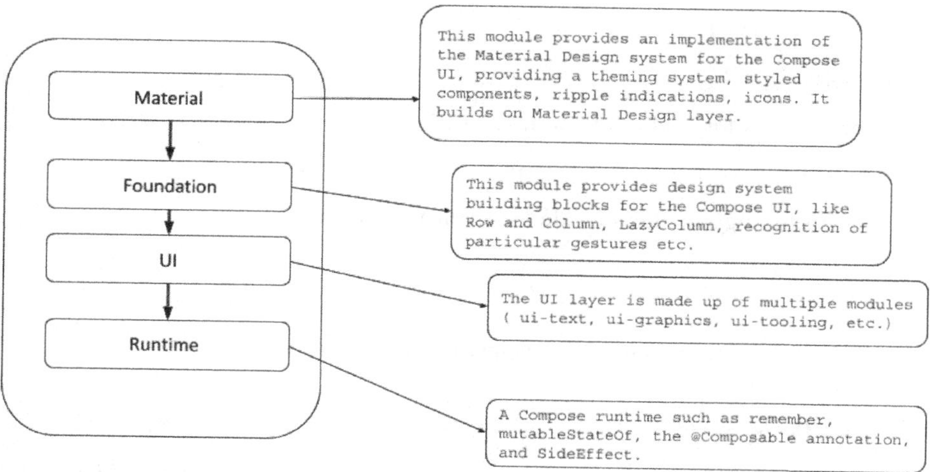

Figure 3.12 – A diagram showing Jetpack Compose Architectural Layers

In **Material**, this module implements the Material Design system for the Compose UI.

Furthermore, it provides a theming system, styled components, and more. **Foundation** is where we have the design system building blocks such as the UI, `Row`, `Column`, and more. The **UI** layer is made of multiple modules that implement the fundamentals of the UI toolkit.

See also

The Compose team is launching Jetpack Compose Composition Tracing, the first alpha that will help developers trace their composition easily; you can read more here:

- `https://medium.com/androiddevelopers/jetpack-Compose-composition-tracing-9ec2b3aea535`
- `https://developer.android.com/jetpack/compose/lifecycle`

Writing UI tests for your Compose views

It is essential to test your code when developing Android applications, especially if your applications have many users. Furthermore, when you write tests for your code, you basically verify the functions, behavior, correctness, and versatility of the Android application. The most popular UI testing tools in Android are Espresso, UI Automator, Calabash, and Detox.

In this book, however, we will use Espresso. The most notable advantages of Espresso are as follows:

- It is easy to set up
- It has highly stable test cycles
- It supports JUnit 4
- It is made purely for Android UI testing
- It is suitable for writing black-box tests
- It supports testing activities outside the application as well

Getting ready

You will need to have completed previous recipes to follow along with this one.

How to do it...

As with the other recipes in this chapter, we will use the new project we created in *Chapter 1, Getting Started with Modern Android Development Skills*:

1. Let's go ahead and navigate into the `androidTest` package in our project folder.

2. Start by creating a new class in the `androidTest` package and call it `LoginContentTest.kt`. In Jetpack Compose, testing is made more accessible, and we need to have unique tags for our views.

3. So, for this step, let's go back to our main package (`com.name.SampleLogin`) and create a new package and call it `util`. Inside `util`, let's create a new class and call it `TestTags`, which will be an object. Here, we will have another object, name it `LoginContent`, and create constant values that we can call in our view:

```
object TestTags {
    object LoginContent {
        const val SIGN_IN_BUTTON = "sign_in_button"
        const val LOGO_IMAGE = "logo_image_button"
        const val ANDROID_TEXT = "community_text"
        const val USERNAME_FIELD = "username_fields"
        const val PASSWORD_FIELD = "password_fields"
    }
}
```

4. Now that we have created the test tags, let's go back to our `LoginContent` and add them to all views in the `Modifier()` so that when we test, it is easier to identify the view using the test tag we have added. See the following code snippet:

```
Image(
    modifier = modifier.testTag(LOGO_IMAGE),
    painter = painterResource(id =
        R.drawable.ic_launcher_foreground),
    contentDescription = "Logo"
)
```

5. Inside our `LoginCotentTest` class, let's now go ahead and set up our testing environment. We will need to create `@get:Rule`, which annotates fields that reference rules or methods that return a rule. Under the rule, let's create `ComposeRuleTest` and initialize it:

```
@get:Rule
val ComposeRuleTest = createAndroidComposeRule<MainActivity>()
```

6. Add the following function to help us set up the content. We should call this function in our `Test` annotated function:

```
private fun initCompose() {
    ComposeRuleTest.activity.setContent {
        SampleLoginTheme {
            LoginContent()
        }
```

```
        }
    }
```

7. Finally, let's go ahead and add our first test. For the tests we will write, we will verify that the views are displayed on the screen as we expect them to be:

```
    @Test
    fun assertSignInButtonIsDisplayed(){
        initCompose()
        ComposeRuleTest.onNodeWithTag(SIGN_IN_BUTTON,
        true).assertIsDisplayed()
    }

    @Test
    fun assertUserInputFieldIsDisplayed(){
        initCompose()
        ComposeRuleTest.onNodeWithTag(USERNAME_FIELD,
        true).assertIsDisplayed()
    }
```

8. `SIGN_IN_BUTTON` and `USERNAME_FIELD` are imported from the test tags that we have created and are already used by only one view, the sign-in button.

9. Go ahead and run the tests, and a dialog will pop up showing the running process; if successful, the tests will pass. In our case, the tests should pass.

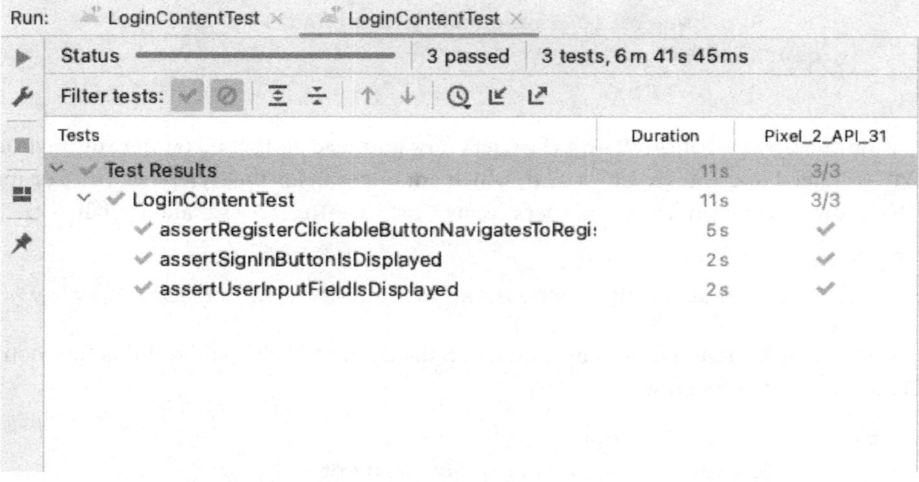

Figure 3.13 – A screenshot showing passing tests

> **Important note**
>
> For these tests, you will not need to add any dependencies; everything we need is already available for our use.

How it works...

We use `createAndroidComposeRule<>()` when accessing an activity. Testing and ensuring your applications display the expected outcome is essential. This is why Android Studio uses the emulator to help developers test their code to ensure their application functions as it would on standard devices.

Furthermore, Android phones come with a developers' option ready for developers to use, making it even easier for the different number of devices that Android supports and helping reproduce bugs that are hard to find in emulators.

When we test our Compose code, we improve our app's quality by catching errors early on in the development process. In this chapter, we touched on creating more views to demonstrate how Jetpack Compose works; furthermore, our test cases need to address user action since we did not implement any.

In a different setting, we can write more crucial tests to confirm the intended action, and we will do this in later chapters. Furthermore, Compose provides testing APIs to find elements, verify their attributes, and perform user actions. Moreover, they also include advanced features such as time manipulation, among others.

Explicitly calling the `@Test` annotation is very important when writing tests since this annotation tells JUnit that the function to which it is attached is to run as a `Test` function. In addition, UI tests in Compose use **Semantics** to interact with the UI hierarchy. And semantics, as the name implies, give meaning to a piece of UI, for example, `.onNodeWithTag`.

A UI portion or element can mean anything from a single Composable to a full screen. If you try to access the wrong node, the semantics tree, which is generated alongside the UI hierarchy, will complain.

There's more...

There are other testing tools as follows:

- **Espresso Test Recorder** provides developers with a faster, interactive way to test their app's everyday user input behavior and visual elements.
- **App Crawler** undoubtedly uses a more hands-off approach to help you test user actions without needing to maintain or write any code. With this tool, you can easily configure your inputs, such as entering your username and password credentials.
- **Monkey** is a command-line device that also stress-tests your app by sending a random flow of user validation/input or tap actions into the device or emulator instance.

To learn more about testing and semantics in Compose, read the following: `https://developer.android.com/jetpack/compose/semantics`.

Writing tests for your ViewModels

Unlike **Model-View-Controller** (**MVC**) and **Model-View-Presenter** (**MVP**), MVVM is the favored design pattern in Modern Android Development because of its unidirectional data and dependency flow. Furthermore, it becomes more accessible to unit test, as you will see in this recipe.

Getting ready

We will use our previous recipe, *Implementing ViewModel and understanding the state in Compose*, to test our logic and state changes.

How to do it...

In this recipe, we will write unit tests to verify our authentication state changes since that is what we have implemented so far:

1. Start by creating a `LoginViewModelTest` class in the `test` package:

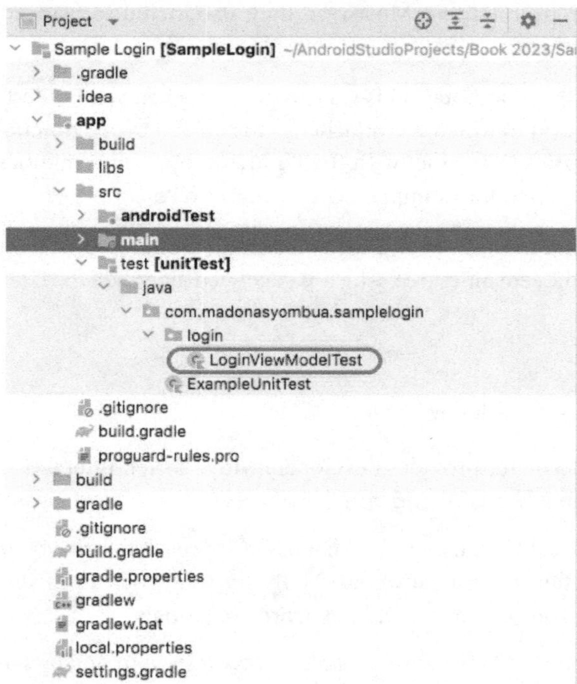

Figure 3.14 – Created unit test

2. We will use the `cashapp/turbine` testing library for coroutine flows to test the flow we have created. Hence, you will need to include the processing code snippet in `build.gradle`:

```
repositories {
  mavenCentral()
}
dependencies {
  testImplementation 'app.cash.turbine:turbine:0.x.x'
}
```

3. Once you have created the class, go ahead and set up `@Before`, which will run before each test:

```
class LoginViewModelTest {
    private lateinit var loginViewModel: LoginViewModel
    @Before
    fun setUp(){
        loginViewModel = LoginViewModel(
            dispatchers =
            SampleLoginDispatchers.createTestDispatchers(
            UnconfinedTestDispatcher()),
            stateHandle = SavedStateHandle()
        )
    }
}
```

4. As you can see, we utilized `SampleLoginDispatchers.createTestDispatchers`. For `UnconfinedTestDispatcher`, you must include the testing dependencies and import, `import kotlinx.coroutines.test.UnconfinedTestDispatcher`.

5. Now that we have our setup ready let us go ahead and create our test, verifying the authentication state changes:

```
@Test
fun `test authentication state changes`() = runTest {...}
```

6. Inside our `Test` function, we will now need to access the `loginViewModel` functions and pass fake values to the parameters:

```
@Test
fun `test authentication state changes`() = runTest {
    loginViewModel.userNameChanged("Madona")
    loginViewModel.passwordChanged("home")
    loginViewModel.passwordVisibility(true)
    loginViewModel.state.test {
        val stateChange = awaitItem()
```

```
            Truth.assertThat(stateChange).isEqualTo(
                AuthenticationState(
                    userName = "Madona",
                    password = "home",
                    togglePasswordVisibility = true
                )
            )
        }
    }
```

7. Finally, go ahead and run the test, and it should pass.

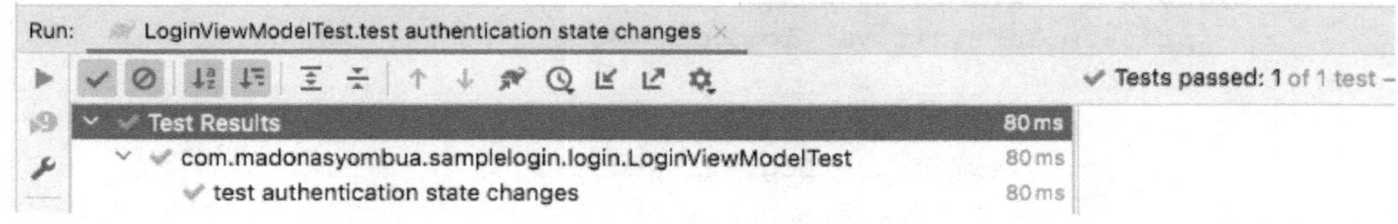

Figure 3.15 – Unit test passing

How it works...

As mentioned before, the most notable advantage of MVVM is being able to write code you can quickly test. In addition, architecture in Android is all about selecting the trade-offs. Each architecture has its pros and cons; based on your company's needs, you might work with a different one.

We create `lateint var loginViewModel` to set up a class for testing, and this is because the logic to be tested is in `ViewModel`.

We use `UnconfinedDispatcher`, which creates an instance of an `Unconfined` dispatcher. That means the tasks it executes are not confined to any particular thread and form an event loop. It is different in that it skips delays, as all `TestDispatcher` instances do. And by default, `runTest()` provides `StandardTestDispatcher`, which does not execute child coroutines immediately.

We use `Truth` for our assertation to help us make more readable code, and the significant advantages of `Truth` are as follows:

- It aligns the actual values to the left
- It gives us more detailed failure messages
- It offers richer operations to help with testing

There are also other alternatives, such as Mockito, Mockk, and more, but in this section, we have used `Truth`. We have also used a library by Cashapp that helps us test coroutine flows. You can learn more about the `turbine` library here: `https://github.com/cashapp/turbine`.

4
Navigation in Modern Android Development

In Android development, navigation is the interaction that allows your Android application users to navigate to, from, and back out from the different screens within your app, an action that is very vital in the mobile ecosystem.

Jetpack navigation has simplified navigation between screens, and in this chapter, we will learn how to implement navigation with a simple view click, from the bottom navigation bar, which is most commonly used, by navigating with arguments, and more.

In this chapter, we'll cover the following recipes:

- Implementing a bottom navigation bar using navigation destinations
- Navigating to a new screen in Compose
- Navigating with arguments
- Creating deep links for destinations
- Writing tests for navigation

Technical requirements

The complete source code for this chapter can be found at `https://github.com/PacktPublishing/Modern-Android-13-Development-Cookbook/tree/main/chapter_four`.

Implementing a bottom navigation bar using navigation destinations

In Android development, having a bottom navigation bar is very common; it helps inform your users that there are different sections in your application. In addition, other apps opt to include a navigation drawer activity, which holds a profile and additional information about the application.

An excellent example of an app that utilizes both – a navigation drawer and bottom navigation – is Twitter. It is also important to mention that some companies prefer to have a top navigation bar as a preference. In addition, others such as Google Play Store have both bottom and drawer navigation.

Getting ready

Create a new Android project with your preferred editor or Android Studio, or you can use any project from previous recipes.

How to do it...

In this recipe, we are going to create a new project and call it `BottomNavigationBarSample`:

1. After creating our new empty `Activity BottomNavigationBarSample` project, we will start by adding the required navigation dependency in `build.gradle`, and then sync the project:

   ```
   implementation 'android.navigation:navigation-compose:2.5.2'
   ```

2. As noticed in a previous new project, when you create a new project, there is code that comes with it, the `Greeting()` function; you can go ahead and delete that code.
3. After deleting that code, let us go ahead and create a `sealed` class in the main package directory and call it `Destination.kt`, where we will define our `route` string, `icon: Int`, and `title: String` for our bottom navigation items:

   ```
   sealed class Destination(val route: String, val icon: Int, val
   title: String) {...}
   ```

   Strictly speaking, we might not need the `sealed` class, but it is a nicer way to implement navigation. A `sealed` class in Kotlin represents a restricted class hierarchy that provides more control over inheritance. Alternatively, you can think of it as a class that, in its value, can have one of the types from a limited set, but it cannot have any other types.

4. Inside the `sealed` class, now let's go ahead and create our destinations. For our sample, we will assume we are creating a budgeting app. Hence, the destinations we can have are `Transactions`, `Budgets`, `Tasks`, and `Settings`. See the next step on how to get the icons; in addition, you will need to import them. For good practice, you can extract the `String` resource and save it in the `String` XML file. You can try this as a small exercise:

```
sealed class Destination(val route: String, val icon: Int, val
title: String) {
    object Transaction : Destination(
        route = "transactions", icon =
            R.drawable.ic_baseline_wallet,
            title = "Transactions"
    )
    object Budgets : Destination(
        route = "budget", icon =
            R.drawable.ic_baseline_budget,
            title = "Budget"
    )
    object Tasks : Destination(route = "tasks", icon =
        R.drawable.ic_add_task, title = "Tasks")
    object Settings : Destination(
        route = "settings", icon =
            R.drawable.ic_settings,
            title = "Settings"
    )
    companion object {
        val toList = listOf(Transaction, Budgets,
        Tasks, Settings)
    }
}
```

5. For the icons, you can access them easily but clicking on the resource folder (`res`), then navigating to **Vector Assets | Clip Art**, which will launch and bring up free icons that you can use, as shown in *Figure 4.1*:

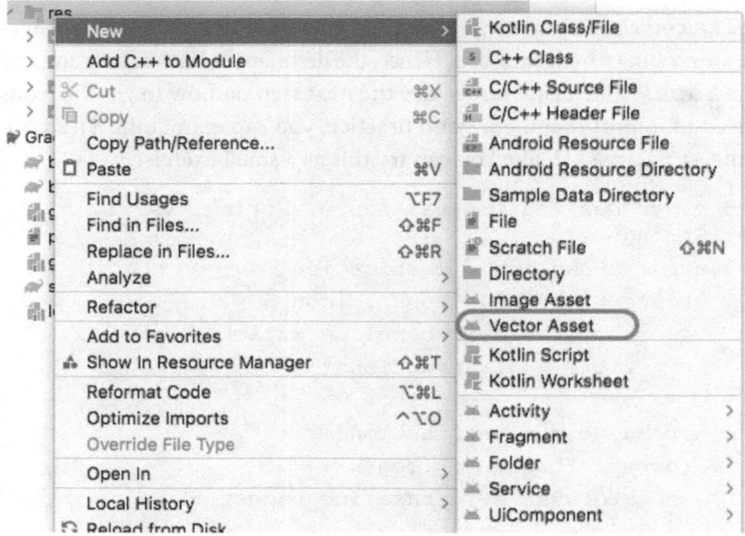

Figure 4.1 – How to access Vector Asset

6. You can also upload an SVG file and access it through **Asset Studio**. For more icons, you can check out this link: `https://fonts.google.com/icons`.

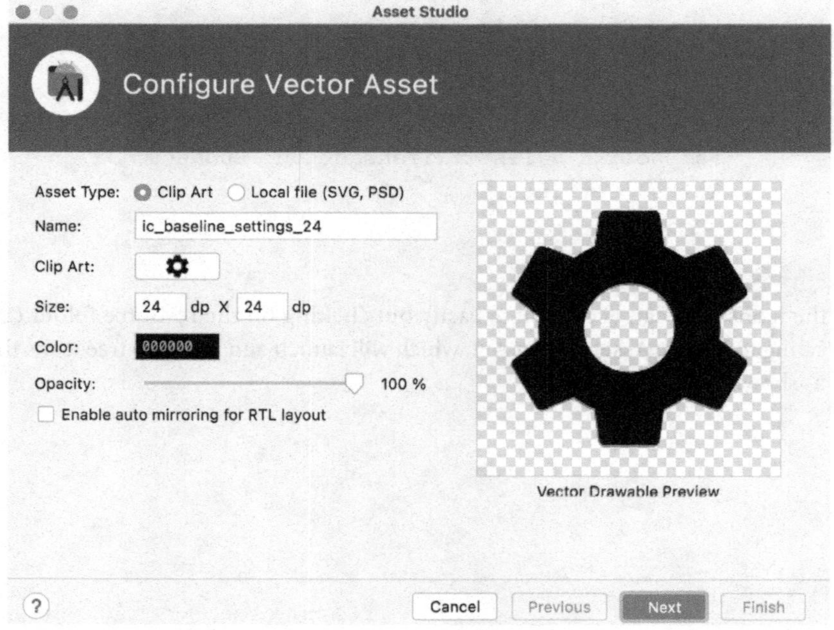

Figure 4.2 – Asset Studio

7. Now, for the destinations we just added, let's go ahead and add dummy text to verify that, indeed, when we navigate, we are on the right screen. Create a new file and name it `AppContent.kt`. Inside `AppContent`, we will add our `Transaction` function, which will be our home screen, where new users enter the app the first time; then later, they can navigate to other screens:

```
@Composable
fun Transaction(){
    Column(
        modifier = Modifier
            .fillMaxSize()
            .wrapContentSize(Alignment.Center)
    ) {
    ...
    }
}
```

8. Go ahead and add the remaining three screens, `Task`, `Budget`, and `Settings`, using the same composable pattern.

9. We now need to create a bottom navigation bar composable and tell the `Composable` function how to react when clicked, and also restore the state when re-selecting a previously selected item:

```
@Composable
fun BottomNavigationBar(navController: NavController, appItems:
List<Destination>) {
    BottomNavigation(
        backgroundColor = colorResource(id =
            R.color.purple_700),
            contentColor = Color.White
    ) {
    ...
    }
}
```

10. Now, let's go to `MainActivity` and create `NavHost` and a few composable functions, `AppScreen()`, `AppNavigation()`, and `BottomNavigationBar()`. Each nav controller must be associated with a single nav host composable because it connects the controller with a nav graph that helps specify the composable directions:

```
@Composable
fun AppNavigation(navController: NavHostController) {
    NavHost(navController, startDestination =
    Destination.Transaction.route) {
        composable(Destination.Transaction.route) {
            Transaction()
```

```
            }
            composable(Destination.Budgets.route) {
                Budget()
            }
            composable(Destination.Tasks.route) {
                Tasks()
            }
            composable(Destination.Settings.route) {
                Settings()
            }
        }
    }
```

11. Finally, let's go ahead and glue everything together by creating another composable function and calling it `AppScreen()`. We will call this function inside `setContent` in the `onCreate()` function:

```
@Composable
fun AppScreen() {
    val navController = rememberNavController()
    Scaffold(
        bottomBar = {
            BottomNavigationBar(navController =
            navController, appItems =
            Destination.toList) },
        content = { padding ->
            Box(modifier = Modifier.padding(padding))
            {
                AppNavigation(navController =
                    navController)
            }
        }
    )
}
```

12. Then, call this created function inside `setContent{}`; the import should be `import androidx.activity.compose.setContent`, based on the fact that sometimes it might happen that you import the wrong one. Run the application. You will notice a screen with four tabs, and when you select a tab, the selected one gets highlighted, as shown in *Figure 4.3*:

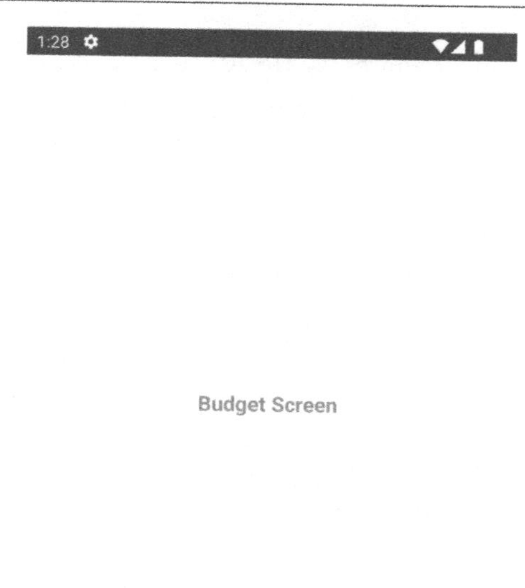

Figure 4.3 – The bottom navigation bar

How it works...

In Compose, navigation has a crucial term called **route**. The key is the string that defines the pathway to your composable. The key basically is the source of truth – or think of it as a deep link that takes you to a specific destination, and each destination should have a unique route.

Furthermore, each destination should consist of a unique key route. In our example, we added icons and a title. The icons, as seen in *Figure 4.3*, show what the bottom navigation entails, and the title describes the specific screen we are browsing at that exact time. In addition, these are optional and only needed for some routes.

`NavController()` is the main API for our navigation component, and it keeps track of every back stack entry for the composables that make up the screens in our application and the state of each screen. We created this using `rememberNavController`: as we mentioned in the previous chapter, `remember`, as the name suggests, remembers the value; in this instance, we are remembering `NavController`:

```
val navController = rememberNavController()
```

`NavHost()`, on the other hand, requires the `NavController()` previously created through `rememberNavController()` and the destination route of the entry point of our graph. In addition, `rememberNavController()` returns `NavHostController`, which is a subclass of `NavController()` that offers some additional APIs that `NavHost` requires.

This is very similar to how Android developers build navigation before composing fragments. The steps include creating a bottom navigation menu with the menu items, as shown in the following code block:

```
<?xml version="1.0" encoding="utf-8"?>
<menu xmlns:android="http://schemas.android.com/apk/res/android">
    <item
        android:id="@+id/transaction_home"
        android:icon="@drawable/card"
        android:title="@string/transactions"/>

    <item
         android:id="@+id/budget_home"
         android:icon="@drawable/ic_shopping_basket_black_
             24dp"
         android:title="@string/budgets"
    />
...
</menu>
```

Then, we create another resource in the `navigation` package that points to the screens (fragments):

```
<?xml version="1.0" encoding="utf-8"?>
<navigation xmlns:android="http://schemas.android.com/apk/res/android"
    app:startDestination="@+id/transaction_home">

    <fragment
        android:id="@+id/transaction_home"
        android:name="com.fragments.TransactionsFragment"
        android:label="@string/title_transcation"
        tools:layout="@layout/fragment_transactions" >
        <action
            android:id="@+id/action_transaction_home_to_
                budget_home"
            app:destination="@id/budget_home" />
    </fragment>
    <fragment
        android:id="@+id/budget_home"
        android:name="com.fragments.BudgetsFragment"
        android:label="@string/title_budget"
```

```
        tools:layout="@layout/fragment_budget" >
        <action
            android:id="@+id/action_budget_home_to_tasks_
                home"
            app:destination="@id/tasks_home" />
    </fragment>
</navigation>
```

Navigating to a new screen in Compose

We will build a register screen prompt on our login page for registering first-time users of our application. This is a standard pattern because we need to save the user's credentials so that the next time they log in to our application, we just log them in without registering again.

Getting ready

You should have completed the previous recipe, *Implementing a bottom navigation bar using navigation destinations*, before getting started with this one.

How to do it...

In this recipe, we will need to use our `SampleLogin` project and add a new screen that users can navigate to if it is their first time using the application. This is a typical use case in many applications:

1. Open your `SampleLogin` project, create a new `sealed` class, and call it `Destination`. To also ensure we maintain great packaging, add this class to `util`. Also, just like the bottom bar, we will have a route, but this time, we do not need any icons or titles:

```
sealed class Destination (val route: String){
    object Main: Destination("main_route")
    object LoginScreen: Destination("login_screen")
    object RegisterScreen:
        Destination("register_screen")
}
```

2. After creating the destinations, we now need to go ahead and add clickable text in `LoginContent` to ask users whether it is their first time using the application. They should click **Register**. Then, we can navigate to `RegisterContent`. You can open the project by checking out the *Technical requirements* section if you need to refer to any step:

```
@Composable
fun LoginContent(
    ...
```

```
        onRegister: () -> Unit
    ) {
    ClickableText(
        modifier = Modifier.padding(top = 12.dp),
        text = AnnotatedString(stringResource(id =
            R.string.register)),
        onClick = { onRegister.invoke() },
        style = TextStyle(
            colorResource(id = R.color.purple_700),
            fontSize = 16.sp
        )
    )
```

3. Now, when you click on `ClickableText`, our clickable text is text that you can click, and it will help users navigate to the registration screen via **First-time user? Sign UP**. Once you click on this, it should navigate to a different screen where users can now sign up, as shown in *Figure 4.4*:

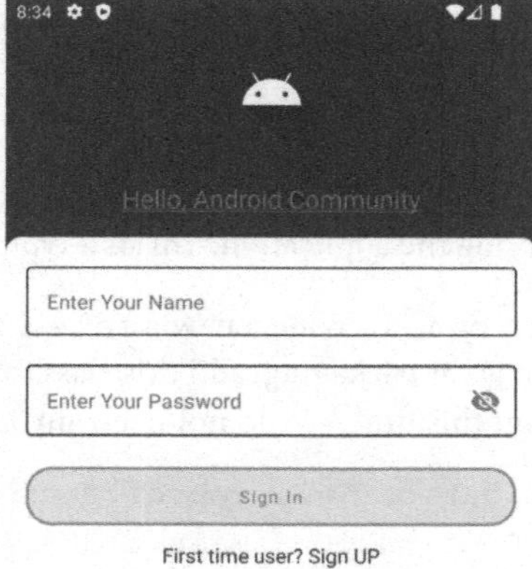

Figure 4.4 – A new Register screen

4. For the **Register** screen, you can get the entire code in the *Technical requirements* section. We will reuse the user input fields that we created and just change the text:

```
@Composable
fun PasswordInputField(
    text: String
) {
    OutlinedTextField(
        label = { Text(text = text) },
...
}
```

5. In `MainActivity`, we will have a `Navigation()` function, as follows:

```
@Composable
fun Navigation(navController: NavHostController) {
    NavHost(navController, startDestination =
    Destination.LoginScreen.route) {
        composable(Destination.LoginScreen.route) {
            LoginContentScreen(loginViewModel =
                hiltViewModel(),
            onRegisterNavigateTo = {
                navController.navigate(
                    Destination.RegisterScreen.route)
            })
        }
        composable(Destination.RegisterScreen.route) {
            RegisterContentScreen(registerViewModel =
                hiltViewModel())

        }

    }
}
```

6. In `PasswordInputField`, we will name each input appropriately for reusability:

```
PasswordInputField(
    text = stringResource(id = R.string.password),
    authState = uiState,
    onValueChanged = onPasswordUpdated,
    passwordToggleVisibility =
        passwordToggleVisibility)
```

7. Moreover, you can also navigate to the previous **Sign in** screen by clicking on the hardware **Back** button.
8. Finally, in `setContent`, we will need to update the code to accommodate the new navigation:

```
@AndroidEntryPoint
class MainActivity : ComponentActivity() {
    override fun onCreate(savedInstanceState: Bundle?)
    {
        super.onCreate(savedInstanceState)
        setContent {
            SampleLoginTheme {
                // A surface container using the
                   'background' color from the theme
                Surface(
                    modifier = Modifier.fillMaxSize(),
                    color =
                       MaterialTheme.colors.background
                ) {
                    val navController =
                      rememberNavController()
                    Navigation(navController =
                      navController)
                }
            }
        }
    }
}
```

Run the code and click on the **Sign up** text, and you should now be taken to a new screen.

How it works...

You will notice that we have just created a different destination entry point, where `ClickableText` is used to navigate to the newly created screen. Furthermore, in order to navigate to a composable destination in the nav graph, you must use `navController.navigate(Destination.RegisterScreen.route)`, and as mentioned earlier, the string represents the destination route.

In addition, `navigate()` adds our destination to the back stack by default, but if we need to modify the behavior, we can easily do that by adding additional nav options to our `navigate()` call.

Suppose you want to work with animations when navigating. In that case, you can easily do that by using the Accompanist library – `https://github.com/google/accompanist` –which offers a group of libraries that aim to supplement Jetpack Compose with features that are required mainly by developers and are not available yet.

You can utilize `enterTransition`, which explicitly specifies the animation that runs when you navigate to a particular destination, whereas `exitTransition` does the opposite:

```
AnimatedNavHost(
    modifier = Modifier
        .padding(padding),
    navController = navController,
    startDestination = Destination.LoginScreen.route,
    route = Destination.LoginScreen.route,
    enterTransition = { fadeIn(animationSpec = tween(2000)) },
    exitTransition = { fadeOut(animationSpec = tween(200))
    }
)
```

You can also use `popEnterTransition`, which specifies the animation that runs when the destination re-enters the screen after going through `popBackStack()`, or `popExitTranstion`, which does the opposite.

> **Important note**
>
> It is crucial to note a good practice that becomes relevant for hoisting the state is when you expose events from your composable functions to callers in your application that know how to handle that logic properly. In addition, under-the-hood navigation is all state-managed.

See also

For more about `AnimatedNavHost`, you can find details here: `https://google.github.io/accompanist/navigation-animation/`.

Navigating with arguments

Passing data between destinations is very vital in Android development. The new Jetpack navigation allows developers to attach data to a navigation operation by defining an argument for a destination. Readers will learn how to pass data between destinations using arguments.

A good use case is, say, you load an API with data and want to show more description on the data you just displayed; you can navigate with unique arguments to the next screen.

Getting ready

We will explore the most common interview project requirement, which is to fetch data from an API and display one screen and add an additional screen for extra points.

Let's assume the API is the GitHub API, and you want to display all organizations. Then, you want to navigate to another screen and see the number of repositories each company has.

How to do it...

For this recipe, we will look at an example of navigating with arguments as a concept since there is little more to do other than create the basic arguments to pass to utilize an already-built project – `SampleLogin`:

1. Let's go ahead and create `SearchScreen`, and this screen will have just a search function, `EditText`, and a column to display the data returned from an API:

```
SearchScreen(
    viewModel = hiltViewModel(),
    navigateToRepositoryScreen = { orgName ->
        navController.navigate(
            Destination.BrowseRepositoryScreen.route +
            "/" + orgName
        )
    }
)
```

2. And now, when setting up navigation to `BrowseRepository`, you will need to add the following code. This piece of code is for passing a mandatory data parameter from one screen to another, but adding the example of passing an optional argument; a default value will help the user:

```
composable(
    route = Destination.BrowseRepositoryScreen.route +
            "/{org_name}",
    arguments = listOf(navArgument("org_name") { type
        = NavType.StringType }),
    enterTransition = { scaleIn(tween(700)) },
    exitTransition = { scaleOut(tween(700)) },
) {
    BrowseRepositoryScreen(
        viewModel = hiltViewModel(),
    )
}
```

We also use the `enter` and `exit` transition for animations. In this recipe, we have just touched on the concept of navigating with arguments, which can be applied to many projects.

How it works...

When you want to pass an argument to the destination, which is something that might be required, you need to explicitly attach it to the route when initiating the `navigate` function call, as you can see in the following code snippet:

```
navController.navigate(Destination.BrowseScreen.route + "/" + orgName)
```

We added an argument placeholder to our route, similar to how we added arguments to a deep link when using the base navigation library.

There is also a list of what the navigation library supports; if you have a different use case, you can look into this document: `https://developer.android.com/guide/navigation/navigation-pass-data#supported_argument_types`.

The Navigation library supports the following argument types:

Type	app:argType syntax	Support for default values	Handled by routes	Nullable
Integer	app:argType="integer"	Yes	Yes	No
Float	app:argType="float"	Yes	Yes	No
Long	app:argType="long"	Yes - Default values must always end with an 'L' suffix (e.g. "123L").	Yes	No
Boolean	app:argType="boolean"	Yes - "true" or "false"	Yes	No
String	app:argType="string"	Yes	Yes	Yes
Resource Reference	app:argType="reference"	Yes - Default values must be in the form of "@resourceType/resourceName" (e.g. "@style/myCustomStyle") or "0"	Yes	No
Custom Parcelable	app:argType="<type>", where <type> is the fully-qualified class name of the `Parcelable`	Supports a default value of "@null". Does not support other default values.	No	Yes
Custom Serializable	app:argType="<type>", where <type> is the fully-qualified class name of the `Serializable`	Supports a default value of "@null". Does not support other default values.	No	Yes
Custom Enum	app:argType="<type>", where <type> is the fully-qualified name of the enum	Yes - Default values must match the unqualified name (e.g. "SUCCESS" to match MyEnum.SUCCESS).	No	No

Figure 4.5 – Navigation support argument type (credit: developers.android.com)

There's more...

There is more to learn about navigation and, for a more thorough way to look into how you can navigate with arguments, retrieve complex data when navigating, and add additional arguments in depth, you can read more here: `https://developer.android.com/jetpack/compose/navigation`.

Creating deep links for destinations

In Modern Android Development, deep links are very vital. A link that helps you navigate directly to a specific destination within an app is called a **deep link**. The `Navigation` component lets you create two types of deep links: **explicit** and **implicit**.

Compose navigation supports implicit deep links, which can be part of your Composable functions. It is also fair to mention there is no huge difference between how you would handle these using XML layouts.

Getting ready

Since we don't have a deep link use case in our application, in this recipe, we will look into how we can utilize the knowledge by learning how to implement implicit deep links.

How to do it...

You can match deep links using a **Uniform Resource Locator** (**URI**), intent actions, or **Multipurpose Internet Mail Extensions** (**MIME**) types. Furthermore, you can easily specify multiple types that match for a deep link single but remember that the URI argument comparison is always prioritized, followed by the intent action, then the MIME type.

Compose has made it easier for developers to work with deep links. The `composable` function accepts a parameter list of `NavDeepLinks`, which can be easily created using the `navDeepLink` method:

1. We will start by making the deep link externally available by adding the appropriate intent filter to our `AndroidManifest.xml` file:

```
<activity>
    <intent-filter>
      ...
      <data android:scheme="https"
      android:host="www.yourcompanieslink.com" />
    </intent-filter>
</activity>
```

2. Now in our `composable` function, we can use the `deepLinks` parameter, specify the list of `navDeepLink`, and then pass the URI pattern:

```
val uri = "www.yourcompanieslink.com"
composable(deepLinks = listOf(navDeepLink { uriPattern = "$uri/
{id}" }))
{...}
```

3. Please note that navigation will automatically deep-link into that composable when another application triggers the deep link.

   Many applications still use `launchMode` when navigating. This is when using the Navigation Jetpack component, as seen in the following code snippet:

```
override fun onNewIntent(intent: Intent) {
    super.onNewIntent(intent)
    navigationController.handleDeepLink(intent)
}
```

4. Finally, you can also utilize `deepLinkPendingIntent` like any other `PendingIntent` to start your Android application at the deep link destination.

> **Important note**
>
> When triggering an implicit deep link, the back stack state depends on when the implicit intent was launched with `Intent.FLAG_ACTIVITY_NEW_TASK`. Furthermore, if the flag is set, the back stack task is cleared and then replaced with the intended deep link destination.

How it works...

In Android development, a deep link refers to a specific destination for the application. For instance, when you invoke the deep link, the link opens up your application's corresponding destination when a user clicks on the specified link.

This refers to where the link is meant to lead once clicked. The explicit deep link is a single instance that uses `PendingIntent` to take users to a specific location within your application. A good use case is when using notifications or app widgets.

There's more...

There is more to learn about deep links; for instance, how to create an explicit deep link. You can learn more about deep links here: `https://developer.android.com/training/app-links/deep-linking`.

Writing tests for navigation

Now that we have created a new screen for our `SampleLogin` project, we need to fix the broken test and add new tests for the UI package. If you can recall, in *Chapter 3, Handling the UI State in Jetpack Compose and Using Hilt*, we did unit tests and not UI tests. This means after adding all the `ViewModel` instances, our UI tests are now broken. In this recipe, we will fix the failing tests and add a navigation test.

Getting ready

In this recipe, you do not need to create any new project; use the already-created project, `SampleLogin`.

How to do it...

You can apply these concepts to test the bottom navigation bar we created. Hence, we will not be writing tests for the `BottomNavigationBarSample` project. Open `SampleLogin` and navigate to the `androidTest` package. We will add tests here for the new `RegisterScreen()` a Composable function, and also fix the broken tests:

1. Let's open the `LoginContentTest` class. Now, let's move the `LoginContent` class to a helper class that we will create to help us with testing the UI logic:

```
@Composable
fun contentLoginForTest(
    uiState: AuthenticationState =
    AuthenticationState(),
    onUsernameUpdated : (String) -> Unit = {},
    onPasswordUpdated :(String) -> Unit = {},
    onLogin : () -> Unit = {},
    passwordToggleVisibility: (Boolean) -> Unit = {},
    onRegisterNavigateTo: () -> Unit = {}
) {
    LoginContent(
        uiState = uiState,
        onUsernameUpdated = onUsernameUpdated,
        onPasswordUpdated = onPasswordUpdated,
        onLogin = onLogin,
        passwordToggleVisibility =
            passwordToggleVisibility,
        onRegister = onRegisterNavigateTo
    )
}
```

2. Inside the `LoginContentTest` class, now, we will replace `LoginContent` with the newly created `contentLoginForTest()` function inside the `initCompose` function:

```
private fun initCompose() {
    composeRuleTest.activity.setContent {
        SampleLoginTheme {
            contentLoginForTest()
            launchRegisterScreenWithNavGraph()
        }
    }
}
```

3. Now that we have fixed the tests, we can now add a `test` tag for our newly created clickable, `TextView`:

```
const val REGISTER_USER = "register_user"
```

4. Once that is done, we now need to create `lateint var NavHostController`, and a `launchRegisterScreenWithNavGraph` function to help us set up the navigation:

```
private fun launchRegisterScreenWithNavGraph() {
    composeRuleTest.activity.setContent {
        SampleLoginTheme {
            navController = rememberNavController()
            NavHost(
                navController = navController,
                startDestination =
                    Destination.LoginScreen.route
            ) {
                composable(Destination.LoginScreen
                .route) {
                LoginContentScreen(
                onRegisterNavigateTo = {
                    navController.navigate(
                        Destination.RegisterScreen
                        .route)
                }, loginViewModel = hiltViewModel())
                }
                composable(
                    Destination.RegisterScreen
                    .route) {
                        RegisterContentScreen(
                            hiltViewModel())
                    }
```

```
            }
        }
    }
}
```

You can call the created function inside the `initCompose` function or in the new test function that we will create.

5. Now, let's create a test function and name it `assertRegisterClickableButtonNavigatesToRegisterScreen()`. In this test case, we will set our route and then use `assert` when the correct `TextView` is clicked; we will navigate to the correct destination:

```
@Test
fun assertRegisterClickableButtonNavigatesToRegisterScreen() {
    initCompose()
    composeRuleTest.onNodeWithTag(
        TestTags.LoginContent.REGISTER_USER)
            .performClick(
    )

    val route =
        navController.currentDestination?.route
    assert(route.equals(
        Destination.RegisterScreen.route))

}
```

6. Finally, run the test, and the UI test should pass, as seen in *Figure 4.6*:

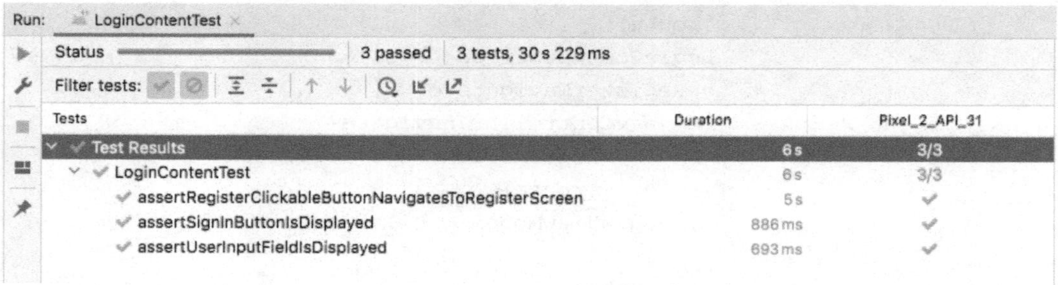

Figure 4.6 – Tests passing

How it works...

We created the `contentLoginForTest` that can help us verify our navigation. That is, when a user enters a valid username and password, they can navigate to a home screen. Furthermore, we created `launchRegisterScreenWithNavGraph()`, a helper function that creates the testing graph for our navigation test case.

If you are using `FragmentScenario`, there are great tips for testing your navigation that you can see here: `https://developer.android.com/guide/navigation/navigation-testing`.

5

Using DataStore to Store Data and Testing

Modern Android Development practices help Android developers create better applications. DataStore is a data storage solution provided by the Android Jetpack library. It allows developers to store key-value pairs or complex objects asynchronously and with consistency guarantees. Data is critical in Android development, and how we save and persist data matters. In this chapter, we will explore using DataStore to persist our data and look at best practices using DataStore.

In this chapter, we'll be covering the following recipes:

- Implementing DataStore
- Adding Dependency Injection to DataStore
- Using Android Proto DataStore versus DataStore
- Handling data migration with DataStore
- Writing tests for our DataStore instance

Technical requirements

The complete source code for this chapter can be found at `https://github.com/PacktPublishing/Modern-Android-13-Development-Cookbook/tree/main/chapter_five`.

Implementing DataStore

When building mobile applications, it is critical to ensure that you persist your data in order to allow for smooth loading, reduce network issues, or even handle data entirely offline. In this recipe, we will look at how to store data in our Android applications using the Modern Android Development Jetpack library called DataStore.

DataStore is a data storage solution for Android applications that enables you to store key-value pairs or any typed objects with protocol buffers. Moreover, DataStore uses Kotlin coroutines and flows to store data consistently, transactionally, and asynchronously.

If you have built Android applications before, you might have used `SharedPreferences`. The new Preferences DataStore aims to replace this old method. It is also fair to say that Preferences DataStore harnesses the power of `SharedPreferences` since they are pretty similar. In addition, Google's documentation recommends that if you're currently using `SharedPreferences` in your project to store data, you consider migrating to the latest DataStore version.

Another way to store data in Android is by using Room. This will be covered in *Chapter 6, Using the Room Database and Testing*; for now, we will just look at DataStore. Moreover, it is essential to note that DataStore is ideal for simple or small datasets and does not have support for partial updates or referential integrity.

How to do it...

Let's go ahead and create a new, empty Compose project and call it `DataStoreSample`. In our example project, we will create a task entry app where users can save tasks. We will allow users to enter only three tasks, then use DataStore to store the tasks and later log the data and see whether it was inserted correctly. An additional exercise to try is to display data when users want to see it:

1. In our newly created project, let's go ahead and delete code that we don't need. In this case, we're referring to the `Greeting(name: String)` that comes with all empty Compose projects. Keep the Preview function since we will use it to view the screen we create.
2. Now, let's go on and add the required dependencies for DataStore and sync the project. Also, note that there are versions of the DataStore library that are specific to RxJava 2 and 3:

```
dependencies {
implementation "androidx.DataStore:DataStore-preferences:1.x.x"
}
```

3. Create a new package and call it `data`. Inside `data`, create a new Kotlin data class and call it `Tasks`.
4. Let's now go ahead and construct our data class with the expected input fields:

```
data class Tasks(
    val firstTask: String,
    val secondTask: String,
    val thirdTask: String
)
```

5. Inside the same package, let's add a `TaskDataSource` enum since we will reuse this project to showcase saving data using Proto DataStore in the *Using Android Proto DataStore versus DataStore* recipe:

```
enum class TaskDataSource {
    PREFERENCES_DATA_STORE
}
```

6. Inside our package, let's go ahead and add a `DataStoreManager` interface. Inside our class, we will have a `saveTasks()` function to save the data and a `getTasks()` function to help us retrieve the saved data. A `suspend` function in Kotlin is simply a function that can be paused and resumed later.

   In addition, the suspend functions can execute long-running operations and await completion without blocking:

```
interface DataStoreManager {
    suspend fun saveTasks(tasks: Tasks)
    fun getTasks(): Flow<Tasks>
}
```

7. Next, we need to implement our interface, so let's go ahead and create a `DataStoreManagerImpl` class and implement the `DataStoreManager`. To refresh your knowledge of Flows, refer to *Chapter 3, Handling the UI State in Jetpack Compose and Using Hilt*:

```
class DataStoreManagerImpl(): DataStoreManager {
    override suspend fun saveTasks(tasks: Tasks) {
        TODO("Not yet implemented")
    }

    override fun getTasks(): Flow<Tasks> {
        TODO("Not yet implemented")
    }
}
```

8. You will notice that once we've implemented the interface, we brought a view to the function, but it says TODO, and nothing has been implemented. To continue with this step, let's go ahead and add DataStore and pass `Preference` in our constructor. We will also need to create the string preference key for each task:

```
class DataStoreManagerImpl(
    private val tasksPreferenceStore:
        DataStore<Preferences>
) : DataStoreManager {
```

```
    private val FIRST_TASK =
        stringPreferencesKey("first_task")
    private val SECOND_TASK =
        stringPreferencesKey("second_task")
    private val THIRD_TASK =
        stringPreferencesKey("third_task")

    override suspend fun saveTasks(tasks: Tasks) {
        tasksPreferenceStore.edit {
        taskPreferenceStore ->
            taskPreferenceStore[FIRST_TASK] =
                tasks.firstTask
            taskPreferenceStore[SECOND_TASK] =
                tasks.secondTask
            taskPreferenceStore[THIRD_TASK] =
                tasks.thirdTask
        }
    }

    override fun getTasks(): Flow<Tasks> {
        TODO("Not yet implemented")
    }
}
```

9. Finally, let's finish our implementation of the `DataStore` section by adding functionality to the `getTasks` function:

```
override fun getTasks(): Flow<Tasks> = tasksPreferenceStore.
data.map { taskPreference ->
    Tasks(
        firstTask = taskPreference[FIRST_TASK] ?: "",
        secondTask = taskPreference[SECOND_TASK] ?:
        "",
        thirdTask = taskPreference[THIRD_TASK] ?: ""
    )
}
```

10. In our `MainActivity` class, let's go on and create a simple UI: three `TextField` and a **Save** button. The **Save** button will save our data, and we can try to log data once everything works as expected. Refer to the *Technical requirements* section of this chapter to get the UI code.

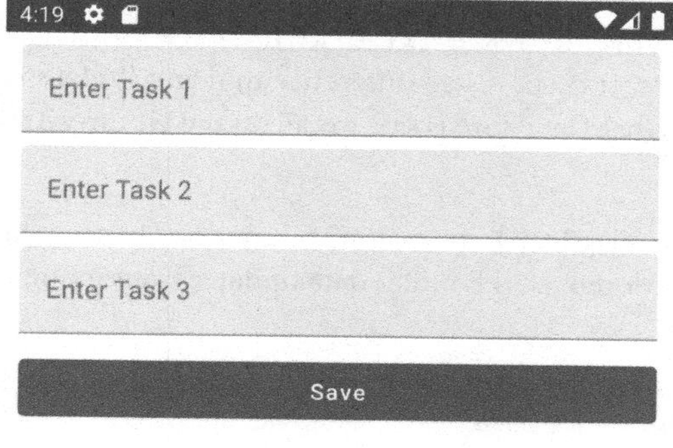

Figure 5.1 – The DataStore UI example

Now that we have our implementation ready, in the following recipe, *Adding Dependency Injection to DataStore*, we will add Dependency Injection and then glue everything together.

How it works...

The new Modern Android Development Jetpack library called Preferences DataStore's main objective is to replace `SharedPreferences`. To implement Preferences DataStore, as you have seen in the recipe, we use a DataStore interface that takes in a `Preference` abstract class, and we can use this to edit and map the entry data. Furthermore, we create keys for the crucial parts of the key-value pairs:

```
private val FIRST_TASK = stringPreferencesKey("first_task")
private val SECOND_TASK = stringPreferencesKey("second_task")
private val THIRD_TASK = stringPreferencesKey("third_task")
```

To save our data in DataStore, we use `edit()`, which is a suspend function that needs to be called from `CoroutineContext`. A key difference in using Preferences DataStore compared to `SharedPreferences` is that DataStore is safe to call on the UI thread since it uses `dispatcher.IO` under the hood.

You also do not need to use `apply{}` or `commit` functions to save the changes, as is required in `SharedPreferences`. Moreover, it handles data updates transactionally. More features are listed in *Figure 5.2*.

Feature	SharedPreferences	PreferencesDataStore	ProtoDataStore
Async API	✅ (only for reading changed values, via listener)	✅ (via `Flow` and RxJava 2 & 3 `Flowable`)	✅ (via `Flow` and RxJava 2 & 3 `Flowable`)
Synchronous API	✅ (but not safe to call on UI thread)	❌	❌
Safe to call on UI thread	❌1	✅ (work is moved to `Dispatchers.IO` under the hood)	✅ (work is moved to `Dispatchers.IO` under the hood)
Can signal errors	❌	✅	✅
Safe from runtime exceptions	❌2	✅	✅
Has a transactional API with strong consistency guarantees	❌	✅	✅
Handles data migration	❌	✅	✅
Type safety	❌	❌	✅ with Protocol Buffers

Figure 5.2 – A list of a sample of Datastore's features taken from developers.android.com

There is more to learn, and it is fair to acknowledge that what we covered in this recipe is just a tiny part of what you can do with DataStore. We will cover more features in the following recipes.

Adding Dependency Injection to DataStore

Dependency Injection is an important design pattern in software engineering, and its use in Android app development can lead to cleaner and more maintainable code. When it comes to DataStore in Android, which is a modern data storage solution introduced in Android Jetpack, adding Dependency Injection can bring several benefits:

- By using Dependency Injection, you can separate the concerns of creating an instance of DataStore from the code that uses it. This means that your business logic code will not have to worry about how to create a DataStore instance and can instead focus on what it needs to do with the data.
- Dependency Injection makes it easier to write unit tests for your app. By injecting a mock DataStore instance into your tests, you can ensure that your tests are not affected by the actual state of the DataStore.
- Dependency Injection can help you break down your code into smaller, more manageable modules. This makes it easier to add new features or modify existing ones without affecting the entire code base.
- By using Dependency Injection, you can easily switch between different implementations of DataStore. This can be useful when testing different types of data storage or when migrating from one storage solution to another.

How to do it...

You need to have completed the previous recipe to continue with this one by executing the following steps:

1. Open your project and add the necessary Hilt dependency. See the *Handling the UI State in Jetpack Compose and Using Hilt* recipe in *Chapter 3* if you need help setting it up.
2. Next, let's go ahead and add our `@HiltAndroidApp` class, and in our `Manifest` folder, add the `.name = TaskApp: android:name=".TaskApp"`:

```
@HiltAndroidApp
class TaskApp : Application()

<application
    android:allowBackup="true"
    android:name=".TaskApp"
    tools:targetApi="31">
...
```

3. Now that we have implemented Dependency Injection, let's go ahead and add `@AndroidEntryPoint` to the `MainActivity` class, and in `DataStoreManagerImpl`, let's go ahead and add the `@Inject constructor`. We should have something similar to the following code snippet:

```
class DataStoreManagerImpl @Inject constructor(
    private val tasksPreferenceStore:
    DataStore<Preferences>
) : DataStoreManager {
```

4. Now, we need to create a new folder and call it `di`; this is where we will put our `DataStoreModule` class. We create a file called `store_tasks` to store the Preference values:

```
@Module
@InstallIn(SingletonComponent::class)
class DataStoreModule {
    private val Context.tasksPreferenceStore :
    DataStore<Preferences> by
    preferencesDataStore(name = "store_tasks")

    @Singleton
    @Provides
    fun provideTasksPreferenceDataStore(
        @ApplicationContext context: Context
    ): DataStore<Preferences> =
        context.tasksPreferenceStore
}
```

5. We will also need to create an `abstract` class for `DataStoreManagerModule` inside our `di` package. In order to reduce the boilerplate code using manual Dependency Injection, our application also supplies the required dependencies to the classes that need them. You can learn more about this in *Chapter 3, Handling the UI State in Jetpack Compose and Using Hilt*:

```
@Module
@InstallIn(SingletonComponent::class)
abstract class DataStoreManagerModule {

    @Singleton
    @Binds
    abstract fun
        bindDataStoreRepository(DataStoreManagerImpl:
            DataStoreManagerImpl): DataStoreManager
}
```

6. Let's now go ahead and create a new package and call it `service`:

```
interface TaskService {
    fun getTasksFromPrefDataStore(): Flow<Tasks>
    suspend fun addTasks(tasks: Tasks)
}

class TaskServiceImpl @Inject constructor(
    private val DataStoreManager: DataStoreManager
) : TaskService {
    override fun getTasksFromPrefDataStore() =
            DataStoreManager.getTasks()

    override suspend fun addTasks(tasks: Tasks) {
        DataStoreManager.saveTasks(tasks)
    }
}
```

7. Let's also ensure we have the required dependencies for the newly created service:

```
    @Singleton
    @Binds
    abstract fun bindTaskService(taskServiceImpl:
    TaskServiceImpl): TaskService
}
```

8. Now that we are done with Dependency Injection and adding all the functionalities required for DataStore, we will go ahead and add a `ViewModel` class and implement functionality to save the data once the user clicks the Save button:

```
fun saveTaskData(tasks: Tasks) {
    viewModelScope.launch {
        Log.d("Task", "asdf Data was inserted
                correctly")
        taskService.addTasks(tasks)
    }
}
```

9. Call the `saveTaskData` function inside the Compose Save button in the Compose view to save our data:

```
TaskButton(onClick = {
    val tasks = Tasks(
        firstTask = firstText.value,
        secondTask = secondText.value,
```

```
        thirdTask = thirdText.value
    )
    taskViewModel.saveTaskData(tasks)},
    text = stringResource(id = R.string.save))
```

10. Lastly, we will need to verify that everything is working, that is, our UI and data storing process. We can verify this, by typing input data in our TextFields and clicking the Save button, and when we log the message it confirms the data is indeed saved.

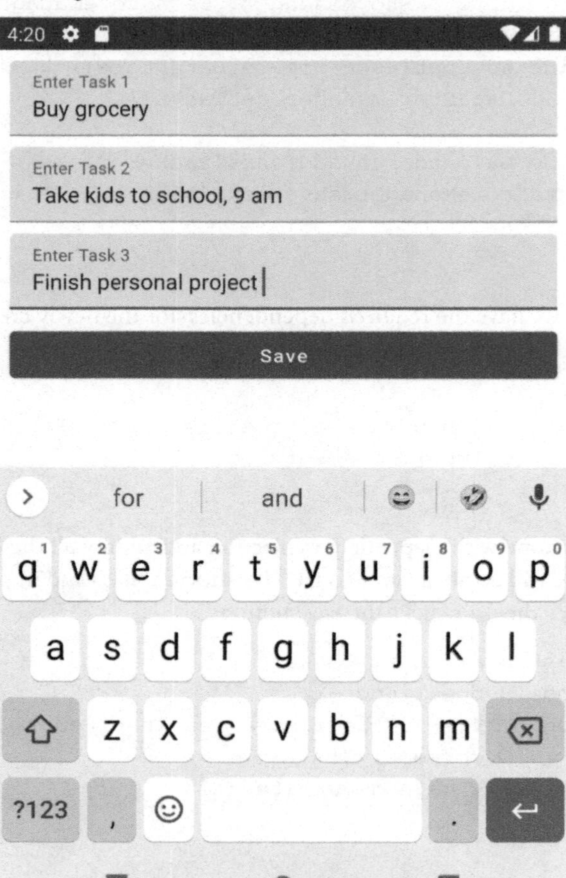

Figure 5.3 – The entry of tasks

11. If you missed it initially, the code for this view can be found in the *Technical requirement* section. Now, you will notice that when we enter the data, as in *Figure 5.4*, we should be able to log the data on our Logcat and verify that our data was inserted correctly.

ariables

Evaluate expression (⏎) or add a watch (⇧⌘⏎)

> firstText = {ParcelableSnapshotMutableState@19852} Buy grocery
> secondText = {ParcelableSnapshotMutableState@19853} Take kids to school, 9 am
> taskViewModel = {TaskViewModel@19854} com.madonasyombua.datastoreexample.TaskViewModel@104d7be
> thirdText = {ParcelableSnapshotMutableState@19855} Finish personal project
⌄ tasks = {Tasks@19856} Tasks(firstTask=Buy grocery, secondTask=Take kids to school, 9 am, thirdTask=Finish personal project)
  > firstTask = "Buy grocery"
    firstTask {java.lang.String} ... get()
  > secondTask = "Take kids to school, 9 am"
    secondTask {java.lang.String} ... get()
  > thirdTask = "Finish personal project"
    thirdTask {java.lang.String} ... get()
  > shadow$_klass_ = {Class@18714} "class com.madonasyombua.datastoreexample.data.Tasks" ... Navigate
    shadow$_monitor_ = 0

Figure 5.4 – The entry of tasks through debugging

12. A log message should also be displayed in the Logcat tab if all is working as expected.

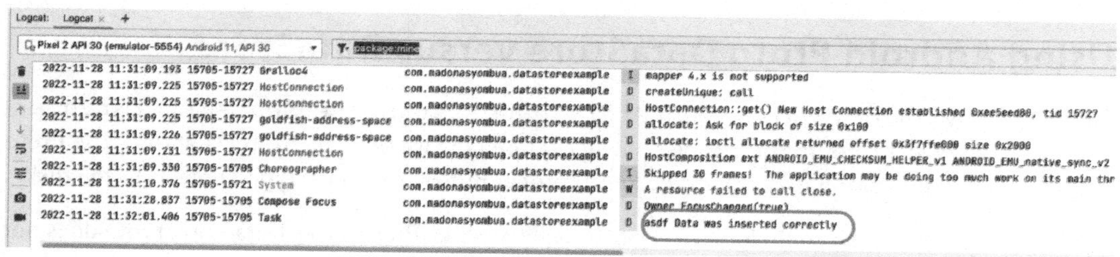

Figure 5.5 – The debug log indicating that data was inserted correctly

How it works...

In this recipe, we opted to use Dependency Injection to supply the required dependencies to specific classes. We've already covered what Dependency Injection is in depth, so we will not explain it again but instead talk about the modules we created.

In our project, we created `DataStoreManagerModule` and `DataStoreModule`, and all we did was supply the required dependencies. We created a file and called it `store_tasks`, which helps us store the Preference values:

```
private val Context.tasksPreferenceStore : DataStore<Preferences> by
preferencesDataStore(name = "store_tasks")
```

By default, DataStore uses coroutines and returns a flow value. Some important rules to remember while using DataStore, as per the documentation, are as follows:

- DataStore requires only one instance for a given file in the same process. Hence, we should never create more than one instance of DataStore.

- Always have the generic `DataStore` type be immutable to reduce unnecessary and hard-to-trace bugs.
- You should never mix the usage of a single-process DataStore and multi-process DataStore in the same file.

There's more...

As an exercise, you can try to add another button and display the saved data in a lazy column or a text field.

See also

There is more to learn about DataStore, and this recipe has only given you an overview of what you can do with DataStore. You can learn more by following the link at `https://developer.android.com/topic/libraries/architecture/datastore`.

Using Android Proto DataStore versus DataStore

Figure 5.2 shows the differences between `PreferencesDataStore`, `SharedPreferences`, and `ProtoDataStore`. In this recipe, we will explore how we can use Proto DataStore. The Proto DataStore implementation uses DataStore and Protocol Buffers to persist typed objects to the disk.

Proto DataStore is similar to Preferences DataStore, but unlike Preferences DataStore, Proto does not use key-value pairs and just returns the generated object in the flow. The file types and structure of the data depend on the schema of the `.protoc` files.

Getting ready

We will use our already created project to show how you can use Proto DataStore in Android. We will also use already created classes and just give the functions different names.

How to do it...

1. We will need to start by setting up the required dependencies, so let's go ahead and add the following to our Gradle app-level file:

```
implementation "androidx.DataStore:DataStore:1.x.x
implementation "com.google.protobuf:protobuf-javalite:3.x.x"
```

2. Next, we will need to add `protobuf` to `plugins` in our `build.gradle` file:

```
plugins {
...
```

```
        id "com.google.protobuf" version "0.8.12"
    }
```

3. We will need to add the protobuf configuration to our build.gradle file to finalize our setup:

```
protobuf {
    protoc {
        artifact = "com.google.protobuf:protoc:3.11.0"
    }

    generateProtoTasks {
        all().each { task ->
            task.builtins {
                java {
                    option 'lite'
                }
            }
        }
    }
}
```

4. Now, inside our package folder, we will need to add our proto file under app/src/main/, then create a new directory and call it proto. You should now have this in your app/src/main/proto file directory:

```
syntax = "proto3";

option java_package =
    "com.madonasyombua.DataStoreexample";
option java_multiple_files = true;

message TaskPreference {
    string first_task = 1;
    string second_task = 2;
    string third_task = 3;
}
```

That was a lot to set up. We can now start adding code to hook everything up.

5. Let's modify classes that might need ProtoDataStore. First, let's add PROTO_DATA_STORE to the TaskDataSource enum class:

```
enum class TaskDataSource {
    PREFERENCES_DATA_STORE,
```

```
    PROTO_DATA_STORE
}
```

6. In `DataStoreManager`, let's add `saveTaskToProtoStore()` and `getUserFromProtoStore()`, and our new interface will look like this:

```
interface DataStoreManager {
    suspend fun saveTasks(tasks: Tasks)
    fun getTasks(): Flow<Tasks>
    suspend fun saveTasksToProtoStore(tasks: Tasks)
    fun getTasksFromProtoStore(): Flow<Tasks>
}
```

7. Since we just modified our interface, we will need to go ahead and add new functionalities to the implementation class. You will also notice that the project will complain once you add the functions:

```
override suspend fun saveTasksToProtoStore(tasks: Tasks) {
    TODO("Not yet implemented")
}

override fun getTasksFromProtoStore(): Flow<Tasks> {
    TODO("Not yet implemented")
}
```

8. As recommended, we will need to define a class that implements `Serializer<Type>`, where the type is defined in the Proto file. The purpose of this serializer class is to tell DataStore how to read and write our data type. So, let's create a new object and call it `TaskSerializer()`:

```
object TaskSerializer : Serializer<TaskPreference> {
    override val defaultValue: TaskPreference =
        TaskPreference.getDefaultInstance()

    override suspend fun readFrom(input: InputStream):
        TaskPreference{
            try {
                return TaskPreference.parseFrom(input)
            } catch (exception:
            InvalidProtocolBufferException) {
              throw CorruptionException("Cannot read
              proto.", exception)
            }
    }

    override suspend fun writeTo(t: TaskPreference,
```

```
        output: OutputStream) = t.writeTo(output)
}
```

9. The `TaskPreference` class is auto-generated, and you can access it directly by clicking on it but cannot edit it. Auto-generated files are not editable unless you change the original file.

```
/.../

package com.madonasyombua.datastoreexample;

/**
 * Protobuf type {@code TaskPreference}
 */
public  final class TaskPreference extends
    com.google.protobuf.GeneratedMessageLite<
        TaskPreference, TaskPreference.Builder> implements
    // @@protoc_insertion_point(message_implements:TaskPreference)
    TaskPreferenceOrBuilder {
  private TaskPreference() {
    firstTask_ = "";
    secondTask_ = "";
    thirdTask_ = "";
  }
  public static final int FIRST_TASK_FIELD_NUMBER = 1;
  private java.lang.String firstTask_;
  /**
   * <code>string first_task = 1;</code>
   * @return The firstTask.
   */
  @java.lang.Override
  public java.lang.String getFirstTask() { return firstTask_; }
  /**
   * <code>string first_task = 1;</code>
   * @return The bytes for firstTask.
   */
  @java.lang.Override
  public com.google.protobuf.ByteString
      getFirstTaskBytes() { return com.google.protobuf.ByteString.copyFromUtf8(firstTask_); }
  /**
   * <code>string first_task = 1;</code>
```

Figure 5.6 – A screenshot showing the auto-generated TaskPreference class

10. Now that we have created our data type class, we need to create a `taskProtoDataStore: DataStore<TaskPreference>` with the context used with DataStore. Hence, inside `DataStoreModule`, let's go ahead and add this code:

```
private val Context.taskProtoDataStore:
DataStore<TaskPreference> by DataStore(
    fileName = "task.pd",
    serializer = TaskSerializer
)


@Singleton
@Provides
fun provideTasksProtoDataStore(
    @ApplicationContext context: Context
):DataStore<TaskPreference> = context.taskProtoDataStore
```

11. Now, let's go back to `DataStoreManagerImpl` and work on the functions that we are yet to implement:

```
override suspend fun saveTasksToProtoStore(tasks: Tasks) {
    taskProtoDataStore.updateData { taskData ->
        taskData.toBuilder()
            .setFirstTask(tasks.firstTask)
            .setSecondTask(tasks.secondTask)
            .setThirdTask(tasks.thirdTask)
            .build()
    }

}

override fun getTasksFromProtoStore(): Flow<Tasks> =
    taskProtoDataStore.data.map { tasks ->
        Tasks(
            tasks.firstTask,
            tasks.secondTask,
            tasks.thirdTask
        )
```

12. In `TaskService`, we will also go ahead and add `getTasksFromProto`, and `getTasks()`:

```
interface TaskService {
    fun getTasksFromPrefDataStore() : Flow<Tasks>
    suspend fun addTasks(tasks: Tasks)
    fun getTasks(): Flow<Tasks>
```

```
    fun getTasksFromProtoDataStore(): Flow<Tasks>
}
```

13. When you implement an interface, at first the class that is being implemented will might show compile error, which will prompt you to override the interface functionalities into the class. Hence, inside the `TaskServiceImpl` class, add the following code:

```
class TaskServiceImpl @Inject constructor(
    private val DataStoreManager: DataStoreManager
) : TaskService {
    override fun getTasksFromPrefDataStore() =
        DataStoreManager.getTasks()

    override suspend fun addTasks(tasks: Tasks) {
        DataStoreManager.saveTasks(tasks)
        DataStoreManager.saveTasksToProtoStore(tasks)
    }

    override fun getTasks(): Flow<Tasks> =
        getTasksFromProtoDataStore()

    override fun getTasksFromProtoDataStore():
        Flow<Tasks> =
        DataStoreManager.getTasksFromProtoStore()
}
```

Finally, now that we have all our data saved, we can Log to ensure the data is as expected on the UI; check out the link with the code in the *Technical requirements* section to see how this is implemented.

> **Important note**
>
> Apple M1 has a reported problem with proto. There is an issue open for this; follow this link to resolve the issue: `https://github.com/grpc/grpc-java/issues/7690`. Hopefully, it will be fixed by the time the book is published. It is important to note that if you use the `DataStore-preferences-core` artifact with Proguard, you have to manually add Proguard rules to your rule file to prevent your already written fields from being deleted. Also, you can follow the same process to Log and check whether the data is inserted as expected.

How it works...

You might have noticed that we stored our custom data type as an instance. That is what Proto DataStore does; it stores data as instances of custom data types. The implementations require us to define a schema using protocol buffers, but it provides type safety.

In Android's Proto Datastore library, the `Serializer<Type>` interface converts objects of a specific type (`Type`) into their corresponding protocol buffer format and vice versa. This interface provides methods for serializing objects to bytes and deserializing bytes back into objects.

Protocol buffers in Android is a language and platform-neutral extensible mechanism for serializing your structured data. Protocol buffers encodes and decodes your data in a binary stream that is really lightweight.

The override val defaultValue is used when defining a property in a data class or a serialized model class. It is part of the Kotlin Serialization library, which is commonly used for serializing and deserializing objects to and from different data formats such as JSON or protocol buffers.

We expose the appropriate property by exposing the flow DataStore data from our stored object and writing a proto DataStore that provides us with an `updateData()` function that transactionally updates a stored object.

The `updateData` function gives us the current state of the data as an instance of our data type and updates it in an atomic read-write-modify operation.

See also

There is more to learn about how to create defined schemas. You can check out the protobuf language guide here: `https://developers.google.com/protocol-buffers/docs/proto3`.

Handling data migration with DataStore

If you have built Android applications before, you might have used `SharedPreferences`; the good news now is that there is support for migration, and you can migrate from `SharedPreferences` to DataStore using `SharedPreferenceMigration`. As with any data, we will always modify our dataset; for instance, we might want to rename our data model values or even change their type.

In such a scenario, we will need a DataStore to DataStore migration; that is what we will be working on in this recipe. The process is pretty similar to the migration from `SharedPreferences`; as a matter of fact, `SharedPreferencesMigration` is an implementation of the `DataMigration` interface class.

Getting ready

Since we just created a new `PreferenceDataStore`, we will not need to migrate it, but we can look at ways to implement a migration in case a need arises.

How to do it...

In this recipe, we will look at how you can utilize the knowledge learned to help you when a need to migrate to DataStore arises:

1. Let's start by looking at the interface that helps with migration. The following code section showcases the `DataMigration` interface, which `SharedPreferencesMigration` implements:

```
/* Copyright 2022 Google LLC.
   SPDX-License-Identifier: Apache-2.0 */

public interface DataMigration<T> {
    public suspend fun shouldMigrate(currentData: T): Boolean
    public suspend fun migrate(currentData: T): T
        public suspend fun cleanUp()
}
```

2. In the `Tasks` data, we might want to change the entries to `Int`; this means changing one of our data types. We will imagine this scenario and try to create a migration based on this. We can start by creating a new `migrateOnePreferencesDataStore`:

```
private val Context.migrateOnePreferencesDataStore :
DataStore<Preferences> by preferencesDataStore(
    name = "store_tasks"
)
```

3. Now, let's go on to implement `DataMigration` and override its functions. You will need to specify your condition for whether the migration should happen. The migration data shows instructions on how exactly the old data is transformed into new data. Then, once the migration is over, clean up the old storage:

```
private val Context.migrationTwoPreferencesDataStore by
preferencesDataStore(
    name = NEW_DataStore,
    produceMigrations = { context ->
        listOf(object : DataMigration<Preferences> {
            override suspend fun
                shouldMigrate(currentData:
                    Preferences) = true

            override suspend fun migrate(currentData:
            Preferences): Preferences {
                val oldData = context
                    .migrateOnePreferencesDataStore
                        .data.first().asMap()
                val currentMutablePrefs =
```

```
                    currentData.toMutablePreferences()

                oldToNew(oldData, currentMutablePrefs)
                return
                   currentMutablePrefs.toPreferences()
            }
            override suspend fun cleanUp() {
                context.migrateOnePreferencesDataStore
                    .edit { it.clear() }
            }
        })
    }
)
```

4. Finally, let's create the `oldToNew()` function, which is where we can add the data we want to migrate:

```
private fun oldToNew(
    oldData: Map<Preferences.Key<*>, Any>,
    currentMutablePrefs: MutablePreferences
) {
    oldData.forEach { (key, value) ->
        when (value) {

            //migrate data types you wish to migrate
            ...
        }
    }
}
```

How it works...

To better understand how `DataMigration` works, we will need to look into the functions that are in the `DataMigration` interface. In our interface, we have three functions, as shown in the following code block:

```
public suspend fun shouldMigrate(currentData: T):
    Boolean
public suspend fun migrate(currentData: T): T
public suspend fun cleanUp()
```

The `shouldMigrate()` function, as the name suggests, establishes whether the migration needs to be performed or not. If, for instance, no migration is done, which means this will return `false`, then no migration or cleanup will occur. Also, it is crucial to note that this function is initialized every time we call our DataStore instance. `Migrate()`, on the other hand, performs the migration.

By chance, if the action fails or does not work as expected, DataStore will not commit any data to the disk. Furthermore, the cleanup process will not occur, and an exception will be thrown. Finally, `cleanUp()`, as it suggests, just clears any old data from previous data storage.

Writing tests for our DataStore instance

Writing tests is crucial in Android development, and in this recipe, we will write some tests for our DataStore instance. To test our DataStore instance or any DataStore instance, we first need to have instrumentation testing set up since we will be reading and writing in actual files (DataStore), and it is vital to verify that accurate updates are being made.

How to do it...

We will start by creating a simple unit test to test our view model function:

1. In our unit test folder, create a new folder and call it `test`, and inside it, go ahead and create a new class called `TaskViewModelTest`:

```
class TaskViewModelTest {}
```

2. Next, we will need to add some testing dependencies:

```
testImplementation "io.mockk:mockk:1.13.3"
androidTestImplementation "io.mockk:mockk-android:1.13.3"
testImplementation "org.jetbrains.kotlinx:kotlinx-coroutines-
test:1.5.2"
```

3. Now that we have added the required dependencies, let's go ahead and create our mock task service class and mock it, then initialize it in the setup:

```
private lateinit var classToTest: TaskViewModel
private val mockTaskService = mockk<TaskService>()
private val dispatcher = TestCoroutineDispatcher()


@Before
fun setUp(){
    classToTest = TaskViewModel(mockTaskService)
}
```

4. Since we use a coroutine, we will set up our dispatcher in `@Before annotation` and clear any stored data in the `@After` annotation using the `Dispatchers.resetMain()`. If you run your tests without setting up a coroutine, they will fail with an error. The module with the `Main` dispatcher failed to initialize. For tests, `Dispatchers.setMain` from the `kotlinx-coroutines-test` module can be used:

```
@Before
fun setUp(){
    classToTest = TaskViewModel(mockTaskService)
    Dispatchers.setMain(dispatcher)
}

@After
fun tearDown() {
    Dispatchers.resetMain()
}
```

5. After that is completed, let's go on and create a new test called `Verify add tasks function adds tasks as needed`. In this test, we will create a `fakeTask`, add those tasks to `saveTaskData`, and ensure data is inserted as expected by checking that we did not store `null`:

```
@Test
fun `Verify add tasks function adds tasks as needed`() =
runBlocking {
    val fakeTasks = Tasks(
        firstTask = "finish school work",
        secondTask = "buy gifts for the holiday",
        thirdTask = "finish work"
    )
    val expected = classToTest.saveTaskData(fakeTasks)

    Assert.assertNotNull(expected)
}
```

Finally, when you run the unit test, it should pass, and you will see a green check mark.

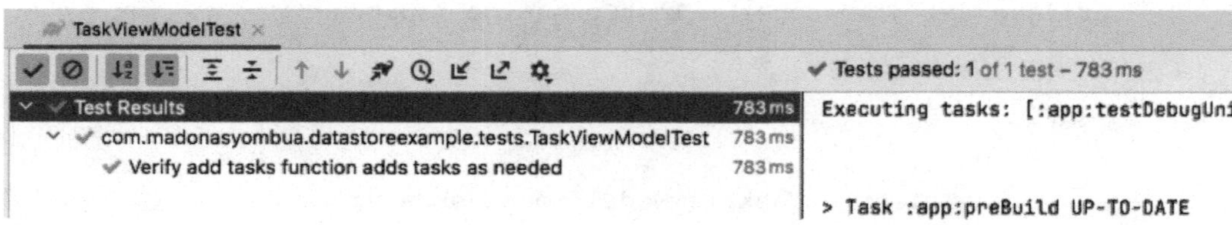

Figure 5.7 – The test passing in the view model

How it works...

There are different mocking libraries used in Android: `Mockito`, `Mockk`, and more. In this recipe, we used `Mockk`, a user-friendly mocking library for Android. `testImplementation "io.mockk:mockk:1.13.3"` is used for unit tests, and `androidTestImplementation "io.mockk:mockk-android:1.13.3"` is used for UI tests.

To test the UI, we will need to follow a pattern, creating a test DataStore instance with default values stored inside it. Then, we create the test subject and verify that the test DataStore values coming from our function match the expected results. We will also need to use `TestCoroutineDispatcher`:

```
private val coroutineDispatcher: TestCoroutineDispatcher =
    TestCoroutineDispatcher()
```

The preceding code performs the execution of the coroutines, which is, by default, immediate. This simply means any tasks scheduled to be run without delays are executed immediately. We also use the same coroutines for our view models. That is also because DataStore is based on Kotlin coroutines; hence we need to ensure our tests have the right setup.

See also

There is more to learn about DataStore. We cannot cover it all in just one chapter. For more information on DataStore, that is, Preference and Proto, you can check out this link: `https://developer.android.com/topic/libraries/architecture/datastore`.

6

Using the Room Database and Testing

Android applications can benefit significantly from storing data locally. The Room persistence library harnesses the power of SQLite. In particular, Room offers excellent benefits for Android developers. Furthermore, Room offers offline support, and the data is stored locally. In this chapter, we will learn how to implement Room, a Jetpack Library.

In this chapter, we'll be covering the following recipes:

- Implementing Room in your applications
- Implementing Dependency Injection in Room
- Supporting multiple entities
- Migrating existing SQL database to Room
- Testing your local database

It is also important to mention there are a couple more libraries are used with Room – for example, RxJava and Paging integration. In this chapter, we will not focus on them but instead on how you can utilize Room to build modern Android apps.

Technical requirements

The complete source code for this chapter can be found at `https://github.com/PacktPublishing/Modern-Android-13-Development-Cookbook/tree/main/chapter_six`.

Implementing Room in your applications

Room is an object-relational mapping library used in Android data persistence and is the recommended data persistence in Modern Android Development. In addition, it is effortless to use, understand and maintain, and harnesses the powers of `SQLiteDatabase`, it also helps reduce boilerplate code, an issue many developers experience when using SQLite. Writing tests is also very straightforward and easy to understand.

The most notable advantage of Room is that it is easy to integrate with other architecture components and gives developers runtime compile checks – that is, Room will complain if you make an error or change your schema without migrating, which is practical and helps reduce crashes.

How to do it...

Let's go ahead and create a new empty compose project and call it `RoomExample`. In our example project, we will create a form intake from users; this is where users can save their first and last names, date of birth, gender, the city they live in, and their profession.

We will save our user data in our Room database, and then later inspect whether the elements we inserted were saved in our database and display the data on the screen:

1. In our newly created project, let's go ahead and delete the unnecessary wanted code – that is, `Greeting(name: String)`, which comes with all empty Compose projects. Keep the preview function, since we will use it to view the screen we create.
2. Now, let's go on and add the needed dependencies for Room and sync the project. We will touch on dependency management using `buildSrc` in *Chapter 12, Android Studio Tips and Tricks to Help You during Development*. You can find the latest version of Room at `https://developer.android.com/jetpack/androidx/releases/room`; we will add `kapt`, which stands for **Kotlin Annotation Processing Tool**, to enable us to use the Java annotation processor with the Kotlin code:

```
dependencies {
implementation "androidx.Room:Room-runtime:2.x.x"
kapt "androidx.Room:Room-compiler:2.x.x"
}

//include kapt on your plugins
plugins {
    id 'kotlin-kapt'
}
```

3. Create a new package and call it `data`. Inside `data`, create a new Kotlin class and call it `UserInformationModel()`. A data class is used to hold data only – in our case, the type of data that we will collect from users will be the first name, last name, date of birth, and so on.

4. By using Room, we use the `@Entity` annotation to give our model a table name; hence, in our newly created `UserInformation` class, let's go ahead and add the `@Entity` annotation and call our table user information:

```
@Entity(tableName = "user_information")
data class UserInformationModel(
    val id: Int = 0,
    val firstName: String,
    val lastName: String,
    val dateOfBirth: Int,
    val gender: String,
    val city: String,
    val profession: String
)
```

5. Next, as in all databases, we need to define a primary key for our database. Hence, in our ID, we will add the `@PrimaryKey` annotation to tell Room that this is our primary key, and it should be autogenerated. If you don't wish to autogenerate, you can set the Boolean to `false`, but this might not be a good idea, due to conflicts that might arise later in your database:

```
@PrimaryKey(autoGenerate = true)
```

6. Now, you should have an entity with a table name, a primary key, and your data types:

```
import androidx.Room.Entity
import androidx.Room.PrimaryKey

@Entity(tableName = "user_information")
data class UserInformationModel(
    @PrimaryKey(autoGenerate = true)
    val id: Int = 0,
    ...
)
```

Inside our data package, let us go ahead and create a new package and call it DAO, which means **data accessible object**. Once that is done, create a new interface and call it `UserInformationDao`; this interface will hold the **create**, **read**, **update**, and **delete** (**CRUD**) functionality – that is, **update**, **insert**, **delete**, and **query**.

We must also annotate our interface with `@Dao` to tell Room that this is our DAO. We use `OnConflictStrategy.REPLACE` on the update and `Insert` functions to help us with a case where we might encounter conflicts in our database. `OnConflictStrategy`, in this case, means that if `Insert` has the same ID, it will replace that data with a particular ID:

```
private const val DEFAULT_USER_ID = 0

@Dao
```

```
interface UserInformationDao {

    @Query("SELECT * FROM user_information")
    fun getUsersInformation():
        Flow<List<UserInformationModel>>

    @Query("SELECT * FROM user_information WHERE id =
        :userId")
    fun loadAllUserInformation(userId: Int =
        DEFAULT_USER_ID): Flow<UserInformationModel>

    @Insert(onConflict = OnConflictStrategy.REPLACE)
    suspend fun insertUserInformation(userInformation:
        UserInformationModel)

    @Update(onConflict = OnConflictStrategy.REPLACE)
    suspend fun updateUserInformation(userInformation:
        UserInformationModel)

    @Delete
    suspend fun deleteUserInformation(userInformation:
        UserInformationModel)
}
```

7. Now that we have our entity and DAO, we will finally create the `Database` class, which extends `RoomDatabase()`. In this class, we will use the `@Database` annotation, pass in the entity that we created, which is the `UserInformation` entity, and give our database a version name, which currently is `one`. We will also specify whether our database schema should be exported or not. So, let's go ahead and create the `Database` abstract class:

```
@Database(entities = [UserInformation::class], version = 1,
exportSchema = false)
abstract class UserInformationDatabase : RoomDatabase() {
    abstract fun userInformationDao():
        UserInformationDao
}
```

8. Finally, we have `Room` set up and ready. Now, we need to add Dependency Injection and our user interface; you can find the code in the *Technical requirements* section. Also, the UI is quite basic at this stage; you can make it a challenge to improve it, as this sample project is just for demonstration purposes.

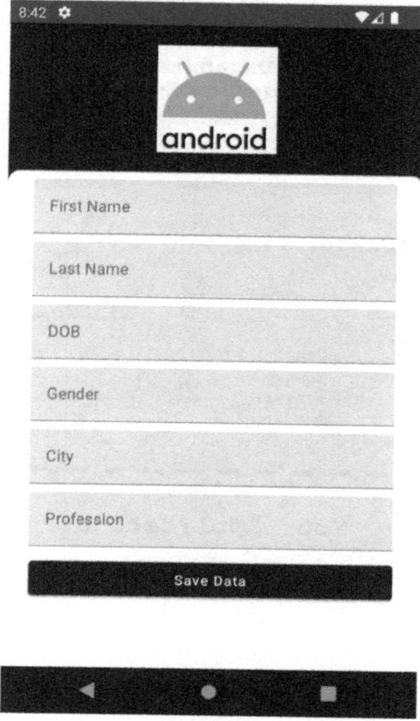

Figure 6.1 – The app's UI

How it works...

The Modern Android Development Room library has three significant components of the Room database:

- The entity
- The DAO
- The database

`Entity` is a table within the database. Room generates a table for each class that has the `@Entity` annotation; if you have used Java before, you can think of the entity as a **plain old Java object** (**POJO**). The entity classes tend to be minor, don't contain any logic, and only hold the data type for the object.

Some significant annotations that map the tables in the database are the foreign keys, indices, primary keys, and table names. There are other essential annotations, such as `ColumnInfo`, which gives column information, and `Ignore`, which, if used, whichever data you wish to ignore will not be persisted by Room.

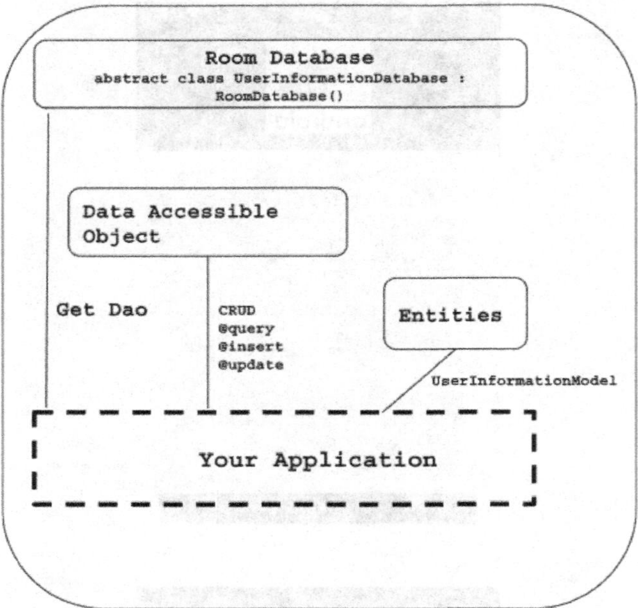

Figure 6.2 – Room DAO

`@DAO` defines the functions that access the database. Think of it like CRUD; if you used SQLite before Room, this is similar to using the cursor objects. Finally, `@Database` contains the database functions and serves as the main entry point for any underlying connection to our application's relational data.

If you need to use this, you annotate with `@Database`, as we did in our database class. In addition, this class extends `RoomDatabase` and includes the list of entities we create. It also contains the abstract method that we create, has no arguments, and returns the class that we annotated with `@Dao`. We run the database by calling `Room.databaseBuilder()`.

Implementing Dependency Injection in Room

As with other recipes, Dependency Injection is vital, and in this recipe, we will walk through how we can inject our `DatabaseModule` and provide the Room database where it is needed.

Getting ready

You will need to have prior knowledge of how Hilt works to be able to follow this recipe step by step.

How to do it...

Open the `RoomExample` project and add Hilt, which is what we will use for Dependency Injection. In *Chapter 3, Handling the UI State in Jetpack Compose and Using Hilt*, we covered Hilt, so we will not discuss it here but just show you how you can use it with Room:

1. Open your project and add the necessary Hilt dependency. See *Chapter 3, Handling the UI State in Jetpack Compose and Using Hilt*, if you need help setting up Hilt or visit `https://dagger.dev/hilt/`.
2. Next, let's go ahead and add our `@HiltAndroidApp` class, and in the `Manifest` folder, add the name of our `HiltAndroidApp`, in our case, `UserInformation`:

```
@HiltAndroidApp
class UserInformation : Application()
<application
    android:allowBackup="true"
    android:name=".UserInformation"
    tools:targetApi="33">
...
```

3. Now that we have Dependency Injection, let's go ahead and add `@AndroidEntryPoint` in the `MainActivity` class, and in our project, let's create a new package and call it `di`. Inside, we will create a new class, `DatabaseModule`, and add our functionalities.
4. In `DatabaseModule`, let's go ahead and create a `provideDatabase()` function, where we will return the `Room` object, add the database name, and ensure we build our database:

```
@Module
@InstallIn(SingletonComponent::class)
class DataBaseModule {

    @Singleton
    @Provides
    fun provideDatabase(@ApplicationContext context:
    Context): UserInformationDatabase {
        return Room.databaseBuilder(
            context,
            UserInformationDatabase::class.java,
            "user_information.db"
        ).build()
    }

    @Singleton
    @Provides
    fun provideUserInformationDao(
```

```
        userInformationDatabase: UserInformationDatabase):
        UserInformationDao {
            return
              userInformationDatabase.userInformationDao()
        }
    }
```

5. Now that we have our Dependency Injection database module set up, we can now start adding the service, which are functions that will help us add user information to the database and get user information from the database. So, let us go ahead and create a new package called `service`. Inside the package, create a new interface, `UserInfoService`, and add the two aforementioned functions:

```
interface UserInfoService {
    fun getUserInformationFromDB():
        Flow<UserInformation>
    suspend fun addUserInformationInDB(
        userInformation: UserInformation)
}
```

6. Since `UserInfoService` is an interface, we will need to implement the functionalities in our `Impl` class, so let us now go ahead and create a new class called `UserInfoServiceImpl` and a singleton class, and then implement the interface:

```
@Singleton
class UserInfoServiceImpl() : UserInfoService {
    override fun getUserInformationFromDB():
        Flow<UserInformation> {
            TODO("Not yet implemented")
    }

    override suspend fun addUserInformationInDB(
        userInformation: UserInformation) {
            TODO("Not yet implemented")
    }
}
```

7. We will need to inject our constructor and pass `UserInformationDao()`, since we will use the insert function to insert the user data:

```
class UserInfoServiceImpl @Inject constructor(
private val userInformationDao: UserInformationDao
): UserInfoService
```

8. Now, we need to add code in our functions that have the TODO in them. Let's go ahead and see the user information first. Using `userInformationDao`, we will call the insert function to tell Room that we want to insert this user information:

```
override suspend fun addUserInformationInDB(
userInformation: UserInformation) {
    userInformationDao.insertUserInformation(
        UserInformation(
            firstName = userInformation.firstName,
            lastName = userInformation.lastName,
            dateOfBirth = userInformation.dateOfBirth,
            gender = userInformation.gender,
            city = userInformation.city,
            profession = userInformation.profession
        )
    )
}
```

9. Then, we need to get the user information from the database; this will visualize a user's data on the screen:

```
override fun getUserInformationFromDB() =
    userInformationDao.getUsersInformation().filter {
        information -> information.isNotEmpty()
    }.flatMapConcat {
        userInformationDao.loadAllUserInformation()
            .map { userInfo ->
                UserInfo(
                    id = userInfo.id,
                    firstName = userInfo.firstName,
                    lastName = userInfo.lastName,
                    dateOfBirth =
                        userInfo.dateOfBirth,
                    gender = userInfo.gender,
                    city = userInfo.city,
                    profession = userInfo.profession
                )
            }
    }
```

10. Finally, we need to ensure that we provide the implementation through Dependency Injection, so let's now go ahead and add the preceding code, then clean the project, run it, and ensure that everything works as expected:

```
@Module
@InstallIn(SingletonComponent::class)
abstract class UserInfoServiceModule {

    @Singleton
    @Binds
    abstract fun bindUserService(
        userInfoServiceImpl: UserInfoServiceImpl):
            UserInfoService
}
```

11. Once you run the project, you should be able to see it launch without issue. We will go ahead and add a function in our `ViewModel` to insert the data in our database; the `ViewModel` will be used in the views that we created:

```
@HiltViewModel
class UserInfoViewModel @Inject constructor(
    private val userInfoService: UserInfoService
) : ViewModel() {

    fun saveUserInformationData(userInfo: UserInfo) {
        viewModelScope.launch {
            userInfoService.addUserInformationInDB(
                userInfo)
        }
    }
}
```

12. We can now inspect the database and see whether it was created correctly. Run the app, and once it's ready in the IDE, click **App Inspection**, as shown in *Figure 6.3*. You should be able to open the Database Inspector.

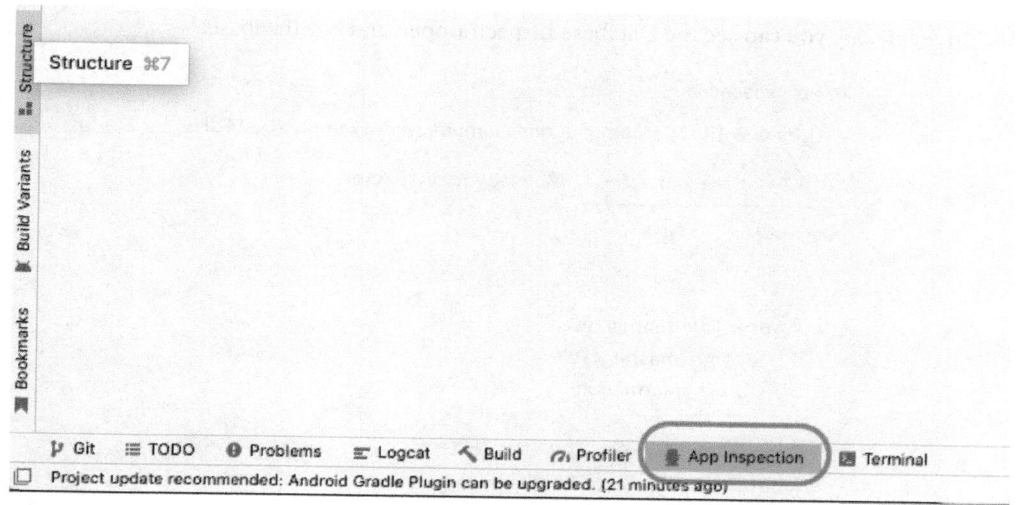

Figure 6.3 – App Inspection

13. Once the Database Inspector is loaded, you should be able to select the currently running Android Emulator, as shown in *Figure 6.4*:

Figure 6.4 – The selected app for app inspection

14. In *Figure 6.5*, you can see the Database Inspector open and our database.

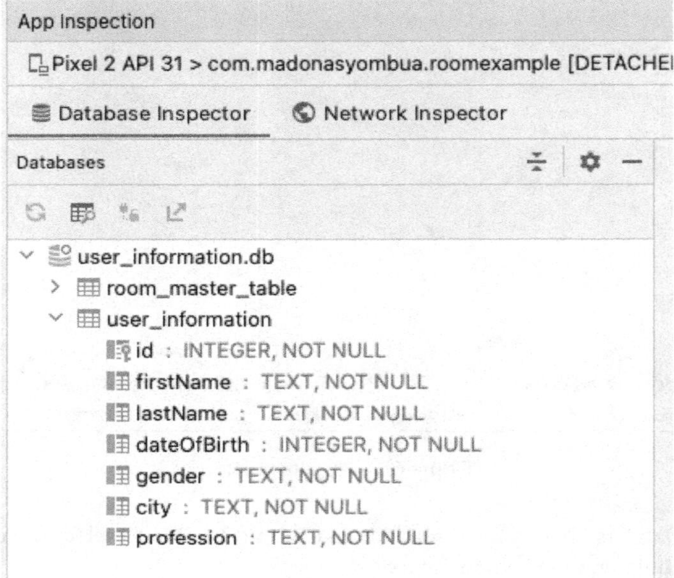

Figure 6.5 – Our user_information database

15. In *Figure 6.6*, you can see that the data we inserted is displayed, which means our insert function works as expected.

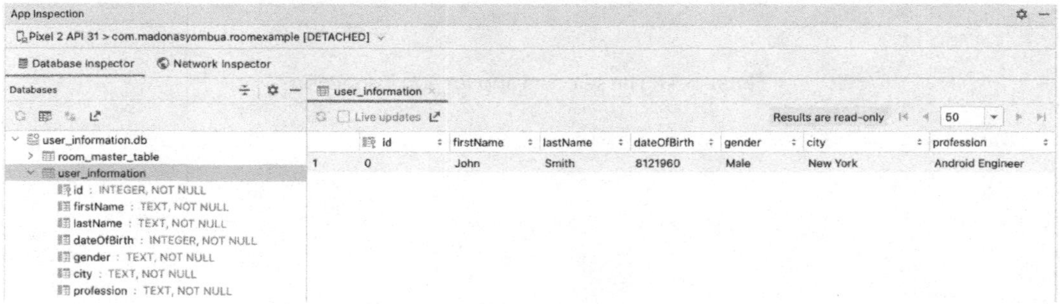

Figure 6.6 – Our database

How it works...

In this recipe, we opted to use Dependency Injection to supply the needed dependencies to specific classes. We covered in depth what Dependency Injection is in previous chapters, so we will not explain it again in this recipe but, instead, talk about the modules we created.

We used the `@Singleton` annotation in Hilt to indicate that `provideDatabase`, which provides an instance of Room, should be created only once during the lifetime of our application, and that this instance should be shared across all the components that depend on it. In addition, when you annotate a class or a binding method with `@Singleton`, Hilt ensures that only one instance of that class or object is created and all the components that need that object will receive the same instance.

It's important to also know that when we use `@Singleton` in Hilt, it is not the same as the Singleton pattern in software design, which can easily be a source of confusion. Hilt's `@Singleton` only guarantees that one instance of a class will be created within the context of a particular component hierarchy.

In our project, we created `DatabaseModule()` and `UserInfoServiceModule()`. In the `DatabaseModule()` class, we have two functions, `provideDatabase` and `provideUserInformationDao`. The first function, `provideDatabase`, returns the `UserInformationDatabase` Room instance, where we get to create the database and build it:

```
fun provideDatabase(@ApplicationContext context: Context):
UserInformationDatabase {
    return Room
        .databaseBuilder(context,
            UserInformationDatabase::class.java,
            "user_information.db")
        .build()
}
```

In `provideUserInformationDao`, we pass `UserInformationDatabase` in the constructor and return the `UserInformationDao` abstract class:

```
fun provideUserInformationDao(userInformationDatabase:
UserInformationDatabase): UserInformationDao {
    return userInformationDatabase.userInformationDao()
}
```

> **Important note**
>
> If you want to lose existing data when you are migrating or if your migration path is missing, you can use the `.fallbackToDestructiveMigration()` function when creating the database.

See also

There is more to learn in Room, and this recipe has only given you a brief overview of what you can do with it. You can learn more by following the link at `https://developer.android.com/reference/androidx/room/package-summary`.

Supporting multiple entities in Room

In this recipe, you will learn how to handle multiple entities in Room. This is useful whenever you have a big project that needs a different data input. An excellent example that we can work with is a budgeting app.

To support multiple entities in Room, you need to define multiple classes that represent your database tables. Each class should have its own annotations and fields that correspond to columns in a table. For instance, a budgeting app might need different types of models, such as the following:

- `BudgetData`
- `ExpenseData`
- `ExpenseItem`

Hence, having multiple entities is sometimes necessary, and knowing how to handle that comes in handy.

Getting ready

To follow along with this recipe, you must have completed the previous recipe.

How to do it ...

You can use any project of your choosing to implement the topics discussed in this recipe. In addition, you can use this example in your pre-existing project to implement the topic.

1. In `RoomExample`, you can add more functionality to the app and try to add more entities, but for this project, let's go ahead and show how you can handle multiple entities in Room.
2. For this example, we will use the sample budgeting App we introduced in an earlier chapter, and since we are working with entities, this will be easier to follow. Let's create a new entity and call it `BudgetData`; the budget data class might have several fields, such as `budgetName`, `budgetAmount`, `expenses`, `startDate`, `endDate`, `notify`, `currency`, and `totalExpenses`; hence, our `BudgetData` data class will look like this:

```
@Entity(tableName = "budgets")
data class BudgetData(
    @PrimaryKey(autoGenerate = true)
    var id: Int = 0,
    var budgetName: String = "",
    var budgetAmount: Double = 0.0,
    var expenses: String = "",
    var startDate: String = "",
    var endDate: String = "",
    var notify: Int = 0,
```

```
    var currency: String = "",
    var totalExpenses: Double
)
```

3. Let's go ahead and add two more entities. First, we will add `ExpenseData`, which might have the following fields and types:

```
@Entity(tableName = "expenses")
data class ExpenseData(
    @PrimaryKey(autoGenerate = true)
    var id: Int = 0,
    var expenseName: String = "",
    var expenseType: String = "",
    var expenseAmount: Double = 0.0,
    @ColumnInfo(name = "updated_at")
    var expenseDate: String = "",
    var note: String = "",
    var currency: String = ""
)
```

4. Then, let's add `ExpenseItem`, which might consist of the following fields:

```
@Entity(tableName = "items")
Data class ExpenseItem(
    @PrimaryKey(autoGenerate = true)
    private var _id: Int
    val name: String
    var type: String?
    val imageContentId: Int
    val colorContentId: Int)
```

5. As you can see, we have three entities; based on these entities, you should create different DAOs for each one:

```
abstract class AppDatabase : RoomDatabase() {
    abstract fun budgetDao(): BudgetDao
    abstract fun itemDao(): ItemDao
    abstract fun expenseDao(): ExpenseDao
}
```

6. At the top of the `AppDatabase` abstract class, we will annotate it with `@Database` and then pass it to all our entities:

```
@Database(
    entities = [ExpenseItem::class, BudgetData::class,
        ExpenseData::class],
```

```
    version = 1
)
@TypeConverters(DateConverter::class)
abstract class AppDatabase  : RoomDatabase() {
    abstract fun budgetDao(): BudgetDao
    abstract fun itemDao(): ItemDao
    abstract fun expenseDao(): ExpenseDao
}
```

7. You can also use embedded objects; the `@Embedded` annotation includes nested or related entities within an entity. It allows you to represent the relationship between entities by embedding one or more related entities in the parent entity:

```
data class ExpenseItem(
...
    @Embedded val tasks: Tasks
  )

data class Tasks(...)
```

In our preceding example, we have annotated the tasks property in the `ExpenseItem` entity with the `@Embedded` annotation. This tells Room to include the fields of the `Tasks` data class within the `ExpenseItem` table, rather than creating a separate table for our `ExpenseItem` entity.

8. Then, the Tasks data class can have the `description`, `priority`, `updatedAt`, and ID:

```
data class Tasks (
    @PrimaryKey(autoGenerate = true)
    var id = 0
    var description: String
    var priority: Int

    @ColumnInfo(name = "updated_at")
    var updatedAt: Date)
```

Hence, the table representing the `ExpenseItem` object will contain additional columns with the newly added fields.

That's it; once you declare the entities in the database and pass them as required, you will have supported multiples entities in your `Database`.

> **Important note**
>
> If your entity has multiple embedded fields of the same type, you can keep each column unique by setting the `Prefix` property; then, Room will add the provided values to the beginning of each column name in the embedded object. Find out more at `https://developer.android.com/`.

How it works...

According to the rules in Room, you can define an entity relationship in three different ways.

- One-to-many relationships or many-to-one relationships
- One-to-one relationships
- Many-to-many relationships

As you have already seen, using entities in one class makes it manageable and easily trackable; hence, this is an excellent solution for Android engineers. A notable annotation is `@Relation`, which specifies where you create an object that shows the relationship between your entities.

There's more...

There is more to learn in Room – for instance, defining relationships between objects, writing asynchronous data accessible object queries, and referencing complex data. It is fair to say we cannot cover everything in just one chapter but offer some guidance to help you navigate building Modern Android applications. For more on Room, visit `https://developer.android.com/training/data-storage/room`.

Migrating an existing SQL database to room

As we mentioned earlier, Room does harness the power of SQLite, and because many applications still use legacy, you might find applications still using SQL and be wondering how you can migrate to Room and utilize the latest Room features.

In this recipe, we will cover the migration of an existing SQL database to Room with step-by-step examples. Furthermore, Room offers an abstraction layer to help with SQLite migrations – that is, by offering the `Migration` class to developers.

How to do it...

Because we did not create a new SQLite database example, since that is not necessary, we will try to emulate a scenario with a dummy sample SQLite database and showcase how you can migrate your existing SQLite database to Room:

1. Since we will be adding Room in an existing SQLite project, you will need to ensure you add the required dependencies. To set this up, refer to the *Implementing Room in your applications* recipe.
2. Next, you will need to go ahead and create a new DAO and entity, since Room requires it. Hence, in this set following the first Room recipe, you can update the model classes to entities. This is pretty straightforward, since mostly what you will do is annotate the classes with `@Entity` and use the table `Names` property to set the name of the table.
3. You must also add `@PrimaryKey` and `@ColumnInfo` annotations for your entity classes. Here is a sample SQLite database:

```
fun onCreate(db: SQLiteDatabase) {

    // Create a String that contains the SQL statement
       to create the items table
    val SQL_CREATE_ITEMS_TABLE =(
            "CREATE TABLE " + ItemsContract.ItemsEntry
                    .TABLE_NAME.toString() + " ("
                    + ItemsContract.ItemsEntry.
                    _Id.toString()
                    + " INTEGER PRIMARY KEY
                    AUTOINCREMENT, "
                    + ItemsContract.ItemsEntry
                    .COLUMN_ITEM_NAME.toString()
                    + " TEXT NOT NULL, "
                    + ItemsContract.ItemsEntry
                    .COLUMN_ITEM_TYPE.toString()
                    + " TEXT NOT NULL, "
                    + ItemsContract.ItemsEntry
                    .COLUMN_ITEM_LOGO.toString()
                    + " INTEGER NOT NULL DEFAULT 0, "
                    + ItemsContract.ItemsEntry
                    .COLUMN_ITEM_COLOR.toString()
                    + " INTEGER NOT NULL DEFAULT 0, "
                    + ItemsContract.ItemsEntry
                    .COLUMN_ITEM_CREATED_DATE
                    .toString() + " DATE NOT NULL
```

```
                    DEFAULT CURRENT_TIMESTAMP);")

    // Execute the SQL statement
    db.execSQL(SQL_CREATE_ITEMS_TABLE)
}
```

However, Room has simplified the process, and we no longer need to create `Contracts`. `Contracts` in Android are a way for developers to define and enforce a set of rules for accessing data within an application. These contracts typically define the structure and schema of the database tables and the expected data types and formats for the data within them. In the case of SQLite on Android, contracts are often used to define the tables and columns of the database, as well as any constraints or relationships between them.

4. Once we have created all our needed entities and DAOs, we can go ahead and create the database. As we saw in the *Implementing Room in your Applications* recipe, we can add all our entities in the `@Database` annotation, and since we are in the first `(1)` version, we can increment the version to `(2)`:

```
val MIGRATION_1_2 = object : Migration(1, 2) {
    override fun migrate(database:
    SupportSQLiteDatabase) {

        //alter items table
        database.execSQL("CREATE TABLE new_items (_id
            INTEGER PRIMARY KEY AUTOINCREMENT NOT
            NULL, name TEXT NOT NULL, type TEXT,
            imageContentId INTEGER NOT NULL,
            colorContentId INTEGER NOT NULL)")
        database.execSQL("INSERT INTO new_items
            (_id,name,type,imageContentId,
            colorContentId)Select_id,name,type,
            imageContentId, colorContentId FROM
            items")
        database.execSQL("DROP TABLE items")
        database.execSQL("ALTER TABLE new_items RENAME
            TO items")

    }
```

5. Then, the important part is ensuring we call `build()` to the Room database:

```
Room.databaseBuilder(
    androidContext(),
    AppDatabase::class.java, "budget.db"
```

```
)
        .addCallback(object : RoomDatabase.Callback() {
            override fun
            onCreate(db:SupportSQLiteDatabase){
                super.onCreate(db)
            }
        })
        .addMigrations(MIGRATION_1_2)
        .build()
```

6. Once your data layer starts using Room, you can officially replace all the `Cursor` and `ContentValue` code with the DAO calls. In our `AppDatabase` class, we have our entities, and our class extends `RoomDatabase()`:

```
@Database(
    entities = [<List of entities>],
    version = 2
)

abstract class AppDatabase : RoomDatabase() {
    abstract fun itemDao(): ItemDao
}
```

   Because Room offers runtime errors, if any error occurs, you will be notified in Logcat.

7. It is fair to say that not everything can be covered in one recipe because SQLite does require a lot of code to set up – for instance, to create queries and handle the cursors – but Room helps to speed these processes up, which is why it is highly recommended.

How it works...

As recommended earlier, migrating a complex database might be hectic and require caution, since it can affect users if pushed to production without thorough testing. It is also highly recommended to use `OpenHelper`, exposed by `RoomDatabase`, for more straightforward or minimal changes to your database. Furthermore, it is worth mentioning that if you have any legacy code using SQLite, it will be written at a high level in Java, so working with a team to find a better solution for the migration is needed.

In your project, you must update the class that extends `SQLiteOpenHelper`. We use `SupportSQLiteDatabase` because we need to update the calls to get the writable and readable database. This is a cleaner database abstraction class to insert and query the database.

> **Important note**
>
> It is important to note that it might be complicated to migrate to a complex database that has many tables and complex queries. However, if your database has minimal tables and no complex queries, migration can be done quickly with relatively small incremental changes in a feature branch. It might be helpful to download the app's database, and you can do so by visiting the following link: `https://developer.android.com/training/data-storage/room/testing-db#command-line`.

Testing your local database

So far, we have ensured that we write tests whenever necessary for our projects. We will now need to go ahead and write tests for our `RoomExample` project, since this is crucial, and you might be required to do so in a real-world scenario. Hence, in this recipe, we will look at a step-by-step guide on writing CRUD tests for our database.

Getting ready

You will need to open the `RoomExample` project to get started with this recipe.

How to do it...

Let's go ahead and first add all the needed Room testing dependencies, and then start writing our tests. For the Hilt test setup, refer to the *Technical requirements* section, where you can find all the required code:

1. You will need to add the following to your `build.gradle`:

```
androidTestImplementation "com.google.truth:truth:1.1.3"
androidTestImplementation "android.arch.core:core-testing:1.1.1"
```

2. After you have added the required dependencies inside the Android test, go ahead and create a new class, calling it `UserInformationDBTest`:

```
class UserInformationDBTest {...}
```

3. Before we can set up our `@Before` function, we will need to create two `lateinit var` instances, which we will initialize in our `@Before` function:

```
private lateinit var database: UserInformationDatabase
private lateinit var userInformationDao: UserInformationDao
```

4. Now, let us go ahead and set up our `@Before` function and create our database, using the in-memory database for testing purposes:

```
@Before
fun databaseCreated() {
    database = Room.inMemoryDatabaseBuilder(
        ApplicationProvider.getApplicationContext(),
            UserInformationDatabase::class.java
    )
        .allowMainThreadQueries()
        .build()

    userInformationDao = database.userInformationDao()
}
```

5. Since we are running and creating the database in memory, we will need to close it after it is done; hence, in our `@After` call, we will need to call `close()` on our database:

```
@After
fun closeDatabase() {
    database.close()
}
```

6. Now that our setup is complete, we will go ahead and start testing our CRUD – that is, inserting, deleting, and updating. Let's go ahead and create an insert test first:

```
@Test
fun insertUserInformationReturnsTrue() = runBlocking {
    val userOne = UserInformationModel(
        id = 1,
        firstName = "Michelle",
        lastName = "Smith",
        dateOfBirth = 9121990,
        gender = "Male",
        city = "New york",
        profession = "Software Engineer"
    )
    userInformationDao.insertUserInformation(userOne)

    val latch = CountDownLatch(1)
    val job = async(Dispatchers.IO) {
        userInformationDao.getUsersInformation()
            .collect {
                assertThat(it).contains(userOne)
                latch.countDown()
```

```
            }
        }

        latch.await()
        job.cancelAndJoin()
    }
```

7. Finally, let us add the `delete` function, and that will wrap up our testing Room for now:

```
    @Test
    fun deleteUserInformation() = runBlocking {
        val userOne = UserInformationModel(
            id = 1,
            firstName = "Michelle",
            lastName = "Smith",
            dateOfBirth = 9121990,
            gender = "Male",
            city = "New york",
            profession = "Software Engineer"
        )

        val userTwo = UserInformationModel(
            id = 2,
            firstName = "Mary",
            lastName = "Simba",
            dateOfBirth = 9121989,
            gender = "Female",
            city = "New york",
            profession = "Senior Android Engineer"
        )
        userInformationDao.insertUserInformation(userOne)
        userInformationDao.insertUserInformation(userTwo)

        userInformationDao.deleteUserInformation(userTwo)

        val latch = CountDownLatch(1)
        val job = async(Dispatchers.IO) {
            userInformationDao.loadAllUserInformation()
                .collect {
                    assertThat(it).doesNotContain(userTwo)
                    latch.countDown()
                }
        }
```

```
        latch.await()
        job.cancelAndJoin()
    }
```

8. When you run the test, they should all pass with a green check mark:

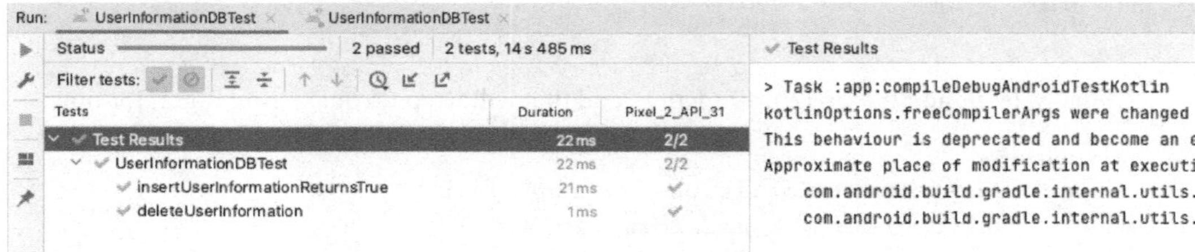

Figure 6.7 – Our tests passing

How it works...

You might have noticed we have used `Truth`, which is a testing framework that provides a fluent and expressive API to write assertions in tests. It is developed by Google, and some of the advantages of using `Truth` include readability, flexibility, and clear error messages. We can easily use a more like natural language constructs – for example, `isEqualTo` and `shouldBe` – which makes the test assertions more intuitive and readable for us developers.

When using the framework, you get a wide range of assertion methods that allow you to test a variety of conditions, including equality, order, and containment. It also allows you to define custom assertion methods, giving you more control over the behavior of your tests.

The `@Before` annotation ensures our `databaseCreated()` function is executed before each class. Our function then creates a database using `Room.inMemoryDatabaseBuilder`, which creates a database in **Random Access Memory** (**RAM**) instead of persistence storage. This means our database will be cleared once the process is killed; hence, in our `@After` call, we close the database:

```
@After
fun closeDatabase() {
    database.close()
}
```

As you might have seen, our tests are in `AndroidTest`, since we launch Room in the main thread and close it after we finish it. The test classes just test the DAO functions – that is, `Update`, `Insert`, `Delete`, and `Query`.

7
Getting Started with WorkManager

In Android, `WorkManager` is an API introduced by Google as part of the Android Jetpack library. It is a powerful and flexible background task scheduling library that allows you to perform deferrable, asynchronous tasks even when your app is not running or the device is in a low-power state.

`WorkManager` provides a unified API to schedule tasks that need to be executed at a specific time or under certain conditions. It takes care of managing and running tasks efficiently, depending on factors such as device idle state, network connectivity, and battery level.

Furthermore, `WorkManager` allows observation of work status and chain creation. This chapter will look into how we can implement `WorkManager` using examples and learn how it works and its use cases.

In this chapter, we'll be covering the following recipes:

- Understanding the Jetpack `WorkManager` library
- Understanding `WorkManager` state
- Understanding threading in `WorkManager`
- Understanding chaining and canceling work requests
- Implementing migration from Firebase `JobDispatcher` to the new recommended `WorkManager`
- How to debug `WorkManager`
- Testing `Worker` implementations

Technical requirements

This chapter utilizes step-by-step examples and does not create a complete project. `WorkManager` is helpful, but because the use case may vary, utilizing examples to see how the code fits your need is an excellent art to learn in programming.

Understanding the Jetpack WorkManager library

WorkManager is one of the most powerful Jetpack libraries, and it is used for persistent work. The API allows observation of persistent status and the ability to create a complex chain of work. When building Android applications, it might be a requirement to have your data persist; if you need help to refresh your knowledge, you can reference *Chapter 6, Using the Room Database and Testing*.

`WorkManager` is the most-recommended API for any background process and is known to handle unique types of ongoing work as shown here:

- **Immediate**: As the name suggests, these are tasks that must be done immediately or completed soon
- **Long-Running**: Tasks that run for a long time
- **Deferrable**: A task that can be rescheduled and can be assigned a different start time and can also run periodically

Some more sample use cases where you can use `WorkManager` are, for instance, if your company wants to create custom notifications, send analytics events, upload images, periodically sync your local data with the network, and more. Furthermore, `WorkManager` is the favored API and is highly recommended as it replaces all previous background scheduling APIs in Android.

There are other APIs that are used for scheduling work. They are deprecated, and in this book, we will not cover them but will mention them since you might encounter them in work with legacy code; they are as follows:

- Firebase Job Dispatcher
- Job Scheduler
- GCM `NetWorkManager`
- `WorkManager`

Getting ready

In this recipe, we will go ahead and look at a simple example of how we can create our own custom notification using `WorkManager`.

You can also use the same concept to send logs or report analytics for your application if you are listening to any logs. We opt for this task because sending notifications to your users is crucial, and most applications do this, compared to uploading images. In addition, with Android 13 and the new API, it's mandatory to request `android.permission.POST_NOTIFICATIONS`.

How to do it...

For this recipe, you do not need to create a project, as the concepts can be used in an already-built project; instead, we will look at examples and walk through the examples with explanations:

1. We will need to ensure we have the required dependency:

```
implementation "androidx.work:work-runtime-ktx:
version-number"
```

   You can get the latest **version number** by following the documentation at `https://developer.android.com/jetpack/androidx/releases/work`.

2. Let us now go ahead and create our notification channel. For this, Google offers a great guide on how you can create one at `https://developer.android.com/develop/ui/views/notifications/channels`, so copy the following code:

```
private fun createCustomNotificationChannel() {
    if (Build.VERSION.SDK_INT >=
    Build.VERSION_CODES.O) {
        val name = getString(
            R.string.notification_channel)
        val notificationDescription = getString(
            R.string.notification_description)
        val importance =
            NotificationManager.IMPORTANCE_DEFAULT
        val channel = NotificationChannel(CHANNEL_ID,
        name, importance).apply {
            description = notificationDescription
        }
        // Register the channel with the system
        val notificationManager: NotificationManager =
            getSystemService(
                Context.NOTIFICATION_SERVICE) as
                    NotificationManager
        notificationManager.createNotificationChannel(
            channel)
    }
}
```

Also, note that creating different channels for separating notification types is possible. As recommended in Android 13, this makes it easier for users to turn them on and off if they do not need them. For example, a user might want to be aware of the latest brands your app is selling, compared to you sending your users info about old existing brands.

3. Now we can create our `workManagerInstance`. Let us think of a scenario where we need to fetch data from our servers every 20 or 30 mins and check whether notifications are available. In that case, we might encounter an issue where users are no longer using our application, which means the application will be put in the background, or the process might even be killed.

   Hence the question becomes how do we fetch the data when the application is killed? This is when `WorkManager` comes to the rescue.

4. We can now create an instance of `WorkManager`:

```
val workManagerInstance = WorkManager.getInstance(application.
applicationContext)
```

5. We will now need to go ahead and set the constraints:

```
val ourConstraints = Constraints.Builder()
    .setRequiredNetworkType(NetworkType.CONNECTED)
    .setRequiresBatteryNotLow(false)
    .build()
```

6. We will also need to set data to pass to the worker; hence we will create new value data, then we will put a string to the endpoint request:

```
val data = Data.Builder()
data.putString(ENDPOINT_REQUEST, endPoint)
```

7. Now we can go ahead and create our `PeriodicWorkRequestBuilder<GetDataWorker>`. In our work, we will set the constraints, set our input data, and pass the `GetDataWorker()` type, which we will create and then build. Furthermore, since we want to be fetching the data every 20 or 30 mins from our server, we use `PeriodicWorkRequestBuilder<Type>()` for that purpose:

```
val job =
    PeriodicWorkRequestBuilder<GetDataWorker>(20,
        TimeUnit.MINUTES)
    .setConstraints(ourConstraints)
    .setInputData(data.build())
    .build()
```

8. We can now finally call `workManagerInstance` and enqueue our job:

```
workManagerInstance
    .enqueue(work)
```

9. We can now go ahead and construct our `GetDataWorker()`. In this class, we will extend the `Worker` class, which will override the `doWork()` function. In our case, however, instead of extending the `Worker` class, we will extend the `CoroutineWorker(context, workerParameters)`, which will help in our case since we will collect this data in a flow. We will also be using Hilt, so we will call `@HiltWorker`:

```
@HiltWorker
class GetDataWorker @AssistedInject constructor(
    @Assisted context: Context,
    @Assisted workerParameters: WorkerParameters,
    private val viewModel: NotificationViewModel
) : CoroutineWorker(context, workerParameters) {

    override suspend fun doWork(): Result {
        val ourEndPoint = inputData.getString(
            NotificationConstants.ENDPOINT_REQUEST)

        if (endPoint != null) {
            getData(endPoint)
        }

        val dataToOutput = Data.Builder()
            .putString(
              NotificationConstants.NOTIFICATION_DATA,
              "Data")
            .build()

        return Result.success(dataToOutput)
    }
```

In our case, we are returning `success`. In our `getData()` function, we pass in the endpoint, and we can assume our data has two or three crucial attributes: the ID, the title, and the description.

10. We can now send notifications:

```
val notificationIntent = Intent(this, NotifyUser::class.java).
apply {
    flags = Intent.FLAG_ACTIVITY_NEW_TASK or
        Intent.FLAG_ACTIVITY_CLEAR_TASK
}
notificationIntent.putExtra(NOTIFICATION_EXTRA, true)
notificationIntent.putExtra(NOTIFICATION_ID, notificationId)
val notifyPendingIntent = PendingIntent.getActivity(
    this, 0, notificationIntent,
```

```
        PendingIntent.FLAG_UPDATE_CURRENT
    )

    val builder = NotificationCompat
        .Builder(context, Channel_ID_DEFAULT)
        .setSmallIcon(notificationImage)
        .setContentTitle(notificationTitle)
        .setContentText(notificationContent)
        .setPriority(NotificationCompat.PRIORITY_HIGH)
        .setContentIntent(notifyPendingIntent)
        .setAutoCancel(true)

    with(NotificationManagerCompat.from(context)) {
        notify(notificationId, builder.build())
    }
```

11. We also need to create a `PendingIntent.getActivity()`, which means when there is a click on the notification, the user will start an activity. For this to happen, we can `getStringExtra(NotificationConstants.NOTIFICATION_ID)` when a notification is clicked and put extras in our intent. This will need to happen in our activity:

```
    private fun verifyIntent(intent: Intent?) {
        intent?.let {
            if (it.hasExtra(
                NotificationConstants.NOTIFICATION_EXTRA)){
                it.getStringExtra(
                NotificationConstants.NOTIFICATION_ID)
            }
        }
    }
```

12. And on our `onResume()`, we can now call our `verifyIntent()` function:

```
    override fun onResume() {
        super.onResume()
        verifyIntent(intent)
    }
```

And that's it; we have custom notifications using our `WorkManager()`.

How it works...

When creating a notification, the `importance` parameter helps determine how to interrupt the user for any given channel, hence why one should specify it in the `NotificationChannel` constructor. If the importance is high and the device is running Android 5.0+, you're going to see a heads-up notification, otherwise, it will just be the icon in the status bar. However, it is essential to note that all notifications, regardless of their importance, appear in a non-interruptive UI at the top of your screen.

The `WorkManager` word is very straightforward, hence removing ambiguity from the API. When using `WorkManager`, `Work` is referenced utilizing the `Worker` class. In addition, the `doWork()` function that we call runs asynchronously in the background thread offered by the `WorkManager()`.

The `doWork()` function returns a `Result{}`, and this result can be `Success`, `Failure`, or `Retry`. When we return the successful `Result{}`, the work will be done and finished successfully. `Failure`, as the name suggests, means the work failed, and then we call `Retry`, which retries the work.

In our `GetDataWorker()`, we pass in `NotificationViewModel` and inject it into our worker using Hilt. Sometimes you might encounter a conflict. The good thing is there is support for such a case with four options for handling any conflict that might occur.

This case is unique to when you are scheduling unique work; it makes sense to tell `WorkManager` what action must be taken when a conflict arises. You can solve this problem easily by using the existing work policy, `ExisitingWorkPolicy`, which has `REPLACE`, `KEEP APPEND`, and `APPEND_OR_REPLACE`.

`Replace`, as the name suggests, replaces the existing work, while `Keep` keeps existing work and ignores new work. When you call *Append*, this adds the new work to the existing one, and finally, `Append or Replace` simply does not depend on the pre-requisite work state.

> **Important note**
>
> `WorkManager` is a singleton, hence it can only be initialized once, that is, either in your app or in the library. And, if you are using any workers with custom dependencies, then you have to provide a `WorkerFactory()` to the config at the time of custom initialization.

There's more...

We can only cover some `WorkManager` steps here. Google has great sample code labs that you can follow through and understand how to use `WorkManager`.

To read more about `WorkManager`, you can use this link: `https://developer.android.com/guide/background/persistent`.

Understanding WorkManager state

In the previous recipe, *Understanding the Jetpack WorkManager library*, we looked into how we can use `WorkManager`. In that recipe, you might have noticed `Work` goes through a series of state changes, and the `doWork` function returns a result.

In this recipe, we will explore states in depth.

How to do it...

We will continue working on an example of how you can apply the concepts learned about in this recipe to your already-built project:

1. You might have noticed we mentioned before that we have three states: `Success`, `Failure`, and `Retry`. `Work` states, however, have different types of processes; we can have a one-time work state, periodic work state, or blocked state:

```
Result
    SUCCESS, FAILURE, RETRY
```

   You can look into this abstract class in more depth by clicking on the result and seeing how it is written.

2. In the first recipe, *Understanding the Jetpack WorkManager library*, we looked into the steps of setting up `WorkManager`. Another great example is downloading files. You can override the `fun doWork()` and check whether your URI is not equal to null and return a success, else failure:

```
override suspend fun doWork(): Result {
    val file = inputData.getString(
        FileParameters.KEY_FILE_NAME) ?: ""
    if (file.isEmpty()){
        Result.failure()
    }

    val uri = getSavedFileUri(fileName = file,
        context = context)
    return if (uri != null){
        Result.success(workDataOf(
            FileParameters.KEY_FILE_URI to
                uri.toString()))
    }else{
        Result.failure()
    }
}
```

3. When handling a state, you can easily check when the state successfully specifies an action, when it failed to perform an action, and finally, when `WorkInfo.State` is equals to `RUNNING`, call `running()`; see the following code snippet:

```
when (state) {
    WorkInfo.State.SUCCEEDED -> {
        success(
            //do something
```

```
        )
    }
    WorkInfo.State.FAILED -> {
        failed("Downloading failed!")
    }
    WorkInfo.State.RUNNING -> {
        running()
    }
    else -> {
        failed("Something went wrong")
    }
}
```

4. The success result returns an instance of `ListenableWorker.Result`, used to indicate that the work was completed successfully.
5. For the mentioned states, you can either use `enqueueUniqueWork()`, which is used for one time, or `PeriodicWorkRequestBuilder`, which is used for periodic work. In our example, we used `PeriodicWorkRequestBuilder<Type>`:

```
WorkManager.enqueueUniqueWork()
WorkManager.enqueueUniquePeriodicWork()
```

How it works...

We always start our request with the *Enqueued* state for the one-time work state, which means the work will run as soon as the constraints are met. Thereafter, we move to *Running*, and if we hit a *Success*, the work is done.

If in any instance, we end up *Running* and we don't hit *Success*, then it means we failed. Then, we will move back to *Enqueued* since we need to retry. *Figure 7.1* and *Figure 7.2* explain the states better for both one-time work and periodic work states.

Finally, if it happens that our enqueued work gets cancelled, then we move it to cancelled.

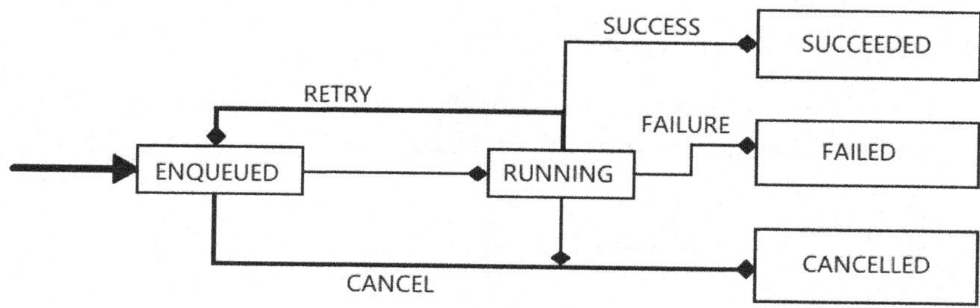

Figure 7.1 – How one-time work requests work

While the preceding image shows the one-time work state, the following diagram depicts the periodic work state.

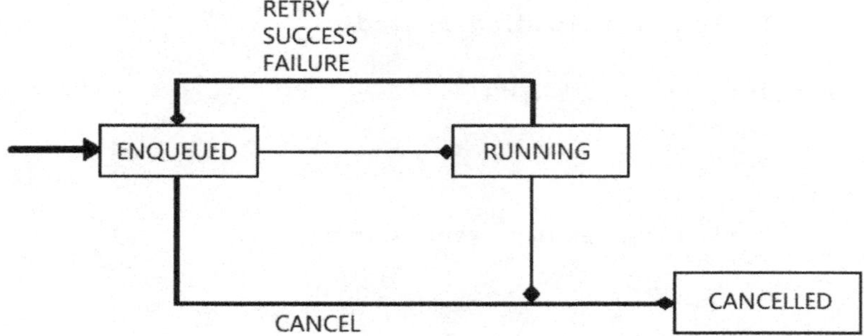

Figure 7.2 – How the periodic work state works

Understanding threading in WorkManager

You can think of `WorkManager` as any process that runs in a background thread. When we use the `Worker()`, and `WorkManager` calls the `doWork()` function, this action works in the background thread. In detail, the background thread comes from the `Executor` specified in the `WorkManager` configuration.

You can also create your own custom executor for your application needs, but if that's not needed, you can use the pre-existing one. This recipe will explore how threading in a `Worker()` works and how to create a custom executor.

Getting ready

In this recipe, since we will be looking at examples, you can follow along by reading and seeing if this applies to you.

How to do it...

Let's learn how threading works in `WorkManager`:

1. In order to configure `WorkManager` manually, you will need to specify your executor. This can be done by calling `WorkManager.initialize()`, then passing the context, and the configuration builder:

```
WorkManager.initialize(
    context,
    Configuration.Builder()
        .setExecutor(Executors.newFixedThreadPool(
```

```
            CONSTANT_THREAD_POOL_INT))
        .build())
```

2. In our earlier example in the previous recipe, *Understanding WorkManager state*, we spoke about a use case where we download files. These files can be in the form of PDF, JPG, PNG, or even MP4. We will look at an example that downloads content 20 times; you can specify how many times you want your content to download:

```
class GetFiles(context: Context, params: WorkerParameters) :
Worker(context, params) {

    override fun doWork(): ListenableWorker.Result {
        repeat(20) {
            try {
                downloadSynchronously("Your Link")
            } catch (e: IOException) {
                return
                    ListenableWorker.Result.failure()
            }
        }

        return ListenableWorker.Result.success()
    }
}
```

3. Currently, if we do not handle the case where the `Worker()` is stopped, it is good practice to ensure that it is dealt with because this is an edge case. To address this case, we need to override the `Worker.onStopped()` method or call `Worker.isStopped` where necessary to free up some resources:

```
    override fun doWork(): ListenableWorker.Result {
        repeat(20) {
            if (isStopped) {
                break
            }

            try {
                downloadSynchronously("Your Link")
            } catch (e: IOException) {
                return
                    ListenableWorker.Result.failure()
            }

        }
```

```
        return ListenableWorker.Result.success()
    }
```

4. Finally, when you stop the worker, the result is entirely ignored until you restart the process again. We used `CoroutineWorker` in our earlier example since `WorkManager` offers support for coroutines, hence why we collected the data in a flow.

> **Important note**
>
> Customizing your executor will require manually initializing `WorkManager`.

How it works...

There is more to learn in the `WorkManager` Jetpack library, and it is fair to acknowledge that it can't all be captured in just a few recipes. For instance, in some scenarios, when providing a custom threading strategy, you should use `ListenableWorker`.

The `ListenableWorker` is a class in the Android Jetpack `WorkManager` library that allows you to perform background work in a flexible and efficient manner. It is a subclass of the `Worker` class and adds the ability to return a `ListenableFuture` from its `doWork()` method, which allows for easier handling of asynchronous operations.

By using `ListenableWorker`, you can create a worker that returns a `ListenableFuture` and register callbacks that will be executed when the future completes. This can be useful for tasks such as network requests or database operations that require asynchronous operations.

The `Worker`, `CoroutineWorker`, and `RxWorker` derive from this particular class. `Worker`, as mentioned, runs in the background thread; `CoroutineWorker` is highly recommended for developers using Kotlin. `RxWorker` will not be touched upon here since Rx by itself is a big topic that caters to users that develop in reactive programming.

See also

Your application might be using Rx. In that case, there are details on how threading works in Rx and how you can use `RxWorker`. See more here: `https://developer.android.com/guide/background/persistent/threading/rxworker`.

Understanding chaining and canceling work requests

In Android development, ensuring you properly handle your application's life cycle is crucial. Needless to say, this also applies to all background work, as a simple mistake can lead to your application draining the user's battery, memory leaks, or even causing the application to crash or suffer from an **application**

not responding (**ANR**) error. This could mean terrible reviews in the Play Store, which will later affect your business and causes stress for developers. How do you ensure this issue is handled well?

This can be done by ensuring all conflicts that arise while using `WorkManager` are appropriately handled or guaranteeing the policy we touched on in the previous recipe is well coded. In this recipe, we will look into chaining and canceling work requests and how to handle long-running work properly.

Say your project requires an order by which the operation should run; `WorkManager` gives you the ability to enqueue and create a chain that specifies multiple dependent tasks, and here you can set the order in which you want the operations to occur.

Getting ready

In this recipe, we will look at an example of how you might chain your work; since this is concept-based, we will look at the example and explain how it works.

How to do it...

To perform chaining using `WorkManager`, follow these steps:

1. In our example, we will assume we have four unique `Worker` jobs to run in parallel. The output of these jobs will be passed to an upload `Worker`. Then, these will be uploaded to our server, like the sample project we had in the *Understanding the Jetpack WorkManager library* recipe.
2. We will have our `WorkManager()` and pass in our context; then we will call `beginWith` and pass a list of our jobs:

```
WorkManager.getInstance(context)
    .beginWith(listOf(job1, job2, job3, job4))
    .then(ourCache)
    .then(upload)
    .enqueue()
```

3. To be able to maintain or preserve all our outputs from our job, we will need to use the `ArrayCreatingInputMerger::class`:

```
val ourCache: OneTimeWorkRequest =
OneTimeWorkRequestBuilder<GetDataWorker>()
    .setInputMerger(ArrayCreatingInputMerger::class)
    .setConstraints(constraints)
    .build()
```

That is about it. There is definitely more to learn, but this serves our purpose.

How it works...

To be able to create the chain of work, we use `WorkManager.beginWith(OneTimeWorkRequest)` or use `WorkManager.beginWith` and pass a list of the one-time work requests that you have specified.

The `WorkManager.beginWith<List<OneTimeWorkRequest>>` operations return an instance of `WorkContinuation`.

We use the `WorkContinuation.enqueue()` function to enqueue our `WorkContinuation` chain. The `ArrayCreatingInputMerger` ensures we pair each key with an array. In addition, the `ArrayCreatingInputMerger` is a class in the Android Jetpack `WorkManager` library that allows you to merge input data from multiple `ListenableWorker` instances into a single array.

Furthermore, if our keys are `unique`, we will get a result of one-element arrays. *Figure 7.3* shows the output:

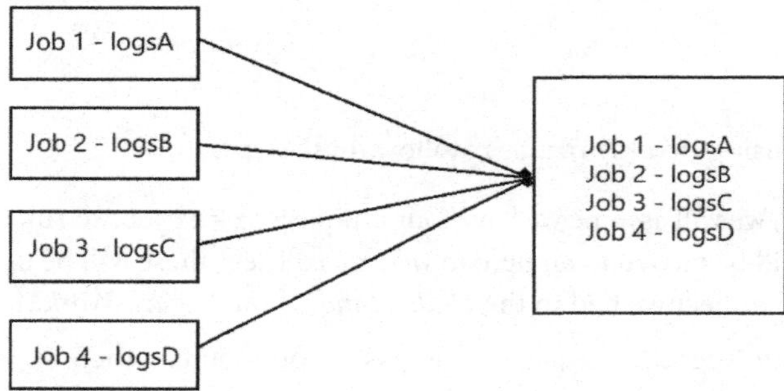

Figure 7.3 – How the array creating input merger works

If we have any colliding keys, then our values will be grouped together in our array, as in *Figure 7.4*.

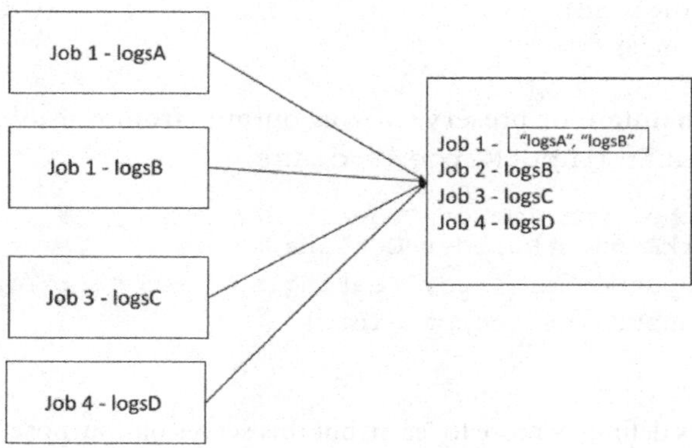

Figure 7.4 – Key collision and result

The rule of thumb is chains of work typically execute sequentially. This is reliant on the work being completed successfully. You might be wondering what happens when the job is enqueued in a chain of several work requests; just like a regular queue, all subsequent work is temporarily blocked until the first work request is completed. Think of it as *first come, first serve*.

See also

You might be wondering how you can support long-running workers; you can learn more at `https://developer.android.com/guide/background/persistent/how-to/long-running`.

Implementing migration from Firebase JobDispatcher to the new recommended WorkManager

In the *Understanding the Jetpack WorkManager library* recipe, we talked about other libraries that are used for scheduling and executing deferrable background work. Firebase `JobDispatcher` is one of the popular ones. If you have used Firebase `JobDispatcher`, you might know it uses the `JobService()` subclass as its entry point. In this recipe, we will look at how you can migrate to the newly recommended `WorkManager`.

Getting ready

We will be looking at how we can migrate from `JobService` to `WorkerManager`. This might apply to your project or not. It is essential to cover it, though, due to the fact that `WorkManager` is highly recommended, and we all have some legacy code. However, if your project is new, you can skip this recipe.

How to do it...

To migrate your Firebase `JobDispatcher` to `WorkManager`, follow these steps:

1. First, you will need to add the required dependency; for this, you can reference the *Understanding the Jetpack WorkManager library* recipe.
2. If you already have Firebase `JobDispatcher` in your project, you might have code similar to the following code snippet:

```
class YourProjectJobService : JobService() {
    override fun onStartJob(job: JobParameters):
    Boolean {
        // perform some job
        return false
    }
```

```
        override fun onStopJob(job: JobParameters):
        Boolean {
            return false
        }
    }
```

3. It is easier if your application utilizes `JobServices()`; then, it will map to `ListenableWorker`. However, if your application is utilizing `SimpleJobService`, then in that case, you should use `Worker`:

```
    class YourWorker(context: Context, params: WorkerParameters) :
        ListenableWorker(context, params) {
        override fun startWork():
        ListenableFuture<ListenableWorker.Result> {
            TODO("Not yet implemented")
        }

        override fun onStopped() {
            TODO("Not yet implemented")
        }
    }
```

4. If your project is using `Job.Builder.setRecurring(true)`, in this case, you should change it to the `PeriodicWorkRequest` a class offered by `WorkManager`. You can also specify your tag, service if the job is recurring, trigger window, and more:

```
    val job = dispatcher.newJobBuilder()
        ...
        .build()
```

5. In addition, to be able to achieve what we want, we will need to input data that will act as the input data for our `Worker`, then build our `WorkRequest` with our input data and the specific constraint. You can reference the *Understanding the Jetpack WorkManager library* recipe, and finally, enqueue the Work Request.

Finally, you can create your work request as either one-time or periodic and ensure you handle any edge cases, such as canceling work.

How it works...

In Firebase `JobDispatcher`, the `JobService.onStartJob()`, which is a function in the `JobSccheduler`, and `startWork()` are called on the main thread. In comparison, in `WorkManager`, the `ListenableWorker` is the basic unit of work. In our example, `YourWorker` implements the `ListenableWorker` and returns an instance of `ListenableFuture`, which helps in signaling work completion. However, you can implement your one-threading strategy based on your application's needs.

In Firebase, the `FirebaseJobBuilder` uses the `Job.Builder` serves as the Jobs metadata. In comparison, `WorkManager` uses `WorkRequest` to perform a similar role. `WorkManager` usually initializes itself by utilizing the `ContentProvider`.

How to debug WorkManager

Any operation that requires working in the background and sometimes making network calls need proper exception handling. This is due to the fact that you do not want your users facing issues and a lack of exception handling coming back to haunt your team or you as a developer.

Hence, knowing how to debug `WorkManager` will come in handy, as this is one of those issues that might last for days if you have a bug. In this recipe, we will look at how to debug `WorkManager`.

Getting ready

To follow this recipe, you must have completed all previous recipes of this chapter.

How to do it...

You might encounter an issue where `WorkManager` no longer runs if it is out of sync. Follow this recipe to debug `WorkManager`:

1. To be able to set up debugging, we will need to first create a custom initialization in our `AndroidManifest.xml` file, that is, by disabling the `WorkManager` initializer:

```
<provider
    ...
    tools:node="remove"/>
```

2. After, we go ahead and set a minimum logging level to debug in our application class:

```
class App() : Application(), Configuration.Provider {
    override fun getWorkManagerConfiguration() =
        Configuration.Builder()
            .setMinimumLoggingLevel(
                android.util.Log.DEBUG)
            .build()
}
```

Once this is done, we will be able to see logs with the prefix `WM-` in our debug level easily, which will make our debugging work much more straightforward, and voila, we can move one step closer to solving our issue.

How it works...

Sometimes it might be helpful just to utilize the verbose `WorkManager` logs to capture any anomalies. In addition, you can enable logging and use your own custom initialization. That is what we do in the first step of our recipe. Furthermore, when we declare our own custom `WorkManager` configuration, our `WorkManager` will be initialized when we call the `WorkManager.getInstance(context)` and not naturally at application startup.

Testing Worker implementations

Testing your `Worker` implementation is crucial, as it helps ensure your code is well handled and your team follows the proper guidelines for writing great code. This will be an integration test, which means we will add our code to the `androidTest` folder. This recipe will look into how to add tests for your worker.

Getting ready

To follow along with this recipe, you need to have completed all previous recipes of this chapter.

How to do it...

Follow these steps to get started with testing `WorkManager`. We will look at examples in this recipe:

1. First, you need to add the testing dependency in your `build.gradle` file:

```
androidTestImplementation("androidx.work:work-testing:$work_
version")
```

   In the scenario where something in the API changes in the future, there's a stable version that you can use, and you can always find that in the documentation by following this link: `https://developer.android.com/jetpack/androidx/releases/work`.

2. We will need to set up our `@Before` function, as provided by Google:

```
@RunWith(AndroidJUnit4::class)
class BasicInstrumentationTest {
    @Before
    fun setup() {
        val context =
            InstrumentationRegistry.getTargetContext()
        val config = Configuration.Builder()
            .setMinimumLoggingLevel(Log.DEBUG)
            .setExecutor(SynchronousExecutor())
            .build()
```

```
            // Initialize WorkManager for instrumentation
               tests.
            WorkManagerTestInitHelper.
                initializeTestWorkManager(context, config)
        }
    }
```

3. Now that we have our `WorkManager` set up, we can go ahead and structure our test:

```
    class GetDataWorker(context: Context, parameters:
    WorkerParameters) : Worker(context, parameters) {
        override fun doWork(): Result {
            return when(endpoint) {
                0 -> Result.failure()
                else -> Result.success(dataOutput)
            }
        }
    }
```

4. You can easily test and verify the states by following this example:

```
    @Test
    @Throws(Exception::class)
    fun testGetDataWorkerHasNoData() {
        ...
        val workInfo =
            workManager.getWorkInfoById(request.id).get()
        assertThat(workInfo.state,
            `is`(WorkInfo.State.FAILED))
    }
```

You can add more tests such as verifying when the state is successful or checking initial delays; you can also go the extra mile and test the constraints and more.

How it works...

The library we use provides excellent support for testing `Worker`. For instance, we have `WorkManagerTestInitHelper` supplied to us through the library. Furthermore, we have the `SynchronousExecutor`, which makes our work as developers easier by ensuring synchronous writing tests is easy. Also, the issue of handling multiple threads, latches, and locks is dealt with.

In our `testGetDataWorkerHasNoData`, we create a request, then enqueue it and wait for the results. We later get the info, then assert when the state is failed, it should fail. You can also test when it is successful.

There's more...

To test worker implementations with different variants, you can follow this link: `https://developer.android.com/guide/background/testing/persistent/worker-impl`.

8

Getting Started with Paging

In Android development, the Paging library helps developers load and display data pages from a larger dataset from local storage or over a network. This can be a common case if your application loads considerable amounts of data for people to read. For instance, a good example is Twitter; you might notice the data refreshes due to the many tweets that people send daily.

Hence, in **Modern Android Development** (**MAD**), Android developers might want to implement the Paging library in their applications to help them with such instances when loading data. In this chapter, you will learn how to utilize the Paging library in your projects.

In this chapter, we'll cover the following recipes:

- Implementing the Jetpack Paging library
- Managing present and loading states
- Implementing your custom pagination in Jetpack Compose
- Loading and displaying paged data
- Understanding how to transform data streams
- Migrating to Paging 3 and understanding the benefits
- Writing tests for your Paging Source

Technical requirements

The complete source code for this chapter can be found at `https://github.com/PacktPublishing/Modern-Android-13-Development-Cookbook/tree/main/chapter_eight`. You will also need to get an API key for `https://newsapi.org/`. `NewsApi` is a worldwide API for news.

Implementing the Jetpack Paging library

The Paging library comes with incredible features for developers. If your codebase is established and extensive, there are other custom ways that developers have created to help them load data efficiently. One notable advantage of Paging is its in-memory caching for your page's data, which ensures your application uses the system resources efficiently while working with the already paged data.

In addition, it offers support for Kotlin coroutine flows and LiveData and has built-in deduplication, which ensures your application uses network bandwidth and resources efficiently, which can help save battery. Finally, the Paging library offers support for error handling, including when refreshing and retrying your data.

Getting ready

In this recipe, we will need to create a new project; if you need to reference a previous recipe for creating a new project, you can visit *Chapter 1, Getting Started with Modern Android Development Skills*.

How to do it...

Let's go ahead and create a new empty Compose project and call it `PagingJetpackExample`. In our example project, we will use the free `NewsApi` to display the news to our users. To get started, check out this link at `https://newsapi.org/docs/get-started`. Also, ensure you get your API for the project, as it is a requirement for this recipe. Follow these steps to get started:

1. Let's go ahead and add the following required dependencies. In addition, since we will be doing a network call, we need to add a library to handle this. As for the correct versioning, check out the *Technical requirements* section for the code and the correct version. We will provide `2.x.x` so you can check compatibility if you are upgrading or already have `Retrofit` in your project and Coil which is a fast, lightweight, and flexible image loading library. It is designed to simplify the process of loading images from various sources (such as network, local storage, or content providers) and displaying them in ImageView or other image-related UI components:

```
//Retrofit
implementation 'com.squareup.retrofit2:retrofit:2.x.x'
implementation 'com.squareup.retrofit2:converter-gson:2.x.x'
//Coil you can also use Glide in this case
implementation 'com.google.accompanist:accompanist-coil:0.x.x'

//Paging 3.0
implementation 'Androidx.Paging:Paging-compose:1.x.x'
```

2. After the project syncs and is ready, go ahead and remove the `Greeting` composable function that comes with the project. You should have just your theme, and your surface should be empty. In addition, for the **user interface** (**UI**) portion of this recipe, you can get the entire code from the *Technical requirements* section.

3. Also, when using an API, developers tend to forget to add the `Android.permission.INTERNET` permission on the manifest, so let's do that now before we forget it:

```
<uses-permission Android:name="Android.permission.INTERNET"/>
```

4. Now, create a package and call it `data`; we will add our model and service files to this package. In addition, ensure you go through the News API **Documentation** section to understand how the API works:

```
data class NewsArticle(
    val author: String,
    val content: String,val title: String ...)
```

5. Let us now create our `NewsArticleResponse` data class, which we will implement in our `NewsApiService` interface. Our API call type is `@GET()`, which means exactly "to get." A more detailed explanation of GET is provided in the *How it works* section. Our call seeks to return a call object containing the data in the form of the `NewsArticleResponse` data class:

```
data class NewsArticleResponse(
    val articles: List<NewsArticle>,
    val status: String,
    val totalResults: Int
)

interface NewsApiService{
    @GET("everything?q=apple&sortBy=popularity&apiKey=
${YOURAPIKEY}&pageSize=20")
    suspend fun getNews(
        @Query("page") page: Int
    ): NewsArticleResponse
}
```

6. Create another class called `NewsArticlePagingSource()`; our class will use `NewsApiService` as the input parameter. When exposing any large datasets through APIs, we need to provide a mechanism to paginate the list of resources. To implement it, we need to pass the type of the Paging key and the type of data to load, which in our case is `NewsArticle`:

```
class NewsArticlePagingSource(
    private val newsApiService: NewsApiService,
): PagingSource<Int, NewsArticle>() {
. . .
}
```

7. Finally, let us go ahead and override `getRefreshKey()` provided by the `PagingSource` and `load()` suspend functions. We will discuss the `load()` and `PagingSource` suspend functions in detail in the *Loading and displaying paged data* recipe:

```
class NewsArticlePagingSource(
    private val newsApiService: NewsApiService,
) : PagingSource<Int, NewsArticle>() {
    override fun getRefreshKey(state: PagingState<Int,
    NewsArticle>): Int? {
        return state.anchorPosition?.let {
        anchorPosition ->
            state.closestPageToPosition(
                anchorPosition)?.prevKey?.plus(1)
                ?: state.closestPageToPosition(
                    anchorPosition)?.nextKey?.minus(1)
        }
    }
    override suspend fun load(params:
    LoadParams<Int>): LoadResult<Int, NewsArticle> {
        return try {
            val page = params.key ?: 1
            val response = newsApiService.getNews(
                page = page)

            LoadResult.Page(
                data = response.articles,
                prevKey = if (page == 1) null else
                    page.minus(1),
                nextKey = if
                    (response.articles.isEmpty()) null
                        else page.plus(1),
            )
        } catch (e: Exception) {
            LoadResult.Error(e)
        }
    }
}
```

8. Now, let's create our repository; a repository is a class that isolates the data sources, such as a web service or a Room database, from the rest of the app. Since we do not have a Room database, we will work with the web service data:

```
class NewsArticleRepository @Inject constructor(
    private val newsApiService: NewsApiService
```

```
) {
    fun getNewsArticle() = Pager(
        config = PagingConfig(
            pageSize = 20,
        ),
        PagingSourceFactory = {
            NewsArticlePagingSource(newsApiService)
        }
    ).flow
}
```

9. We will use Hilt for Dependency Injection in our project and build the required modules that will be supplied. For this section, you can reference the steps in *Chapter 3, Handling the UI State in Jetpack Compose and Using Hilt*, on how to add Hilt to your project and also how to create the required modules. In addition, you can access the entire code through the *Technical requirements* section if you get stuck:

```
@Module
@InstallIn(SingletonComponent::class)
class RetrofitModule{

    @Singleton
    @Provides
    fun provideRetrofitInstance(): NewsApiService =
    Retrofit.Builder()
        .baseUrl(BASE_URL)
        .addConverterFactory(
            GsonConverterFactory.create())
        .build()
        .create(NewsApiService::class.java)
}
```

10. Finally, after we have implemented our `PagingSource`, we can go ahead and create a `Pager` which typically refers to a `ViewPager` in our ViewModel and specify our page size. This can range based on the project's needs or preferences. Furthermore, when using Paging 3.0, we don't need to individually handle or convert any data to survive the screen configuration changes because this is done for us automatically.

    We can simply cache our API result using `cachedIn(viewModelScope)`. In addition, to notify of any change to the `PagingData`, you can handle the loading state using a `CombinedLoadState` callback:

```
@HiltViewModel
class NewsViewModel @Inject constructor(
    private val repository: NewsArticleRepository,
```

```
) : ViewModel() {
    fun getNewsArticle():
        Flow<PagingData<NewsArticle>> =
            repository.getNewsArticle().cachedIn(
                viewModelScope)
}
```

11. Finally, when you run the application, you should see a display like *Figure 8.1*, showing the author's name, image, and content. We also wrap the content since this example is just for learning purposes; you can take it as a challenge to improve the UI and display more details:

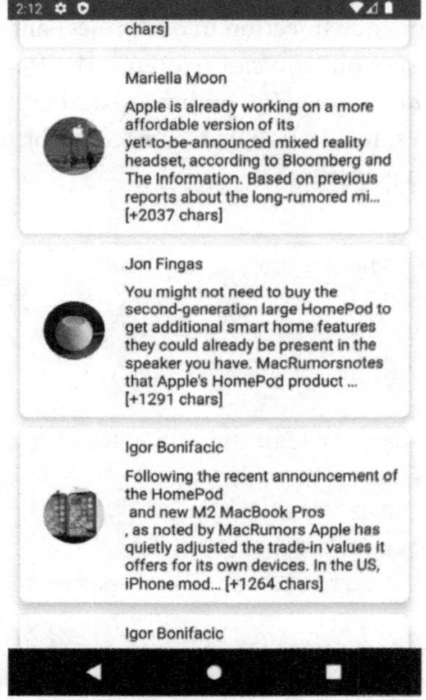

Figure 8.1 – The news article being loaded using the Paging 3 library

How it works...

In Android development, a retrofit request typically refers to a network request made using the Retrofit library, a popular HTTP client library for Android.

Here are some common types of Retrofit requests and their usage:

- GET: This request is used to retrieve data from a server. It is the most common type of request used in Android apps and is often used to retrieve data to populate a UI element such as a list or a grid.

- `POST`: This request is used to submit data to a server. It is commonly used to create new resources on the server, such as a new user account or a new post.
- `PUT`: This request is used to update an existing resource on the server. It is commonly used to update a user's account information or to modify an existing post.
- `DELETE`: This request is used to delete a resource on the server. It is commonly used to delete a user account or to remove a post.
- `PATCH`: This request partially updates an existing resource on the server. It is commonly used when only a small portion of the resource needs to be updated rather than updating the entire resource with a `PUT` request.

When making Retrofit requests, developers typically define an interface that describes the endpoint and the request parameters. Retrofit then generates a client implementation for that interface, which can be used to make the actual network calls.

By using Retrofit, developers can abstract away many of the low-level details of network requests, making it easier and more efficient to communicate with a server from an Android app. For examples about Retrofit, check out the following link `https://square.github.io/retrofit/`.

The Paging library ensures it adheres to the recommended Android architecture patterns. Furthermore, its components are the `Repository`, `ViewModel`, and `UI` layers. The following diagram shows how Paging components operate at each layer and how they work together in unison to load and display your paged data:

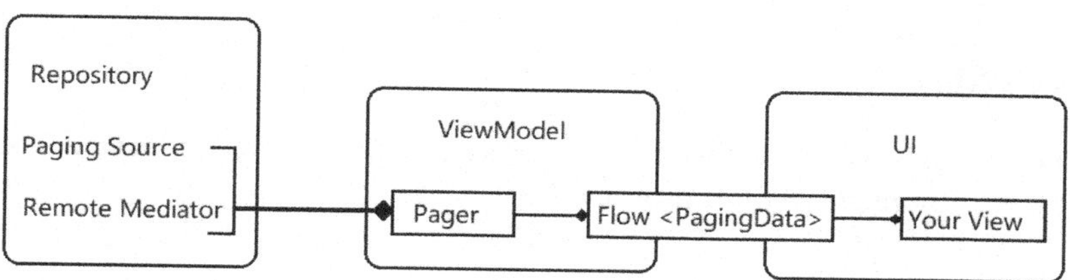

Figure 8.2 – The Paging library architecture

The `Paging Source` component is the main component in the `Repository` layer, as seen in *Figure 8.2*. The object usually declares a source for each piece of data and also handles how to retry data from that source. If you noticed, that is precisely what we did in our example:

```
class NewsArticleRepository @Inject constructor(
    private val newsApiService: NewsApiService
) { . . .
```

We create our Retrofit `builder()` object that contains our base URL of the API, which we defined in the `Constant` class, `const val BASE_URL = "https://newsapi.org/v2/"`, and we use the `Gson` converter to convert our JSON API response. We then declare the `apiService` variable that we will use to connect the Retrofit `builder()` object with our interface and complete our retrofit module.

> **Important note**
>
> It is recommended for anyone using the Paging Library to migrate to Paging 3 due to its improvements and because some functionalities are hard to handle using Paging 2.

Managing present and loading states

The Paging library offers the loading state information to users through its load state object, which can have different forms based on its current loading state. For example, if you have an active load, then the state will be `LoadState.Loading`.

If you have an error state, then the state will be a `LoadState.Error`; and finally, there might be no active load operation, and this state is called the `LoadState.NotLoading`. In this recipe, we will explore the different states and get to understand them; the example demonstrated here can also be found at the following link: `https://developer.android.com/topic/libraries/architecture/paging/load-state`. In this example, we assume your project uses legacy code, which utilizes XML for the view system.

Getting ready

To follow along with this recipe, you need to have completed the code in the previous recipe. You can also skip this if it is not required in your project.

How to do it...

We will not create a new project in this recipe but rather a step-by-step look at how we can access the loading state with a listener or present the loading state with an adapter. Follow along with these steps to get started:

1. When you want to access the state, pass this information to your UI. You can easily use the `loadedStateFlow` stream of the `addLoadStateListener` function provided by `PagingDataAdapter`:

```
lifecycleScope.launch {
    thePagingAdapter.loadStateFlow.collectLatest {
        loadStates ->
    progressBar.isVisible = loadStates.refresh is
```

```
            LoadState.Loading
        retry.isVisible = loadState.refresh !is
            LoadState.Loading
        errorMessage.isVisible = loadState.refresh is
            LoadState.Error
    }
}
```

2. For our example, we will not look into the `addLoadStateListener` function since this is used with an adapter class, and with the new Jetpack Compose, this is barely performed since there is more of a push to use the Jetpack Compose UI-based applications.
3. Filtering the load state steam might make sense based on your application's specific event. This ensures that your app UI is updated at the correct time to avoid issues. Hence, using coroutines, we wait until our refresh load state is updated:

```
lifecycleScope.launchWhenCreated{
    yourAdapter.loadStateFlow
        .distinctUntilChangedBy { it.refresh }
        .filter { it.refresh is LoadState.NotLoading }
        .collect { binding.list.scrollToPosition(0) }
}
```

How it works...

When getting updates from `loadStateFlow` and `addLoadStateListener()`, these are guaranteed to be synchronous, and they update the UI as needed. This simply means in the Paging 3 library for Android, `LoadState.Error` is a state that indicates an error has occurred while loading data from a `PagingSource`.

In Paging 3 library for Android, `LoadState.NotLoading` is a state that indicates that the `PagingDataAdapter` is not currently loading any data and that all available data has been loaded.

When a `PagingDataAdapter` is first created, it starts in the `LoadState.NotLoading` state. This means that no data has been loaded yet, and the adapter is waiting for the first load to occur.

After the first load, the adapter may transition to a different load state depending on the current state of the data loading process. However, once all available data has been loaded, the adapter will transition back to the `LoadState.NotLoading` state.

`LoadState.NotLoading` can be used to inform the UI that the data-loading process is complete and that no further data will be loaded unless the user initiates a refresh or other action.

To handle this state, you can register a listener for changes to the `LoadState` in the `PagingDataAdapter` and update the UI accordingly. For example, you could display a message to the user indicating that all data has been loaded or disable any "load more" buttons or gestures.

There's more...

You can learn more about the state and how to better handle Paging by following this link: `https://developer.android.com/topic/libraries/architecture/paging/load-state`.

Implementing your custom pagination in Jetpack Compose

The Paging library has incredible features for developers, but sometimes you encounter challenges and are forced to create custom pagination. At the beginning of the chapter, we talked about complex code bases having or creating pagination.

In this recipe, we will look into how we can achieve this with a simple list example and how you can use this example to create custom pagination in your application.

Getting ready

In this recipe, we will need to create a new project and call it `CustomPagingExample`.

How to do it...

In our example project, we will try to create a student profile card and use custom pagination to load the profiles in Jetpack Compose.

1. For this recipe, let us go ahead and add the `lifecycle-ViewModel` dependency since we will need it:

```
implementation "Androidx.lifecycle:lifecycle-viewmodel-
compose:2.x.x"
```

2. Let's go ahead and create a new package and call it `data`. In our `data` package, we will add the items we will display on our card. For now, we will just display the student's `name`, `school`, `and major`:

```
data class StudentProfile(
    val name: String,
    val school: String,
    val major: String
)
```

3. Now that we have our `data` class, we will go ahead and build our repository, and since, in our example, we are not using an API, we will use our remote data source, and we can try to load, say, 50 to 100 profiles. Then, inside `data`, add another class and call it `StudentRepository`:

```
class StudentRepository {
```

```
    private val ourDataSource = (1..100).map {
        StudentProfile(
            name = "Student $it",
            school = "MIT $it",
            major = "Computer Science $it"
        )
    }

    suspend fun getStudents(page: Int, pageSize: Int):
    Result<List<StudentProfile>> {
        delay(timeMillis = 2000L) //the delay added is
            just to mimic a network connection.
        val start = page * pageSize

        return if (start + pageSize <=
        ourDataSource.size) {
            Result.success(
                ourDataSource.slice(start until start
                    + pageSize)
            )
        } else Result.success(emptyList())
    }
}
```

4. Now that we have created our repository let us go ahead and create our custom pagination. We will do this by creating a new interface and calling it `StudentPaginator`:

```
interface StudentPaginator<Key, Student> {
    suspend fun loadNextStudent()
    fun reset()
}
```

5. Since `StudentPaginator` is an interface, we must create a class to implement the two functions we just created. Now, let us go ahead and create `StudentPaginatorImpl` and implement our interface:

```
class StudentPaginatorImpl<Key, Student>(

) : StudentPaginator<Key, Student> {
    override suspend fun loadNextStudent() {
        TODO("Not yet implemented")
    }

    override fun reset() {
        TODO("Not yet implemented")
```

```
    }
}
```

6. Next, you will need to work on what you need to handle in the `StudentPaginator` implementation class. For instance, in our constructor, we will need to create a key to listen to the `load`, `request`, `error`, `success`, and `next key`, and then finally, on the `reset()` function, be able to reset our pagination. You can view the complete code in the *Technical requirements* section. You might also notice it looks similar to the Paging Source in the first recipe of this chapter:

```
class StudentPaginatorImpl<Key, Student>(
    private val key: Key,
    private inline val loadUpdated: (Boolean) -> Unit,
    private inline val request: suspend (nextKey: Key)
    ->
. . .
) : StudentPaginator<Key, Student> {
    private var currentKey = key
    private var stateRequesting = false

    override suspend fun loadNextStudent() {
        if (stateRequesting) {
            return
        }
        stateRequesting = true
     . . .
    }
    override fun reset() {
        currentKey = key
    }
```

7. Let's go ahead and create a new package and call it `uistate`. Inside `uistate`, we will create a new data class and call it `UIState` to help us handle the UI state:

```
data class UIState(
    val page: Int = 0,
    val loading: Boolean = false,
    val studentProfile: List<StudentProfile> =
        emptyList(),
    val error: String? = null,
    val end: Boolean = false,
)
```

8. Now let's go ahead and finalize our `ViewModel` `init` in Kotlin is the block that we use for our initialization. We also create `val ourPaginator` that we declare to the `StudentPaginatorImpl` class and handle the inputs with the data we need for our UI:

```
class StudentViewModel() : ViewModel() {
    var state by mutableStateOf(UIState())
    private val studentRepository =
        StudentRepository()
    init {
        loadStudentProfile()
    }

    private val ourPaginator = StudentPaginatorImpl(
        key = state.page,
        loadUpdated = { state = state.copy(loading =
            it) },
        request = { studentRepository.getStudents(it,
            24) },
        nextKey = { state.page + 1 },
        error = { state = state.copy(error =
            it?.localizedMessage) },
        success = { student, newKey ->
            state = state.copy(
                studentProfile = state.studentProfile
                    + student,
                page = newKey,
                end = student.isEmpty()
            )
        }
    )

    fun loadStudentProfile(){
        viewModelScope.launch {
            ourPaginator.loadNextStudent()
        }
    }
}
```

9. Finally, in our `MainActivity` class, we now load the student profile on our card and display it on the screen, as shown in *Figure 8.3*. A tremendous additional exercise to try out is to use Dependency Injection on the sample project to enhance your Android skills. You can utilize *Chapter 3, Handling the UI State in Jetpack Compose and Using Hilt*, for adding Dependency Injection and also to try writing tests for the `ViewModel` class:

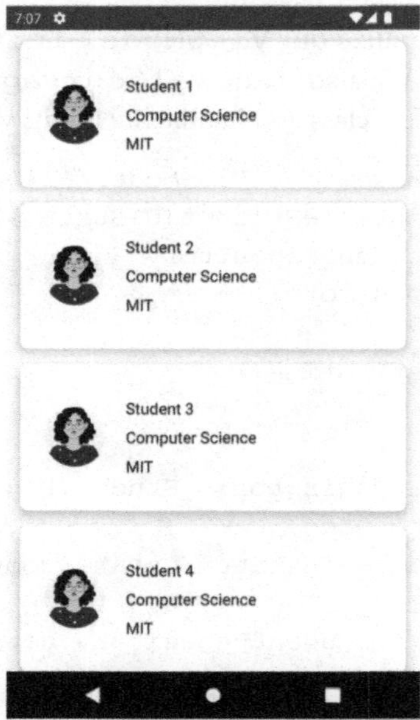

Figure 8.3 – The data loaded on a lazy column

In *Figure 8.4* you will see a progress loading symbol when you scroll down to **Student 4** and so on, which can be great when you have huge loads of data:

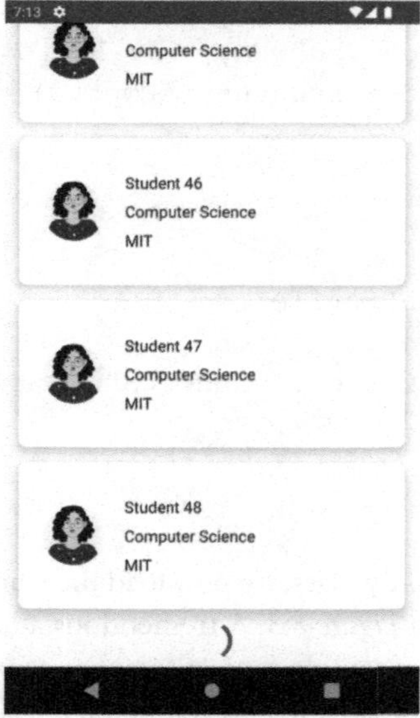

Figure 8.4 – Our data being loaded

How it works...

You might experience issues once you get a list, and it might be tough to notify single items. However, you can easily make your pagination; in our project, we simulate a remote data source but remember that you can use any API for this example.

Our primary focus is the `StudentPaginatorImpl` class – you will notice we pass in a key, a `loadUpdated` value, and a request which is a suspend function that returns a result from our `Student` type; we also pass the `nextkey`, which tells us where we are. Then, in case of an error, we have the throwable error and a `suspend` value, `success`, which gives us the `success` result:

```
class StudentPaginatorImpl<Key, Student>(
    private val key: Key,
    private inline val loadUpdated: (Boolean) -> Unit,
    private inline val request: suspend (nextKey: Key) ->
        Result<List<Student>>,
    private inline val nextKey: suspend (List<Student>) ->
        Key,
    private inline val error: suspend (Throwable?) -> Unit,
    private inline val success: suspend (items:
        List<Student>, newKey: Key) -> Unit
) : StudentPaginator<Key, Student> {
```

So when we override our function from the `loadNextStudent()` interface, we first check our current state request and return our initial value as `false`, but we update it after our status check. We also ensure that we reset the key by setting the `currentKey` to the `nextKey`.

```
currentKey = nextKey(studentProfiles)
success(studentProfiles, currentKey)
loadUpdated(false)
```

This makes it easy if you ever need to customize an item in your `LazyColumn`, ensuring you have great lists.

The `loadStudentProfile()` function has a `viewModelScope.launch {...}`. A ViewModel scope is defined for each ViewModel in our application. In addition, any coroutine launched in this scope is auto-canceled if the ViewModel is cleared.

You might be wondering what a ViewModel is. To help refresh your knowledge, you can look into *Chapter 3, Handling the UI State in Jetpack Compose and Using Hilt*.

Loading and displaying paged data

There are essential steps to consider when loading and displaying paged data. In addition, the Paging library provides tremendous advantages for loading and displaying large, paged datasets. A few steps you must have in mind is ensuring you first define a data source, your Paging Source set up streams if needed, and more.

In this recipe, we will look at how loading and displaying paged data works.

How to do it...

You need to have completed the *Implementing the Jetpack Paging library* recipe to be able to follow along with the explanation of this recipe:

1. You might have noticed in our first recipe that we override `load()`, a method that we use to indicate how we retrieve the paged data from our corresponding data source:

```
override suspend fun load(params: LoadParams<Int>):
LoadResult<Int, NewsArticle> {
    return try {
        val page = params.key ?: 1
        val response = newsApiService.getNews(page =
            page)

        LoadResult.Page(
            data = response.articles,
            prevKey = if (page == 1) null else
                page.minus(1),
            nextKey = if (response.articles.isEmpty())
                null else page.plus(1),
        )
    } catch (e: Exception) {
        LoadResult.Error(e)
    }
}
```

2. We start refreshing at page `1` if `val page = params.key ?: 1` is undefined when we override `getRefreshKey()`; we try to find the page key of the closest page to the anchor position from either our previous key or the next key. We also need to ensure we handle cases where we might have some `null` values:

```
override fun getRefreshKey(state: PagingState<Int,
NewsArticle>): Int? {
    return state.anchorPosition?.let { anchorPosition
        ->
```

```
            state.closestPageToPosition(anchorPosition)?
                .prevKey?.plus(1)
                ?: state.closestPageToPosition(
                    anchorPosition)?.nextKey?.minus(1)
        }
    }
```

How it works...

When using the Paging library, you can specify the position of the first item to be displayed on the screen using the `anchorPosition` parameter. In addition, `anchorPosition` is an optional parameter that you can pass to the `PagingItems` composable function, which is used to display paged data. The `anchorPosition` parameter is used to specify the position of the first item to be displayed on the screen when the composable is first rendered.

The `LoadParams` object carries the information about the load operation to be performed. In addition, it knows about the key to be loaded and the number of items to be displayed on the UI. Furthermore, to better understand how the `load()` function receives the key for each specific load and updates it, review the following diagram:

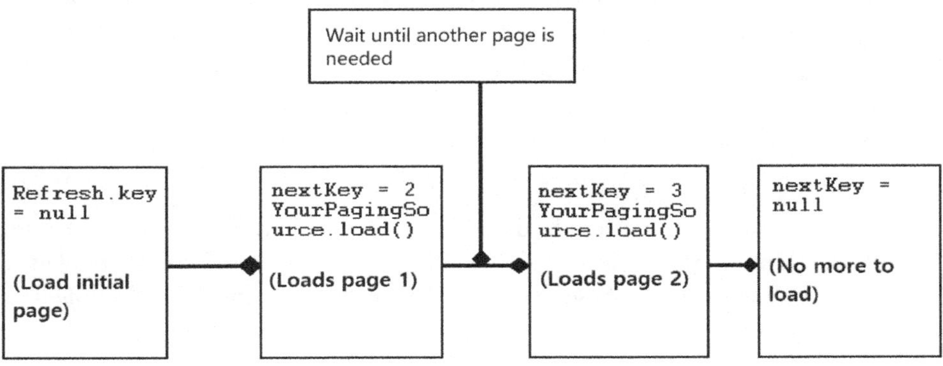

Figure 8.5 – How load() uses and updates the key

Understanding how to transform data streams

When writing any code dealing with Paging, you need to understand how you can transform the data stream as you load it to your users. For instance, you may need to filter a list of items or even convert the items to a different type before you can feed the UI with the data.

Hence, ensuring you apply transformation directly to the stream data lets you keep your repository and UI logic separated cleanly. In this recipe, we will try to understand how we can transform data streams.

Getting ready

To follow along, you must be familiar with the primary usage of the Paging library; hence make sure you have read the previous recipes in this chapter.

How to do it...

In this recipe, we will perform the following steps:

1. Look into how we can apply the essential transformation.
2. Convert and filter the data.
3. Handle separators in the UI and convert the UI model.

   The recipe is helpful to you if you are already using Paging in your application.

4. First, we need to place the transformation inside a `map{PagingData ->}`. A map in Kotlin applies the given lambda function to each element and returns a list of the lambda results:

```
yourPager.flow
    .map { PagingData ->
        // here is where the transformations are
            applied to the items in the paged data.
}
```

5. Second, when we want to convert the data or filter, once we have access to our `PagingData` object, we can use `map()` again on each item separately in the paged list. A typical use case is when you want to map a database or network layer object onto an object that might be used in the UI layer specifically:

```
yourPager.flow
    .map { PagingData ->
        PagingData.map { sports -> SportsModel(sports)
        }
}
```

6. We will need to place the filter operation inside the map because the filter applies to the `PagingData` object. Then once the data is filtered out from our `PagingData`, the new instance is paged to the UI layer and displayed:

```
yourPager.flow
    .map { PagingData ->
```

```
        PagingData.filter { sports ->
            !sports.displayInUi }
}
```

7. Finally, when handling separators in the UI or converting the UI model, the most significant steps are ensuring that you do the following:

   I. Convert the UI models to accommodate your separator items.

   II. Transform the data dynamically and add the separators between presenting and loading the data.

   III. Update the UI to handle the separator items better.

How it works...

The `PagingData` is encapsulated in a reactive stream; what this means is that before loading the data and displaying it to the users, you can incrementally apply the transform to the data. Transforming data streams can be crucial when you have a complex application, and handling this situation in advance might help ensure your application scales better and help minimize the complexity of your data growth.

See also

It is fair to acknowledge that this recipe cannot cover all the information you need to know about transforming the data stream. That said, if you encounter an issue and want to learn more, you can always reference the following link to learn more about how you can handle separators in the UI and more: `https://developer.android.com/topic/libraries/architecture/paging/v3-transform`.

Migrating to Paging 3 and understanding the benefits

You might be using the old Paging version, in this case, Paging 2 or 1, and you might be required to migrate to utilize the benefits Paging 3 offers. Paging 3 offers enhanced functionality and ensures it addresses the most common challenges people experience using Paging 2.

In this recipe, we will look into how you can migrate to the latest recommended Paging library.

Getting ready

If your application is already using Paging 3, then you can skip this recipe; this step-by-step migration guide is intended for users currently using the older versions of the Paging library.

How to do it...

Migrating from old versions of the Paging library might seem complex due to the fact that each application is unique, and complexities might vary. In our example, however, we will touch on a low-level kind of migration since our example application does not need any migration.

To perform migration from old Paging libraries, follow these steps:

1. The first step is to replace the refresh keys, and this is because we need to define how refreshing resumes from the middle of loading data. We will do this by first implementing `getRefreshKey()`, which maps the correct initial key using `PagingState.anchorPosition` as the recent index:

```
override fun getRefreshKey(PagingState: PagingState): String? {
    return PagingState.anchorPosition?.let { position
        ->
          PagingState.getClosestItemToPosition(
              position)?.id
    }
}
```

2. Next, we need to ensure we replace the positional data source:

```
override fun getRefreshKey(PagingState: PagingState): Int? {
    return PagingState.anchorPosition
}
```

3. If you are using the old Paging library, the paged data uses `DataSource.map()`, `mapByPage`, `Factory.map()`, and `Factory.mapByPage`. In Paging 3, however, all these are applied as operators to `PagingData`.

4. Finally, to ensure you migrate from `PageList`, which is in Paging 2, you will need to migrate to `PagingData`. The most notable change is that `PagedList.Config` is not `PagingConfig`. In addition, the `Pager()` exposes an observable `Flow<PagingData>` with its flow:

```
val yourFlow = Pager(
    PagingConfig(pageSize = 24)
) {
    YourPagingSource(yourBackend, yourQuery)
}.flow
    .cachedIn(viewModelScope)
```

How it works...

To ensure your migration is complete and successful, you must make sure you migrate all the significant components from Paging 2. This includes the `DataSource` classes, `PagedList`, and `PagedListAdapter` if your application uses it. Furthermore, some Paging 3 components work well with other versions, which simply means it is backward compatible.

The most notable change to `PagingSource` in Paging 3 is that it combines all the loading functions into one, now called `load()` in `PagingSource`. This ensures there is no redundancy in the code because the loading logic is often identical to the old API. In addition, the loading function parameters in Paging 3 now use the `LoadParams` sealed class, which has subclasses for each load type.

In `PagedList`, which is used in Paging 2, when you migrate, you might use `PagingData` and `Pager`. When you start to use `PagingData` from Paging 3, you should ensure that the configuration is moved from the old `PagedList.Config` to `PagingConfig`.

Writing tests for your Paging Source

Writing tests for your implementations is crucial. We will write unit tests for our `PagingSource` implementation in this recipe to test our logic. Some tests that might be worth writing are checking when news Paging load failure happens.

We can also test the success state and more. You can follow the pattern to write tests for your project or use case.

Getting ready

To follow this recipe step by step, you need to have followed the *Implementing the Jetpack Paging library* recipe, and you need to use the `PagingJetpackExample` project.

How to do it...

Open `PagingJetpackExample` and follow along with this project to add unit tests:

1. Add the following testing libraries to your `build.gradle` app:

```
testImplementation 'org.assertj:assertj-core:3.x.x'
testImplementation "org.mockito:mockito-core:3.x.x"
testImplementation 'Androidx.arch.core:core-testing:2.x.x'

testImplementation 'org.jetbrains.kotlinx:kotlinx-coroutines-
test:1.x.x'
```

2. After adding the dependencies, create a new package and call it `data` in your `test` package in the project structure. You can reference the *Understanding the Android project structure* recipe in *Chapter 1, Getting Started with Modern Android Development Skills,* if you need help finding the folder.

3. Create a test class and call it `NewsArticlePagingSourceTest`.

4. Inside the class, let's go ahead and add `Mock` to mock our `ApiService` interface and create a `lateinit var newsApiService` that we will initialize at our `@Before` step:

```
@Mock
private lateinit var newsApiService: NewsApiService
lateinit var newsPagingSource: NewsArticlePagingSource
```

5. Now let's go ahead and create our `@Before` so we can run our `CoroutineDispatchers`, which is used by all standard builders such as async, and launch to our `@Before` step too:

```
@Before
fun setup() {
    Dispatchers.setMain(testDispatcher)
    newsPagingSource =
        NewsArticlePagingSource(newsApiService)
}
```

6. The first test we will need to write is to check when a failure happens. Hence let's go ahead and set up our test. A `403` response is a forbidden status code indicating the server understood your request but did not authorize it:

```
@Test
fun `news article Paging Source load failure http error`() =
runBlockingTest {
    //setup
    val error = HttpException(
        Response.error<ResponseBody>(
            403, "some content".toResponseBody(
                "plain/text".toMediaTypeOrNull())
        )
    ) . . .
```

7. To continue our test, we will need to use `Mockito.doThrow(error)`:

```
Mockito.doThrow(error)
    .`when`(newsApiService)
    .getNews(
        1
    ). . .
```

8. Then, finally, we trigger `PagingSource.LoadResult.Error` and pass in the type, then assert:

```
//assert
assertEquals(
    expectedResult, newsPagingSource.load(
        PagingSource.LoadParams.Refresh(
            key = null,
            loadSize = 1,
            placeholdersEnabled = false
        )
    )
)
```

9. You can add two more additional tests and then add `tearDown` to clean up the coroutines:

```
@After
fun tearDown() {
    testDispatcher.cleanupTestCoroutines()
}
```

How it works...

We use `Mock` in unit tests, and the general idea is based on the notion that the objects under tests might have dependencies on other complex objects. Based on this, it is much easier to isolate the behavior of the object we want by mocking the object, which ensures it has the same behavior as our real object and makes testing easier:

```
@Mock
private lateinit var newsApiService: NewsApiService
```

Our `lateinit var newsPagingSource: NewsArticlePagingSource` is used for late initialization, and we initialize it on our `@Before` function.

9
Building for Large Screens

We can all agree now that we live in a world with foldable phones, a technology we never anticipated, due to their growing demand and popularity. Ten years ago, if you had told a developer we would have foldable phones, no one would have believed it due to the ambiguity of screen complexity and the transfer of information.

However, now the devices are here with us. And since some of these devices run on the Android operating system, it's vital to know how we developers will build our applications to cater to foldability, along with the number of Android tablets we're now seeing on the market. The support for large screens seems now mandatory, and in this chapter, we will look at supporting large screens in the new Modern Android Development.

In this chapter, we'll be covering the following recipes:

- Building adaptive layouts in Modern Android Development
- Building adaptive layouts using `ConstraintLayouts`
- Handling large-screen configuration changes and continuity
- Understanding activity embedding
- Material Theming in Compose
- Testing your applications on a foldable device

Technical requirements

The complete source code for this chapter can be found at `https://github.com/PacktPublishing/Modern-Android-13-Development-Cookbook/tree/main/chapter_nine`.

Building adaptive layouts in Modern Android Development

When building the UI for your application in Modern Android Development, it is fair to say that you should consider ensuring the application is responsive to different screen sizes, orientations, and form factors. Finally, developers can now remove the lock in portrait mode. In this recipe, we will utilize ideas we learned from previous recipes and build an adaptive app for different screen sizes and orientations.

Getting ready

We will be using the cities application to create a traveler profile, and our screen should be able to change based on different screen sizes and support foldable devices and tablets. To get the entire code, check out the *Technical requirements* section.

How to do it...

For this recipe, we will create a new project, and this time, instead of picking the empty Compose Activity template, we will pick empty Compose Activity (`Material 3`). `Material 3` seeks to improve our application's look and feel in Android. It includes updated theming, components, and great features, such as Material You personalization using dynamic color:

1. Let's start by creating an Empty Compose Activity (`Material3`) project and calling it `Traveller`; note that you can call your project anything you wish.

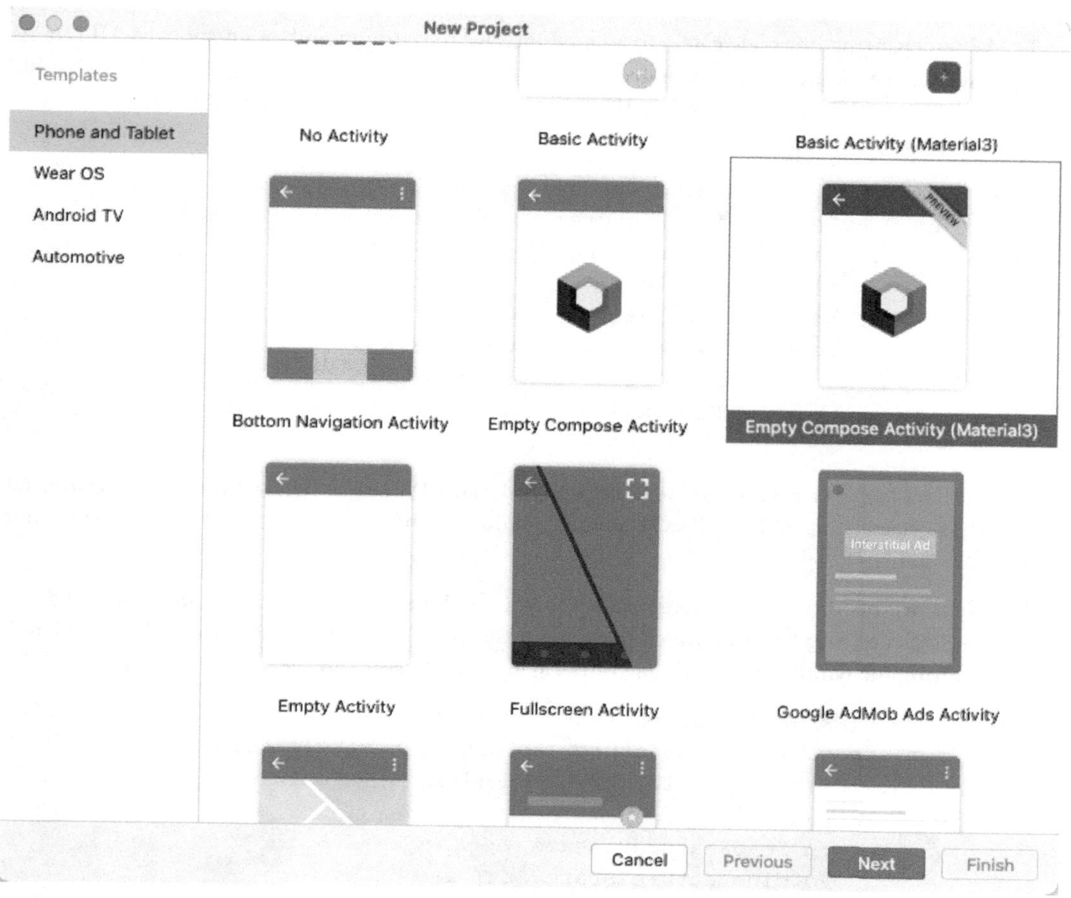

Figure 9.1 – Creating a new Empty Compose Activity (Material3) project

Complex applications utilize responsive UI, and in most cases, ensuring you choose the right navigation type for your application comes in handy. The Material library offers navigation components to developers, such as the bottom navigation, navigation drawer, and navigation rail. You can get the starter code for these in the *Technical requirements* section.

2. Add the following dependency, and check the project for the correct version number, `1.1.0`:

```
implementation "androidx.compose.material3:material3-window-
size-class:1.1.0"
```

3. When ensuring our code caters to adaptability, we have to remember a responsive UI retains data when a phone is rotated, folded, or unfolded. The most crucial part is ensuring we handle the posture. We will create a function, `cityPosture`, that takes `FoldingFeature` as input and returns a Boolean:

```
@OptIn(ExperimentalContracts::class)
fun cityPosture(foldFeature: FoldingFeature?): Boolean {
    contract { returns(true) implies (foldFeature !=
        null) }
    return foldFeature?.state ==
        FoldingFeature.State.HALF_OPENED &&
            foldFeature.orientation ==
                FoldingFeature.Orientation.VERTICAL
}
```

We handle the state based on the three provided states. We also annotate it with the experimental class because this API is still experimental, which means it can change in the future and is not very stable.

4. Next, we need to cover `isSeparating`, which listens to the `FLAT` *fully open* and the `isSeparating` Boolean, which calculates whether `FoldingFeature` should be considered, splitting the window into multiple physical areas that users can see as logically separate:

```
@OptIn(ExperimentalContracts::class)
fun separating(foldFeature: FoldingFeature?): Boolean {
    contract { returns(true) implies (foldFeature !=
        null) }
    return foldFeature?.state ==
        FoldingFeature.State.FLAT &&
            foldFeature.isSeparating
}
```

5. We will also create a sealed interface, `DevicePosture`. This is a Jetpack Compose UI component that allows you to detect a device's posture or orientation, such as whether the device is in portrait or landscape mode:

```
sealed interface DevicePosture {
    object NormalPosture : DevicePosture

    data class CityPosture(
        val hingePosition: Rect
    ) : DevicePosture

    data class Separating(
        val hingePosition: Rect,
```

```
        var orientation: FoldingFeature.Orientation
    ) : DevicePosture
}
```

6. In our `MainActivity`, we now need to ensure we calculate the window size:

```
val windowSize = calculateWindowSizeClass(activity = this)
```

7. Then, we will ensure we handle all sizes well by creating `postureStateFlow`, which will listen to our `DevicePosture` and act when `cityPosture` is either folded, unfolded, or normal:

```
val postureStateFlow = WindowInfoTracker.getOrCreate(this).
windowLayoutInfo(this)
. . .
when {
    cityPosture(foldingFeature) ->
      DevicePosture.CityPosture(foldingFeature.bounds)

    separating(foldingFeature) ->
      DevicePosture.Separating(foldingFeature.bounds,
        foldingFeature.orientation)

    else -> DevicePosture.NormalPosture
}
    }
. . .
    )
```

8. We now need to get set up with a foldable testing virtual device. You can repeat the steps from the first chapter on how to create a virtual device if you need a refresher; otherwise, you should go ahead and create a foldable device. The arrow in *Figure 9.2* shows how you will control the foldable screens.

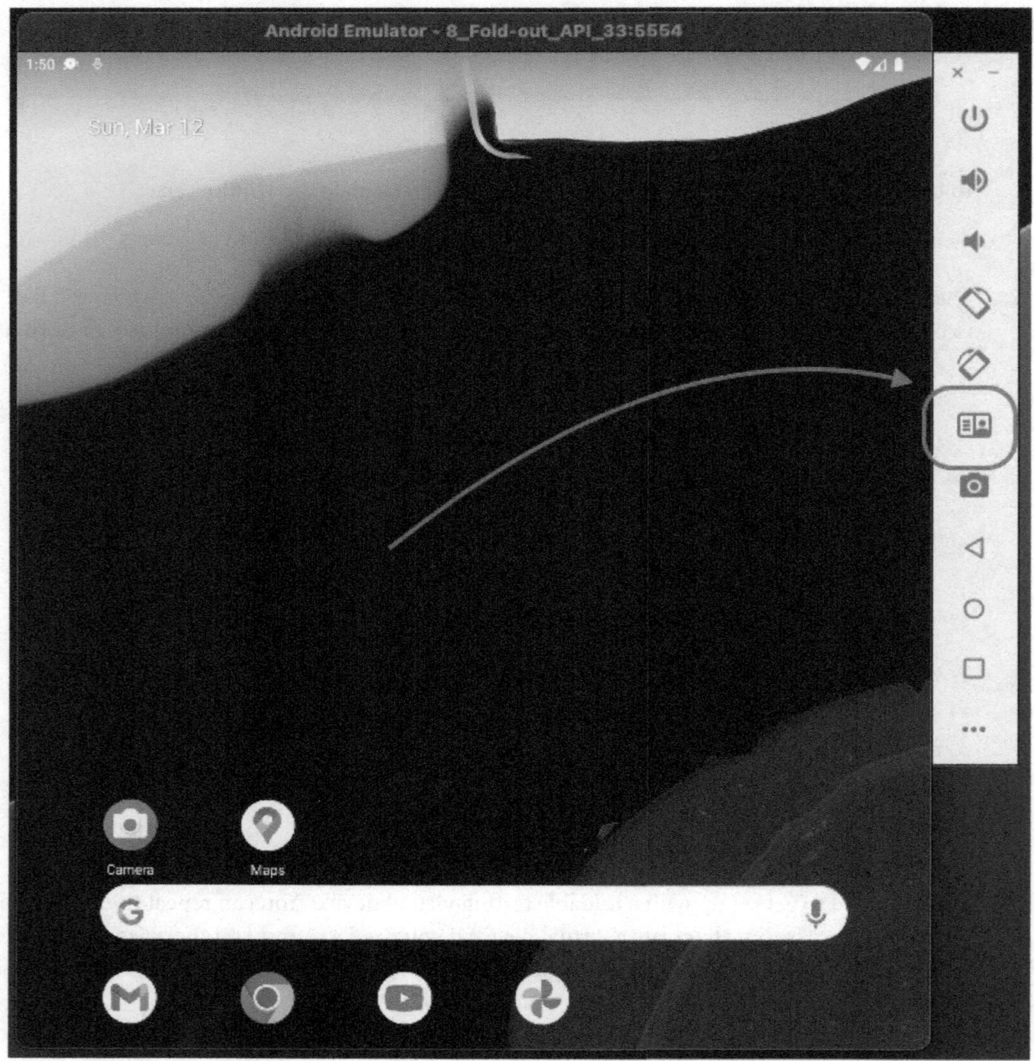

Figure 9.2 – The foldable controls

9. Then, finally, when you run the app, you will see that it changes based on folded and unfolded states, working well. *Figure 9.3* shows when the state is folded.

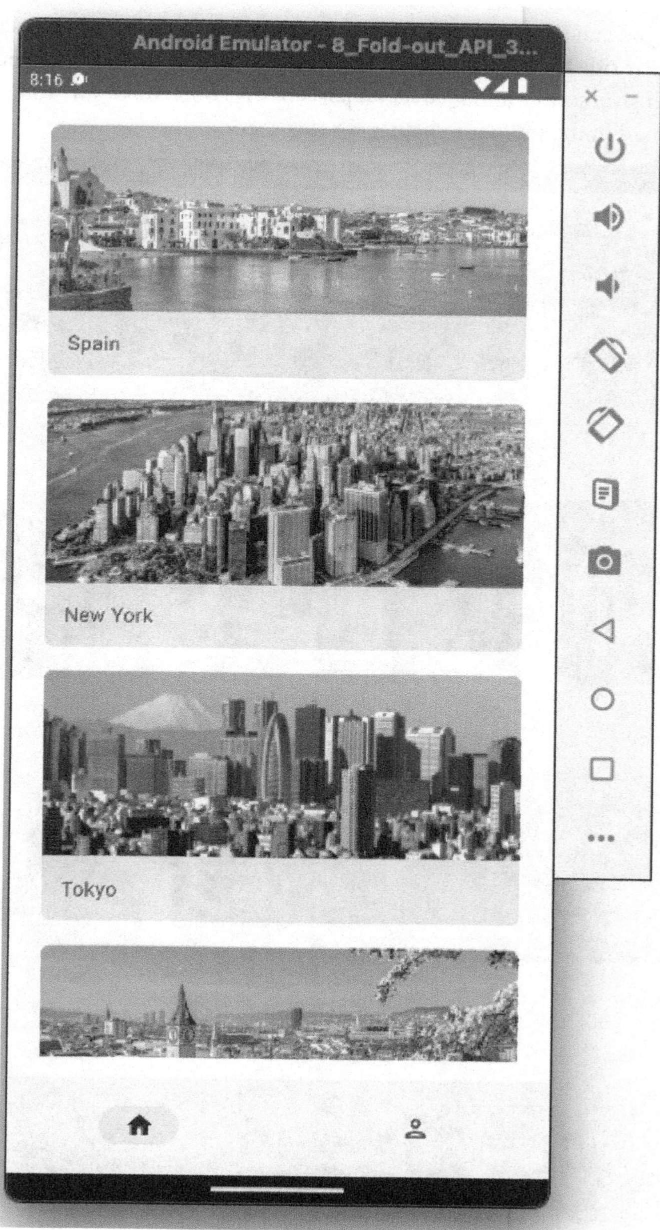

Figure 9.3 – The folded state

10. In *Figure 9.4*, you can see that we changed the bottom navigation and now have our navigation drawer set to the side for more straightforward navigation. It should be acknowledged that this project is extensive, so we cannot cover all parts of the code. Make sure to utilize the Compose concepts learned in the previous chapter for this section.

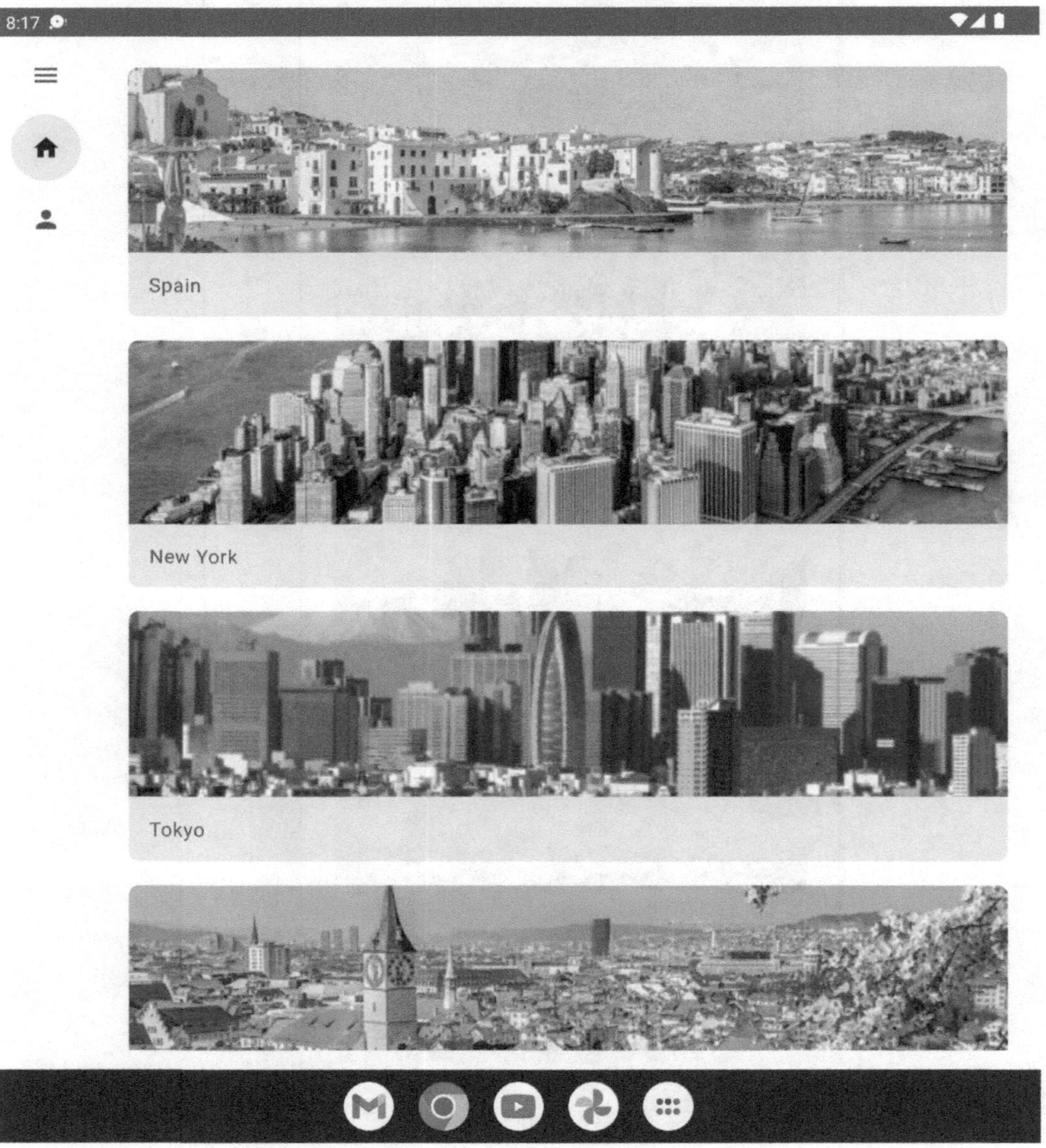

Figure 9.4 – The full-screen state (not folded)

Note that when you expand the navigation drawer, you can see all items, and you should be able to navigate easily.

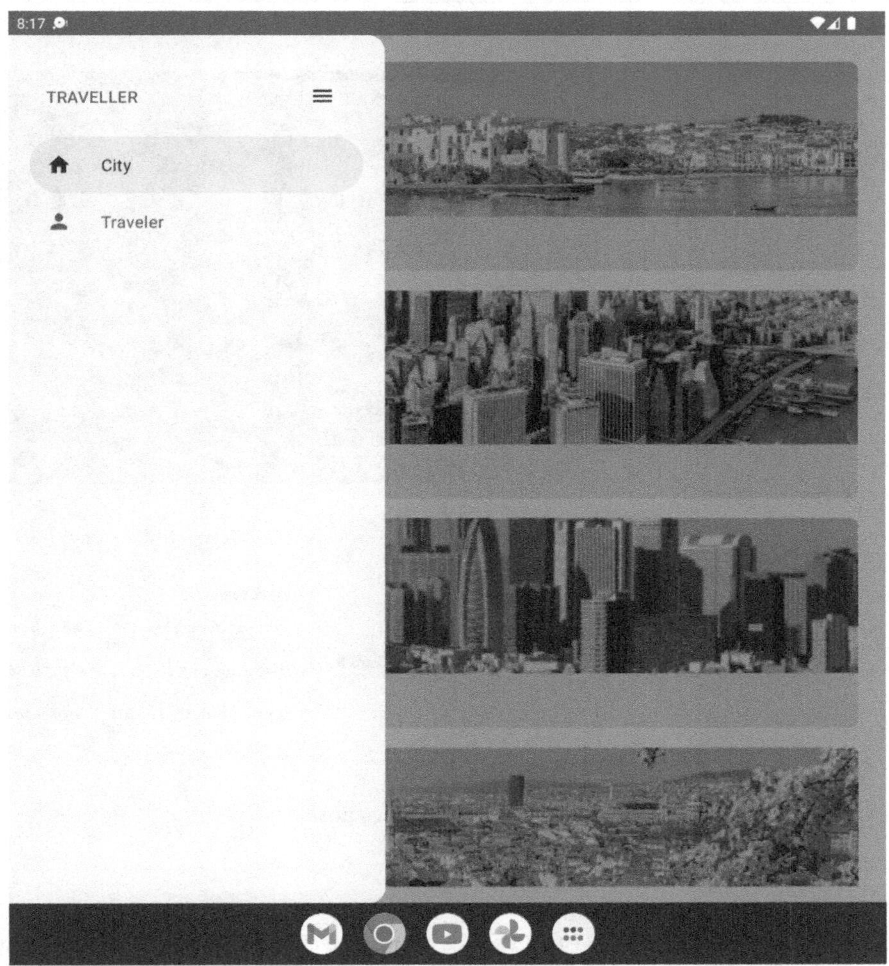

Figure 9.5 – The navigation drawer open

You can also see on the side panel a more descriptive view of your UI, which helps debug issues.

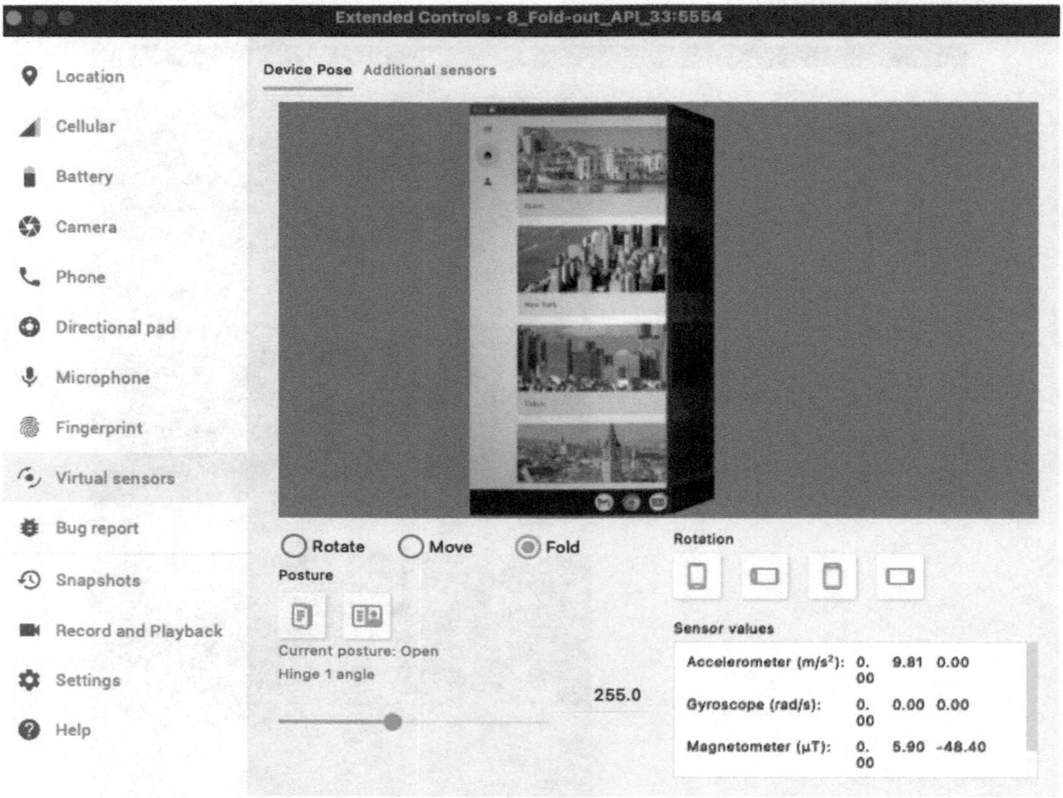

Figure 9.6 – The device pose

> **Important note**
>
> The code base for this project is vast and hence, cannot be covered in just one recipe; you can find the full code in the *Technical requirements* section.

How it works...

We covered the bottom navigation in *Chapter 4, Navigation in Modern Android Development*. In this chapter, however, we use it to showcase how your application can change as the screen changes if your application is installed on a foldable device, which is very important in Modern Android Development.

The navigation rail is used for medium-screen sizes, whereas the navigation drawer, just like in the old way of writing applications, is used as a side drawer and is suitable for large-screen devices. `FoldFeature` is a built-in Jetpack Compose UI component that allows you to create a folding animation effect when you click on it.

Here are the steps to use `FoldFeature` in your Android app. You can also customize `FoldFeature` by providing the necessary parameters:

- `foldableState`: This state controls the folding and unfolding of `FoldFeature`. You can create a `FoldState` instance using the `rememberFoldState()` function.
- `foldedContent`: Content will be displayed when `FoldFeature` is folded.
- `expandedContent`: This is the content that will be displayed when `FoldFeature` is in its expanded state.
- `foldingIcon`: This is the icon that will be displayed to indicate the folding state of `FoldFeature`.

A foldable device has the ability to be in various states and postures. The Jetpack `WindowManager` library's `WindowLayoutInfo` class, which is what we use in our example, provides us with the following details. `state` helps describe the folded state the device is in. When the phone is fully opened, then the state is either `FLAT` or `HALF_OPENED`. We also get to play around with `orientation`, which is the orientation of the hinge.

The hinge can be either `HORIZONTAL` or `VERTICAL`. We have `occlusionType`, and this is the value that is `FULL` when the hinge hides part of the display. Otherwise, the value is `NONE`. Finally, we have `isSeparating`, which becomes valid when the hinge creates two logical displays.

Building adaptive layouts using ConstraintLayouts

Jetpack Compose, a declarative UI toolkit to build great UIs, is ideal to implement and design screen layouts that adjust automatically by themselves and render content well across different screen sizes.

This can be useful to consider when building your application, since the chance of it being installed in a foldable device is high. Furthermore, this can range from simple layout adjustments to filling up a foldable space that looks like a tablet.

Getting ready

You need to have read the previous chapters to follow along with this recipe.

How to do it...

For this recipe, we will build a separate composable function to show you how to use `ConstraintLayout` in the same project instead of creating a new one:

1. Let's go ahead and open `Traveller`. Add a new package and call it `constraintllayoutexample`. Inside the package, create a Kotlin file, called `ConstraintLayoutExample`, and then add the following dependency to the project:

```
implementation "Androidx.constraintlayout:constraintlayout-
compose:1.x.x"
```

2. In our example, we will create a fun `AndroidCommunity()` and use `ConstraintLayout` to create `title`, `aboutCommunity`, and `AndroidImage` references:

```
@Composable
fun AndroidCommunity() {
    ConstraintLayout {
        val (title, aboutCommunity, AndroidImage) =
            createRefs()
  ...
}
```

3. `createRefs()`, which means *create references*, simply creates a reference for each composable in our `ConstrainLayout`.

4. Now, let us go ahead and create our title text, `aboutCommunity`, and `AndroidImage`:

```
Text(
    text = stringResource(id =
        R.string.Android_community),
    modifier = Modifier.constrainAs(title) {
        top.linkTo(parent.top)
        start.linkTo(parent.start)
        end.linkTo(parent.end)
    }
     .padding(top = 12.dp),
    style = TextStyle(
        color = Color.Blue,
        fontSize = 24.sp
    )
)
```

5. Our title text has a modifier that has constraints defined, and if you have used XML before, you may notice that this works exactly how XML works. We provide constraints using the `constrainAs()` modifier, which, in our case, takes the references as a parameter and lets

us specify its constraints in the body lambda. Hereafter, our constraints are specified using `linkTo(...)` or other methods, but in this case, we will use `linkTo(parent.top)`.

We can now connect the parts together using a similar style, in addition, ensure you check the *Technical requirements* section for the entire code:

```
Text(
    text = stringResource(id =
       R.string.about_community),
    modifier = Modifier.constrainAs(aboutCommunity) {
        top.linkTo(title.bottom)
        start.linkTo(parent.start)
        end.linkTo(parent.end)
        width = Dimension.fillToConstraints
    }
        .padding(top = 12.dp, start = 12.dp,
            end = 12.dp),
    style = TextStyle(
        fontSize = 18.sp
    )
)
```

6. Then, we build the image:

```
Image(
    painter = painterResource(id =
        R.drawable.Android),
    contentDescription = stringResource(id =
        R.string.Android_image),
    modifier = Modifier.constrainAs(AndroidImage) {
        top.linkTo(aboutCommunity.bottom,
            margin = 16.dp)
        centerHorizontallyTo(parent)
    }
)
. . .
```

7. Finally, to run this part of the code, you can run the `@Preview` section:

```
@Preview(showBackground = true)
@Composable
fun ShowAndroidCommunity() {
    TravellerTheme() {
        AndroidCommunity()
    }
}
```

8. When you run the application, it should render and adapt well to the screen sizes. For instance, if the state is full (which means not folded), data should be displayed on the entire screen (see *Figure 9.7*).

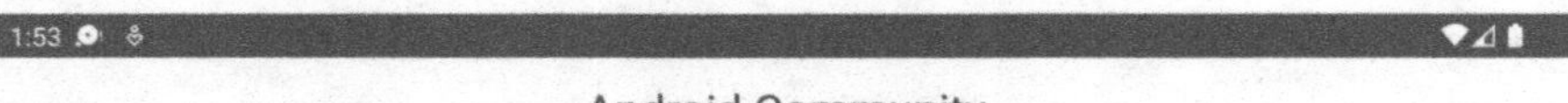

1:53
Android Community
Welcome to the Android community! The key to any community is communication. Like many projects, Android communicates through mailing lists. Because Android is an extremely large project with many components, we have many discussion forums, each focusing on a different topic. View the available groups and join any that seem interesting to you. If you're a user looking for help with the Android UI or an Android device, details on Android updates or security issues, or how to build apps for Android, see the list of resources below.

Figure 9.7 – The full screen of the not folded state

9. In *Figure 9.8*, you can see a version of the data when the screen is folded and how it adapts to the specified dimensions.

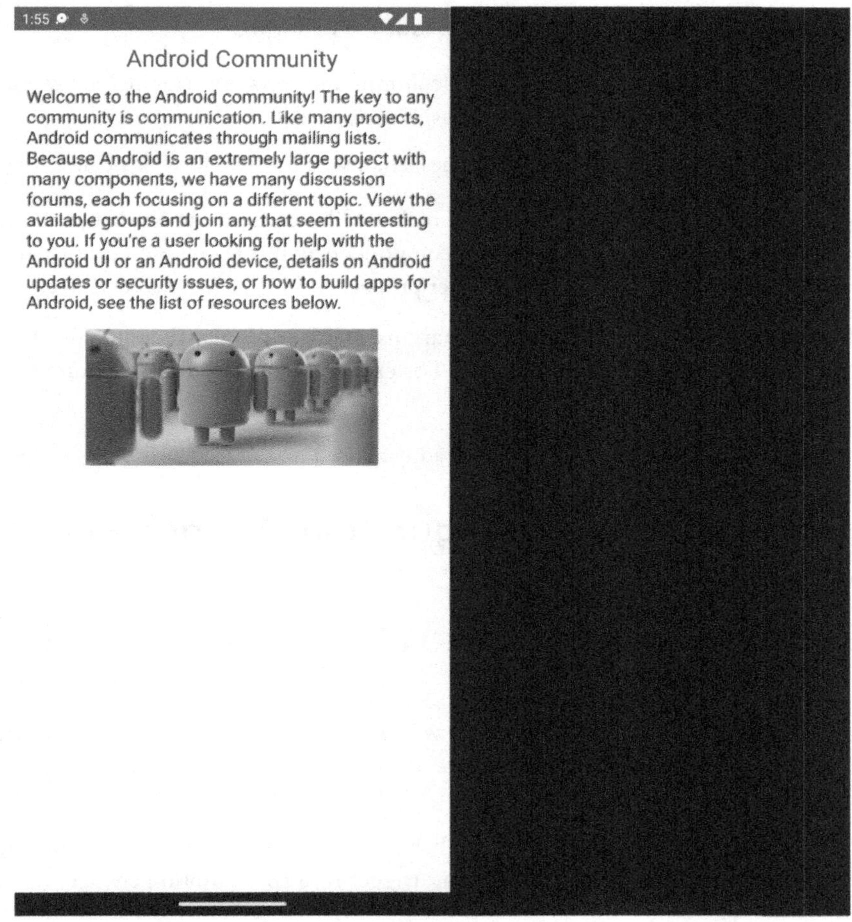

Figure 9.8 – The folded state

How it works...

We use modifiers to adjust the spacing between components and use dimension resources to define the margin between an image and `aboutCommunity`. Our layout will adjust based on the screen size to look good on both small and large screens.

We also use `ConstraintLayout`, which is a layout manager that allows us to create complex layouts with a flat view hierarchy. It also has built-in support for responsive layouts to create different layouts for different screen sizes and orientations.

The best use cases for `ConstraintLayout` include the following:

- When you want to avoid nesting multiple columns and rows; this can include when you want to position your elements on screen for easier code readability
- Utilizing it when you need to use guidelines, chains, or barriers in your positioning

We mentioned modifiers in previous chapters, which are like attributes in XML layouts. They allow us to apply different styles and behaviors to the components in our layout. You can use modifiers to change your component's size, position, and other properties, based on the screen size.

In our example, we use dynamic padding and margins, and you can use them to adjust the spacing between components based on the screen size. For example, you can use a modifier to add more padding to a component on larger screens.

This allows you to create responsive layouts that adjust based on the screen size.

Handling large-screen configuration changes and continuity

Android devices undergo various configuration changes during their operation. Some of the most notable, or standard, ones include the following:

- **Screen orientation change**: This occurs when a user rotates a device's screen, triggering a configuration change. This is when the device switches from portrait to landscape mode or vice versa.
- **Screen size change**: This is when a user changes the screen size of a device – for example, by plugging or unplugging an external display, triggering a configuration change.
- **Language or locale change**: This is when a user changes the language or locale of a device, triggering a configuration change. This can affect the formatting of text and dates, among other things.
- **Theme change**: This is when a user changes a device's theme, triggering a configuration change. This can affect the appearance of the UI.
- **Keyboard availability change**: This is when a user attaches or detaches a keyboard from a device, triggering a configuration change. This can affect the layout of the UI, and so on.

In this recipe, we will look at leveraging this knowledge to better handle screen size changes when dealing with foldable devices.

Getting ready

In the first recipe, *Building adaptive layouts in Modern Android Development,* we discussed different state configurations and how to handle them better. In this recipe, we will learn how to use the already provided `rememberFoldableState` function in Jetpack Compose to handle screen changes in foldable devices.

How to do it...

Let's use the already created `Traveller` project for this example; you will not need to create a new project:

1. To be able to use `rememberFoldableState`, we will need to import it into our project:

```
import Androidx.window.layout.FoldableState
```

2. Then, we will create a new `val/ property foldableState` and initialize it with our `rememberFoldableState`:

```
val foldState = rememberFoldableState()
```

3. Using the `foldState` object, we can get information about foldable devices, make our application respond to the correct state, and display data as needed. The three states available are STATE_FLAT, STATE_HALF_OPENED, and `STATE_CLOSED`:

```
when (foldState.state) {
    FoldableState.STATE_FLAT -> {
        // Our Device is flat (unfolded)do something
    }
    FoldableState.STATE_HALF_OPENED -> {
        //Our Device is partially folded. Do something
    }
    FoldableState.STATE_CLOSED -> {
        //Our Device is fully folded do something
    }
}
```

4. We can then use this information to adjust our UI accordingly, such as showing or hiding certain elements based on the foldable state or specified position. Also, we can create two different layouts for when the device is folded and when it is unfolded:

```
val isFolded = foldState.state == FoldableState.STATE_CLOSED

if (isFolded) {
    // Create our layout for when the device is folded
```

```
    } else {
        // Create our layout for when the device is
            unfolded
    }
```

And that's it; this will help solve the foldable state if you have a complex UI system that needs better handling.

How it works...

Handling significant screen configuration changes, especially with foldable devices, can be challenging in Android Jetpack Compose. Here are some tips that can help you use the Configuration API. It allows you to get information about a device's screen configuration, such as screen size, orientation, and foldable state. You can use this information to adjust your UI accordingly.

Compose's layout system makes it easy to create responsive UIs that can adapt to different screen sizes and aspect ratios. Use flexible layouts such as columns and rows to create a UI that can scale up or down as needed.

The `rememberFoldableState` function lets you get information about a device's foldable state and adjust your UI accordingly. For example, you can use this function to create two different layouts, one for when the device is folded and one for when it is unfolded.

Testing your app with different screen configurations is also essential to ensure that it works properly. You can use the Android emulator or physical devices to test your app.

Understanding activity embedding

In Jetpack Compose, activity embedding refers to the process of including a composable function within the context of an activity. This allows you to create custom views that can integrate seamlessly with existing Android activities.

To embed a composable function within an activity, you can use the `setContent` method of the activity. This method accepts a composable function as a parameter, which can be used to define the activity's layout.

Getting ready

You need to have completed the previous recipes to follow along.

How to do it...

Let's look at an example of embedding a composable function in an activity:

```
class MainActivity : AppCompatActivity() {
    override fun onCreate(savedInstanceState: Bundle?) {
        super.onCreate(savedInstanceState)
        setContent {
            MyCustomView()
        }
    }
}

@Composable
fun MyCustomView() {
    Text(text = "Hello, Android Community!")
}
```

In this example, the `setContent` method embeds the `MyCustomView` composable function within `MainActivity`. When the activity is created, the `MyCustomView` function will be called to generate the activity's layout.

How it works...

The `MyCustomView` function is defined as a composable function using the `@Composable` annotation. This allows the function to be called multiple times without causing any side effects. In this case, the function simply displays a `Text` composable with the text `Hello, Android Community!`.

By embedding composable functions within activities, you can create custom views that can be easily integrated into your Android app. This can be especially useful to create reusable components or customize the layout of existing activities.

Material Theming in Compose

Material Theming in Compose is a design system introduced by Google that provides guidelines and principles to design user interfaces. Material Theming helps designers create interfaces that are consistent, easy to use, and visually appealing. Some key features of Material Theming in Jetpack Compose include the following:

- **Color palettes**: A set of predefined color palettes that can be used to create consistent and visually appealing interfaces. Jetpack Compose provides a `MaterialTheme` composable that allows you to apply a color palette to your entire app.

- **Typography**: A set of typography styles that can create a consistent and easy-to-read interface. Jetpack Compose provides a `Typography` composable that allows you to apply a typography style to your text.
- **Shapes**: A set of shapes that can create consistent and visually appealing components. Jetpack Compose provides a `Shape` composable that allows you to apply a shape to your components.
- **Icons**: A set of icons that can be used to create consistent and recognizable interfaces. Jetpack Compose provides an `Icon` composable that allows you to use Material icons in your app.

By using Material Theming in Jetpack Compose, you can create interfaces that are consistent, easy to use, and visually appealing. Material Theming in Jetpack Compose helps you focus on designing your app's functionality, while the design system takes care of the visual details.

Getting ready

To be able to follow along, you need to have worked on previous recipes.

How to do it...

Many applications still do not use `Material 3`, but if you build a new application from scratch, it is highly recommended you go with `Material 3`. One thing to note is when you create a project, `Material 3` does not come pre-installed; this means you need to go ahead and update the Material libraries yourself to `Material 3`.

Let's see an example of implementing `Material 3` theming in Jetpack Compose for your Android applications:

1. You will need to add the required `Material 3` dependencies to your app's `build.gradle` file:

```
implementation 'Androidx.compose.material3:material3:1.0.0-
alpha14'
```

2. Then, you will need to declare your app theme:

```
@Composable
fun MyAppMaterialTheme(content: @Composable () -> Unit) {
    MaterialTheme(
        colorScheme = /**/,
        typography = /**/,
        shapes = /**/,
        content = content
    )
}
```

3. Finally, you can use your theme in the entire application:

```
@Composable
fun MyApp() {
    MyAppMaterialTheme {}
}
```

In this example, we've used Material 3 colors, typography, and shapes to create a consistent and visually appealing interface. We've also used Material 3 icons to enhance the user experience. Finally, we've wrapped our app's content in the MyAppMaterialTheme composable to apply the Material 3 theme.

How it works...

Here's how Material 3 works in Jetpack Compose. Material 3 introduces new and updated components, such as AppBar, BottomNavigation, and TabBar, which can be used in Jetpack Compose using the Androidx.compose.material3 package. These components have updated design and functionality, and they follow the Material 3 guidelines.

Material 3 also introduces a new theming system that allows for more customization and flexibility – that is, in Jetpack Compose, Material 3 theming can be applied using the MaterialTheme3 composable. This composable allows you to customize the color scheme, typography, and shapes of your app, and it also provides new options to customize the elevation and shadows of your components.

The icons are now modern and easily accessible, which is a big plus for us developers. Finally, Material 3 introduces a new typography system that provides updated styles and guidelines for typography in your app. In Jetpack Compose, Material 3 typography can be applied using the Material3Typography object, which provides several predefined styles for your text.

By using Material 3 in Jetpack Compose, you can create modern and visually appealing interfaces that follow the latest design guidelines. Also note that Material 3 components, theming, icons, and typography can all be used together to create a cohesive and consistent design system for your app.

See also...

There is much to cover in Material Design, and trying to cover all components in a single recipe will not do it justice. To learn more about the components and how to ensure your application follows the Material Design guideline, read more here: https://material.io/components.

Testing your applications on a foldable device

Testing your apps on foldable devices is essential to ensure they work correctly and provide an excellent user experience. In this recipe, we will look at some tips to test your apps on foldable devices in Jetpack Compose.

Getting ready

You will need to have done the previous recipes. You can access the entire code in the *Technical requirements* section.

How to do it...

Here are some tips to test your applications on foldable devices:

- **Use an emulator**: You can use the Android emulator to test your app on foldable devices without buying a physical device. The emulator provides a range of foldable device configurations that you can use to test your app.
- **Use real devices**: Testing your app on an actual foldable device can provide a more accurate representation of how your app will work on these devices. If you have access to a foldable device, it's highly recommended to test your app on it.
- **Test different screen modes**: Foldable devices come in different screen modes, such as single-screen, dual-screen, and extended screens. It's essential to test your app on different screen modes to ensure it works correctly in all modes.
- **Test with different screen sizes**: Foldable devices come in different sizes, so it's crucial to test your app on different screen sizes to ensure it works well on all devices.
- **Test app transition**: Testing your app's transition between different screen modes can help you identify any issues with an app's layout or behavior. Make sure to test all the transition modes, such as fold, unfold, and hinge.
- **Use automated testing**: Automated testing can help you test your app on different screen sizes, modes, and orientations more efficiently. You can use tools such as Espresso or UI Automator to write automated tests for your app.

How it works...

Overall, testing your app on foldable devices requires careful consideration of a device's unique features and abilities. By following these tips, you can ensure that your app is optimized for foldable devices and provides an excellent user experience.

10

Implementing Your First Wear OS Using Jetpack Compose

Wear OS is an operating system developed by Google for smartwatches and other wearable devices. There are several reasons why creating Wear OS for Android is essential in our Modern Android Development. First, this means expanding the Android ecosystem; Wear OS extends the Android ecosystem by allowing developers to create apps and services that can be accessed through a smartwatch or other wearable device.

This expands the reach of Android and creates new opportunities for developers and users. In addition, it provides seamless integration with Android smartphones, allowing users to easily access notifications, calls, and other information on their smartwatches, hence providing a more convenient and efficient way for users to interact with your application.

Let's not forget the most notable apps that can benefit from this are health and fitness tracking apps, including heart rate monitoring, step tracking, and workout tracking. This allows users to track their fitness goals and stay motivated to achieve them. Finally, Wear OS allows users to customize their smartwatch with different watch faces, apps, and widgets. This provides a personalized experience that meets individual needs and preferences.

Wearable technology is a rapidly growing market, and as the technology continues to evolve, Wear OS has the potential to become a key player in the wearable technology market. Wear OS is still very new, and in this chapter, we will explore simple basic examples as many of the APIs might change in the future. Therefore, getting an idea of how it works and how to create cards, buttons, and show lists will be helpful.

In this chapter, we'll be covering the following recipes:

- Getting started with your first Wear OS in Android Studio
- Creating your first button
- Implementing a scrollable list
- Implementing cards in Wear OS (`TitleCard` and `AppCard`)
- Implementing a chip and a toggle chip
- Implementing `ScalingLazyColumn` to showcase your content

Technical requirements

The complete source code for this chapter can be found at `https://github.com/PacktPublishing/Modern-Android-13-Development-Cookbook/tree/main/chapter_ten`.

Getting started with your first Wear OS in Android Studio

The Android OS is used worldwide, and one of the use cases is Wear OS (by *wear*, we mean smartwatches). This is good news for Android developers because this means more jobs. Furthermore, many applications now have to support Wear OS, such as Spotify, fitness tracking apps, heart monitoring apps, and more, which implies more use cases will arise, and companies will adopt building for *Wear OS* even if it's only for notification purposes. Therefore, this chapter will explore how to get started.

Getting ready

In this recipe, we will look into getting started with Wear OS and how to set up your virtual watch testing environment.

How to do it...

To create your first project on Wear OS in Jetpack Compose, follow these steps:

1. First, create a new Android project in Android Studio and ensure you have the latest version of Android Studio and the Wear OS SDK installed.

2. Then, following the procedure of creating your first application, *Chapter 1, Getting Started with Modern Android Development Skills,* pick **Wear OS** instead of **Phone and Tablet**, as shown in *Figure 10.1*.

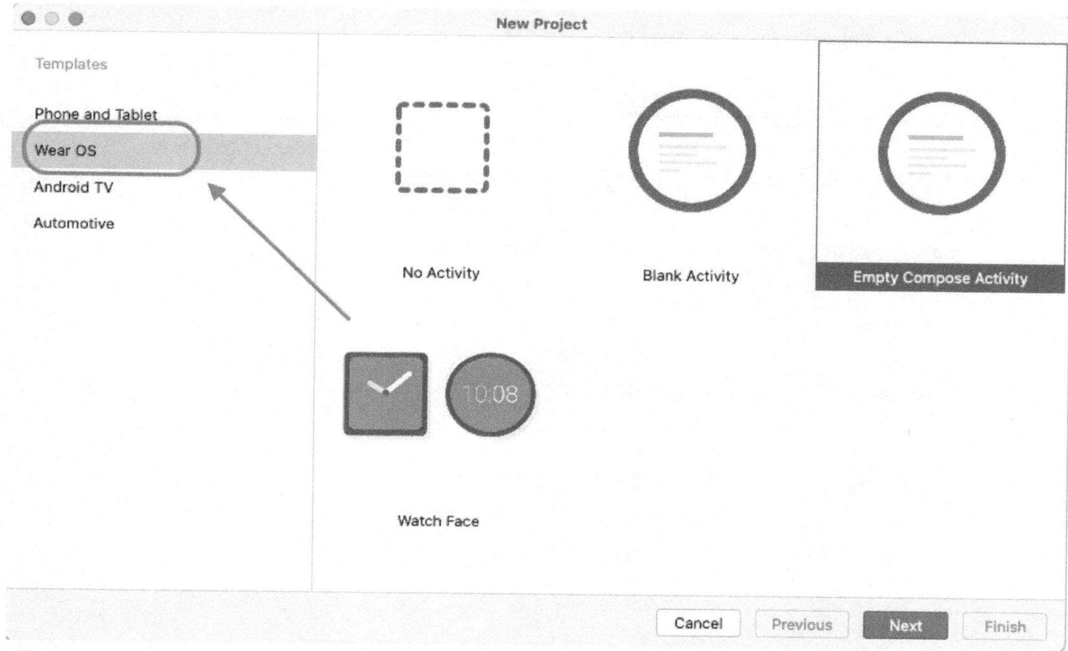

Figure 10.1 – Selecting Wear OS

3. Choose **Empty Compose Activity** (see *Figure 10.1*); as you might know, it is much better to use Compose while building for Wear OS since Google recommends this. Then, hit **Next**, and name your Wear OS project `WearOSExample`. You will notice it uses a minimum SDK of `API 30: Android 11.0 (R)`.

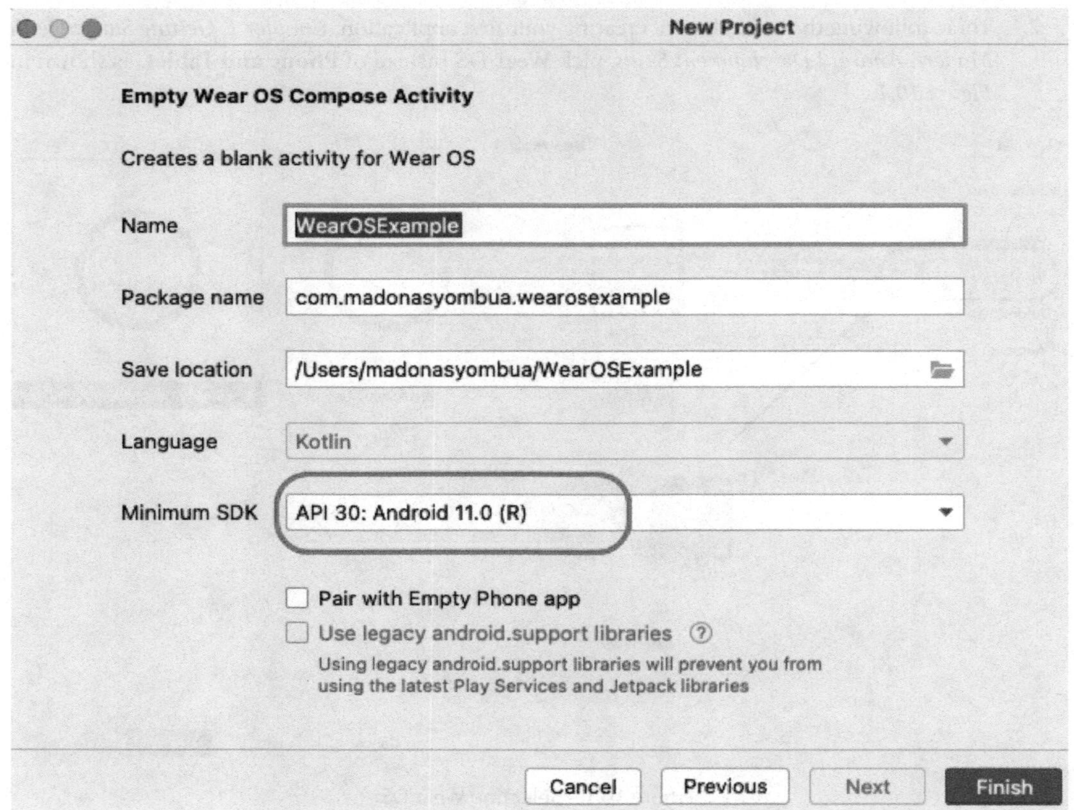

Figure 10.2 – Minimum SDK version

4. Click **Finish**, and you should be able to see a sample code template provided for you.
5. Now, let's go ahead and get our virtual Wear OS testing device set up to run the already provided code template. Navigate to **Tools | Device Manager**, then create a new device. If you need help in this section, refer to *Chapter 1*, *Getting Started with Modern Android Development Skills*.

6. Now, see *Figure 10.3* to choose your Wear OS virtual testing device. Note that you can also choose either a round, square, or rectangular device. We will use round.

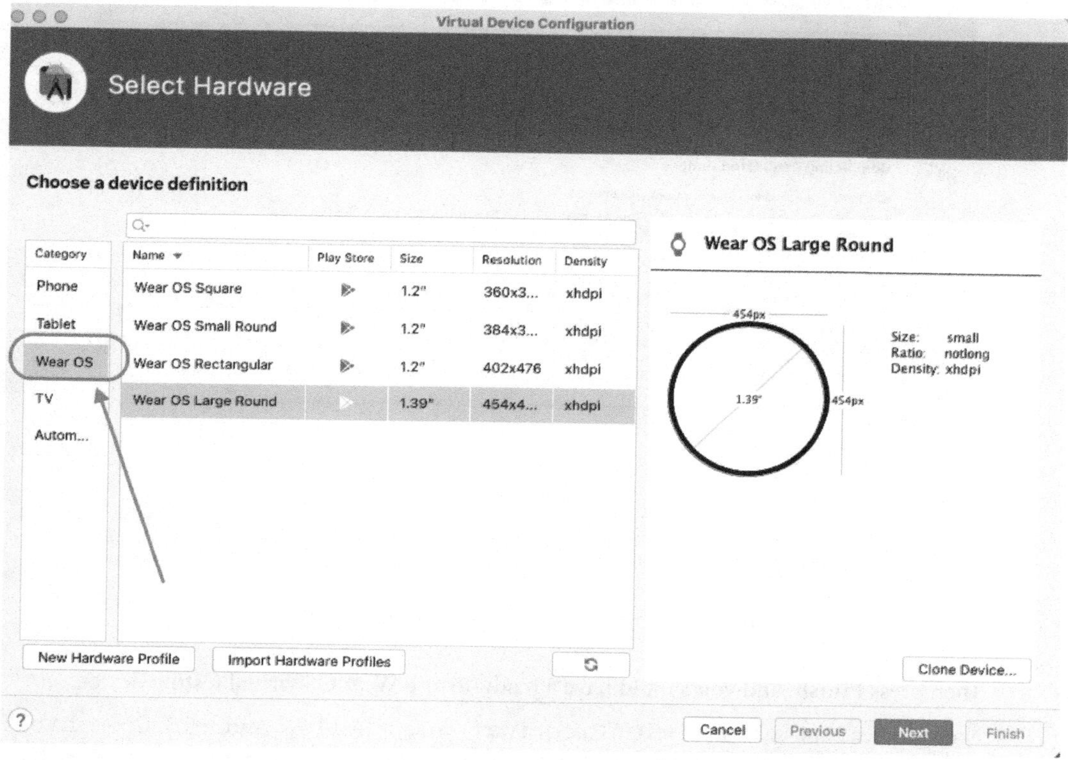

Figure 10.3 – Wear OS virtual device set up

7. Hit **Next**, then download the system image – in our case, **R**, which is API level 30.

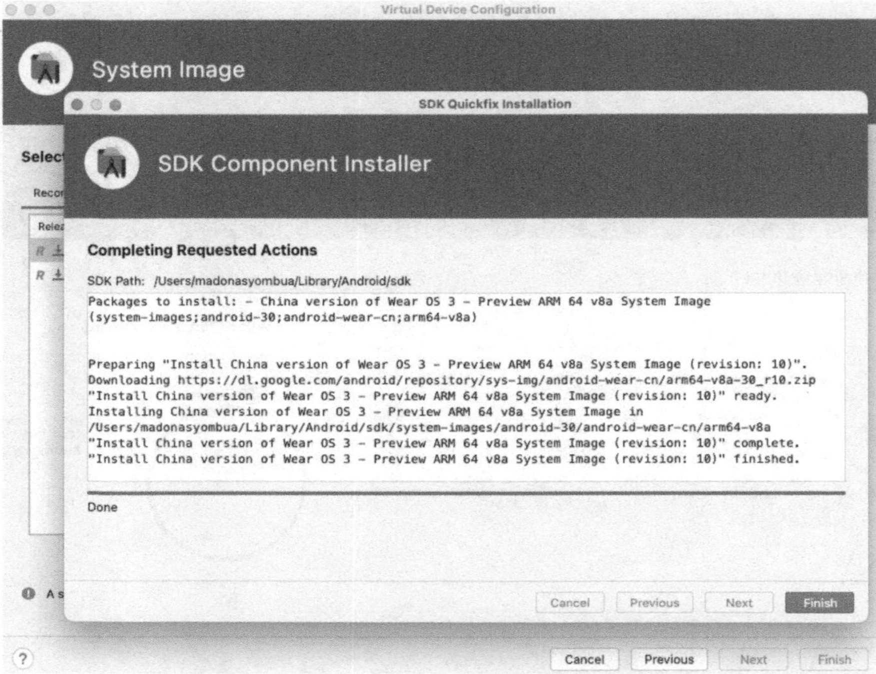

Figure 10.4 – Installing the system image for testing

8. Then press **Finish**, and you should have a ready-to-use Wear OS virtual testing device.
9. Now, go ahead and change the text in `Greeting()` to say `"Hello, Android Community"` in the code template and run, and you should have something similar to *Figure 10.5*. If everything is installed correctly, you should not have a build error.

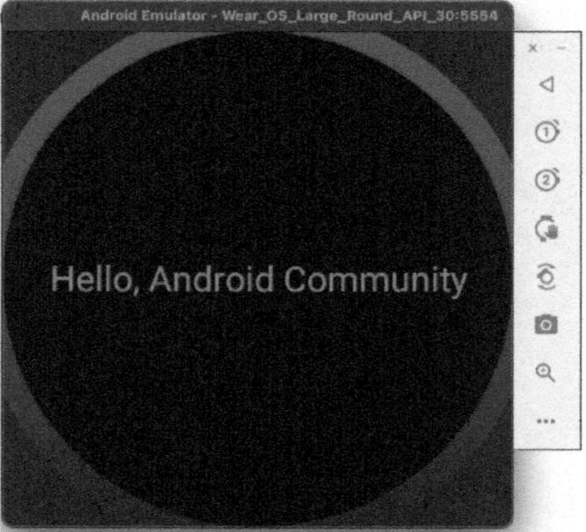

Figure 10.5 – Displaying a greeting on a Wear OS virtual device

10. Also, ensure you change the text on the round string resource too.

That's it, you have successfully set up your first Wear OS, and we were able to run the already provided `Greeting()`. In the following recipe, we will look at creating a simple button.

How it works...

You will notice the template looks precisely how you'd build Android applications, the only difference being the libraries used. The template uses Compose, which makes our work easier while developing since we will be using most of the concepts that we learned in previous chapters.

The following is a comparison to help you know the difference between the Wear OS dependency and the standard dependency:

Wear OS Dependency(androidx.wear.*)	**Comparison**	**Standard Dependency**(androidx.*)
androidx.wear.compose:compose-material	***instead of***	androidx.compose.material:material ,
androidx.wear.compose:compose-navigation	***instead of***	androidx.navigation:navigation-compose
androidx.wear.compose:compose-foundation	***in addition to***	androidx.compose.foundation:foundation

Figure 10.6 – Different types of dependencies (source: developer.android.com)

Creating your first button

In this recipe, we will create our first button in Wear OS to explore the principles and best practices of building in Wear OS.

Getting ready

You need to have completed the previous recipe to get started on this one. We will be building upon our already created `WearOSExample` project.

How to do it...

To create your first button on Wear OS in Jetpack Compose, you can follow these steps:

1. Using the already-created project, we will be adding a new button. Let's go ahead and remove some of the already provided code, `fun Greeting(greetingName: String)`:

```
@Composable
fun Greeting(greetingName: String) {
    Text(
        modifier = Modifier.fillMaxWidth(),
        textAlign = TextAlign.Center,
        color = MaterialTheme.colors.primary,
        text = stringResource(R.string.hello_world, greetingName)
    )
}
```

Figure 10.7 – A screenshot showing what to be deleted

2. Removing the `Greeting()` function called in `WearOSExampleTheme` will complain; go ahead and remove that too.
3. Then create a new `Composable` function that will define your button. You can use the `Button` function provided by Jetpack Compose:

```
@Composable
fun SampleButton() {
    Button(
        onClick = { /* Handle button click */ },
        modifier = Modifier.fillMaxWidth()
    ) {
        Text("Click me")
    }
}
```

4. Then, call the new function in our `WearApp()` function:

```
@Composable
fun WearApp() {
    WearOSExampleTheme {
        /* If you have enough items in your list, use
           [ScalingLazyColumn] which is an optimized
           version of LazyColumn for wear devices with
           some added features. For more information,
           see d.android.com/wear/compose./
        */
        Column(
            modifier = Modifier
                .fillMaxSize()
                .background(
                    MaterialTheme.colors.background),
            verticalArrangement = Arrangement.Center
        ) {
```

```
            SampleButton()
        }
    }
}
```

5. Then, in our activity, call the `setContent` method with your button's `Composable` function as the parameter:

```
class MainActivity : ComponentActivity() {
    override fun onCreate(savedInstanceState: Bundle?)
    {
        super.onCreate(savedInstanceState)
        setContent {
            WearApp()
        }
    }
}
```

6. You can also utilize the already provided `Preview` function to view the changes. You will notice that we explicitly specify the device, `@Preview(device = Devices.WEAR_OS_SMALL_ROUND, showSystemUi = true)`:

```
@Preview(device = Devices.WEAR_OS_SMALL_ROUND, showSystemUi =
true)
@Composable
fun DefaultPreview() {
    WearApp()
}
```

7. Run your Wear OS app, and you should see your button displayed on the screen, as shown in *Figure 10.8*:

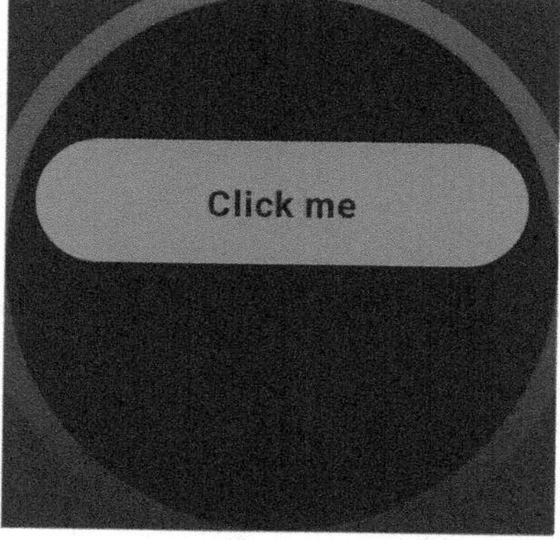

Figure 10.8 – A button in Wear OS

8. Let's look at another example, which is a button with an icon; this is pretty similar to the first button, but in this case, we will just be adding an icon instead of text.
9. Create a new function called `SampleButton2()` and add the following code:

```
@Composable
fun SampleButton2(
) {
    Row(
        modifier = Modifier
            .fillMaxWidth()
            .padding(bottom = 10.dp),
        horizontalArrangement = Arrangement.Center
    ) {

        Button(
            modifier = Modifier.size(
                ButtonDefaults.LargeButtonSize),
            onClick = { /* Handle button click */ },
        ) {
            Icon(
                imageVector =
                    Icons.Rounded.AccountBox,
                contentDescription = stringResource(
                    id = R.string.account_box_icon),
                modifier = Modifier
                    .size(24.dp)
                    .wrapContentSize(
                        align = Alignment.Center)
            )
        }
    }
}
```

10. Finally, comment out `SampleButton`, add `SampleButton2`, and run; you should see something similar to *Figure 10.9*:

Figure 10.9 – A button with an icon in Wear OS

> **Important note**
>
> It is important to note that the Wear OS platform has some unique considerations when it comes to designing and testing apps, such as the smaller screen size and the need to optimize battery life. It's essential to test your app on an actual device to ensure it works as expected on Wear OS.

How it works...

Judging from your previous knowledge of Compose, everything we have worked on so far should look familiar. In our example, we're using `SampleButton` and `WearOSExampleTheme` from the Wear OS Compose library to create a button that's designed specifically for Wear OS devices.

`SampleButton` takes in an `onClick` lambda that gets called when the button is clicked and a modifier that sets the size of the button based on what we specify, which, in our example, is a simple `fillMaxWidth()`.

We're using `horizontalArrangement` in the column to center our button and using the `MaterialTheme` color to paint the background. In the case of Wear OS, Google recommends using the default material wear shapes; these are already optimized for non-round and round devices, which makes our work easier as developers. See the following link for more information on shapes: `https://developer.android.com/reference/kotlin/androidx/wear/compose/material/Shapes`.

Finally, we're using the `Text` composable to display the button text, which is vital since it tells users what the button's intended use is.

Implementing a scrollable list

Implementing a scrollable list is essential for creating an effective and user-friendly Android app that meets the needs of your users. A scrollable list allows you to display a large amount of information on a small screen, which can be beneficial, especially in a tiny device such as a watch. By scrolling through the list, users can quickly and easily access all of the items without navigating to different screens or pages.

Users expect a smooth and responsive scrolling experience when interacting with lists. Implementing a scrollable list with optimized performance can help ensure the app feels fast and responsive to the user. Scrollable lists can be customized to suit a variety of use cases and design requirements. You can adjust the layout, appearance, and behavior of the list to fit your app's specific needs and provide a unique user experience. In this recipe, we will look at how you can implement a scrollable list in Wear OS.

Getting ready

You need to have completed the previous recipe to get started on this one. We will be using our already created `WearOSExample` project to continue this part.

How to do it...

Follow these steps to build a scrollable list in Wear OS using Jetpack Compose:

1. In your `MainActivity.kt` file, let's create a new `Composable` function containing your scrollable list. You can call it anything you like, but for this example, we'll call it `WearOSList`.
2. Another option is to create a new package to organize our code better and call the package `components`. Inside `components`, create a new Kotlin file and call it `WearOsList`.
3. In our `WearOSList` function, we will need a list of strings for our example; we can just create sample dummy data to showcase an example:

```
@Composable
fun WearOSList(itemList: List<String>) {. . .}
```

4. Inside our `WearOSList` function, create `ScalingLazyColumn`, which is optimized for Wear OS. This will be the container for our scrollable list. We will talk about `ScalingLazyColumn` later in the chapter:

```
@Composable
fun  WearOSList(itemList: List<String>) {
    ScalingLazyColumn() {
        // TODO: Add items to the list here
    }
}
```

Building for Wear OS might be challenging due to content size, hence the need to be familiar with Wear's best practices.

5. For our items, we will create a new `Composable` function called `WearOSListItem`, which will just have a `text` since we are just showcasing a text:

```
@Composable
fun WearOSListItem(item: String) {
    Text(text = item)
}
```

6. For our data, we will create a dummy list, so go ahead and add the following in the `WearApp()` function:

```
val itemList = listOf(
        "Item 1",
        "Item 2",
        "Item 3",
        "Item 4",
        "Item 5",
        . . .
)
```

7. Finally, comment out the two buttons we created, call `WearOSList`, pass in `itemList`, and run the application:

```
{
    // SampleButton()
    //SampleButton2()
    WearOSList(
        itemList = itemList,
        modifier = contentModifier
    )
}
```

8. You should see a list similar to *Figure 10.10*:

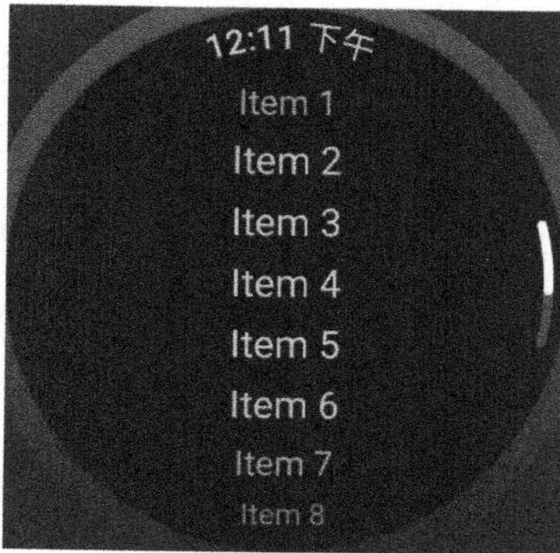

Figure 10.10 – Scrollable list of items

How it works...

In this example, we're using `WearOsList` and `WearOSExampleTheme` from the Wear OS Compose library to create a list that's designed specifically for Wear OS devices.

We start by creating a `WearOSList` composable that takes in a list of items as a parameter. Inside `ScalingLazyColumn`, we use the `items` function to iterate through the list of items and create a `WearOSListItem` for each.

The `WearOSListItem` composable has a `Composable text` function.

Implementing Cards in Wear OS (TitleCard and AppCard)

When building for Wear OS, we have two significant cards that we need to consider: `AppCard` and `TitleCard`. A good use case for cards would be **Notification** and **Smart Reply**. If you use a wearable device, you might know what these are; if you don't use a wearable device, you can look them up, but in this recipe, we will also explore examples.

Furthermore, if you create a Notification card, you intend to provide a quick and easy way to view and respond to notifications from your apps. When a notification arrives, it appears as a card on your watch face, which you can then swipe away or tap to open and interact with the notification.

As for Smart Reply cards, this feature uses machine learning to suggest responses to messages you receive based on the context of the message. These cards appear as a response option to notifications and allow you to quickly send a message without needing to type it out manually.

Both Notification and Smart Reply cards are essential because they provide an efficient and streamlined way to manage notifications and respond to messages without having to pull out your phone constantly. They allow you to stay connected while on the go and keep you informed of important information without disrupting your daily routine, which is why Wear OS is here to stay, and knowing how to build for it will come in handy. In this recipe, we will create a simple card and see how to handle navigation in Wear OS.

Getting ready

You will need to have completed the previous recipes to continue with this recipe.

How to do it...

Here's an example of creating a card in Wear OS using Jetpack Compose. Open the `WearOSExample` project and code along:

1. Inside the `components` package, let's create a new Kotlin file and call it `MessageCardExample`.

2. Inside `MessageCardExample`, create a new composable function called `MessageCard`:

```
@Composable
fun MessageCard(){. . .}
```

3. We must now call `AppCard()` since this is what we want. `AppCard` takes in `appName`, `time`, `title`, and more, as shown in *Figure 10.11*. This means you can customize your `AppCard ()` to fit your needs:

```
@Composable
public fun AppCard(
    onClick: () -> Unit,
    appName: @Composable () -> Unit,
    time: @Composable () -> Unit,
    title: @Composable () -> Unit,
    modifier: Modifier = Modifier,
    appImage: @Composable (() -> Unit)? = null,
    backgroundPainter: Painter = CardDefaults.cardBackgroundPainter(),
    appColor: Color = MaterialTheme.colors.onSurfaceVariant,
    timeColor: Color = MaterialTheme.colors.onSurfaceVariant,
    titleColor: Color = MaterialTheme.colors.onSurface,
    contentColor: Color = MaterialTheme.colors.onSurfaceVariant,
    content: @Composable () -> Unit,
) {
    Card(
        onClick = onClick,
        modifier = modifier,
        backgroundPainter = backgroundPainter,
        enabled = true,
    ) {
```

Figure 10.11 – AppCard composable function

4. This makes our work easier as developers since we know exactly what we need when building, thereby increasing developer productivity:

```
@Composable
fun MessageCard() {
    AppCard(
        onClick = { /*TODO*/ },
        appName = { /*TODO*/ },
        time = { /*TODO*/ },
        title = { /*TODO*/ }) {
        }
}
```

5. Now, let's go ahead and implement our `AppCard()` and send a message to our users. For our example, we will hardcode the data, but if you have an endpoint, you can pull data and display it as needed:

```
@Composable
fun MessageCard() {
    AppCard(
        modifier = Modifier
            .fillMaxWidth()
            .padding(bottom = 8.dp),
        appImage = {
            Icon(
                modifier = Modifier
                    .size(24.dp)
                    .wrapContentSize(
                        align = Alignment.Center),
                imageVector = Icons.Rounded.Email,
                contentDescription = stringResource(
                    id = R.string.message_icon)
            )
        },
        onClick = { /*Do something*/ },
        appName = {  stringResource(
            id = R.string.notification_message) },
       time = {  stringResource(id = R.string.time) },
       title = { stringResource(
           id = R.string.notification_owner) }) {
       Text(text = stringResource(
           id = R.string.hi_android))
       }
}
```

6. In `MainActivity`, comment out other composable functions, for now add `MessageCard()`, and run it:

Figure 10.12 – AppCard with a notification

How it works...

`TitleCard` and `AppCard` are both used to display information on Wear OS, but they have different purposes. In our example, we use `AppCard()`, but as you can see in *Figure 10.13*, `TitleCard()` takes in several inputs that are similar to `AppCard()`:

```
@Composable
public fun TitleCard(
    onClick: () -> Unit,
    title: @Composable () -> Unit,
    modifier: Modifier = Modifier,
    time: @Composable (() -> Unit)? = null,
    backgroundPainter: Painter = CardDefaults.cardBackgroundPainter(),
    titleColor: Color = MaterialTheme.colors.onSurface,
    timeColor: Color = MaterialTheme.colors.onSurfaceVariant,
    contentColor: Color = MaterialTheme.colors.onSurfaceVariant,
    content: @Composable () -> Unit,
) {
    Card(
        onClick = onClick,
        modifier = modifier,
        backgroundPainter = backgroundPainter,
        enabled = true,
    ) {
```

Figure 10.13 – TitleCard input

You can use `TitleCard()` to display information that is relevant to the current context, such as the name of a song that is playing or the title of a movie that is being watched. It is typically displayed at the top of the screen and can be dismissed by swiping it away. A good example is Spotify.

When using `AppCard()`, you can display information about an app that is currently running, such as the name of the app and a brief description of what it does, as we did in our example. It is typically displayed on a smaller card that can be tapped to open the app. That is why it has `onClick{/**TODO*/}`, which can lead to more information.

When deciding whether to use `TitleCard()` or `AppCard()`, you should consider the following factors:

- The amount of information that you need to display
- The relevance of the information to the current context
- The desired user experience

If you need to display a lot of information, `TitleCard()` may be a better option. If you only need to display a small amount of information, `AppCard()` may be a better option. If you want the information to be relevant to the current context, `TitleCard()` may be a better option. If you want the information displayed on a smaller card that can be tapped to open the app, `AppCard()` may be a better option.

Implementing a chip and a toggle chip

In this recipe, we will explore significant Wear components; a chip and a toggle chip are both used to display and interact with data.

A **chip** is a small, rectangular element that can be used to display text, icons, and other information. It is typically used to display items that are related or that have a common theme.

A **toggle chip** is a component that can be used to represent a binary value. It is typically used to represent things such as on/off, yes/no, or true/false.

It is fair to mention that you can use these components in your regular application, and we will explore them more in *Chapter 11*. When deciding which component to use, you should consider the following factors:

- The type of data that you want to display
- The type of interaction that you want to enable
- The look and feel that you want to achieve

Getting ready

We will be using our already-created project for this section.

How to do it...

We will create a chip and a toggle chip in this recipe. Follow these steps:

1. Let's go ahead and build our first chip; inside the `components` package, create a Kotlin file and call it `ChipExample.kt`.
2. Inside the file, create a composable function called `ChipWearExample()`.
3. Now, let's go ahead and call the `Chip()` composable function. You can also use the `Chip` component to display dynamic information. To do this, you can use the `modifier` property to specify a function that will be called to update the information displayed on the chip:

```
@Composable
fun ChipWearExample(){
    Chip(
        modifier = Modifier
            .fillMaxWidth()
```

```
                .padding(bottom = 8.dp),
            onClick = { /*TODO */ },
            label = {
                Text(
                    text = stringResource(
                        id = R.string.chip_detail),
                    maxLines = 1,
                    overflow = TextOverflow.Ellipsis
                )
            },
            icon = {
                Icon(
                    imageVector = Icons.Rounded.Phone,
                    contentDescription = stringResource(
                        id = R.string.phone),
                    modifier = Modifier
                        .size(24.dp)
                        .wrapContentSize(
                            align = Alignment.Center)
                )
            },
        )
    }
```

4. In `MainActivity`, go ahead and comment out the existing `Composable` functions, add `ChipWearExample()`, and run the app:

Figure 10.14 – A chip with a message

5. Now, let's go ahead and create a toggle chip; inside our `component` package, create a Kotlin file and call it `ToggleChipExample`.

6. Inside `ToggleChipExample`, create a `Composable` function and call it `ToggleChipWearExample()`. We will use the `ToggleChip()` component:

```
@Composable
fun ToggleChipWearExample() {
    var isChecked by remember { mutableStateOf(true) }
        ToggleChip(
            modifier = Modifier
                .fillMaxWidth()
                .padding(bottom = 8.dp),
            checked = isChecked,
            toggleControl = {
                Switch(
                    checked = isChecked
                )
            },
            onCheckedChange = {
                isChecked = it
            },
            label = {
                Text(
                    text = stringResource(
                        id = R.string.alert),
                    maxLines = 1,
                    overflow = TextOverflow.Ellipsis
                )
            }
        )
}
```

7. Finally, run the code, and you should be able to toggle the chip on and off depending on whether you want to get any notifications or not:

Figure 10.15 – A toggle chip

How it works...

To implement a chip in Wear OS Jetpack Compose, we need to use the already provided `Chip()` component. The `Chip()` component is stadium shaped and has a maximum height designed to take no more than two lines of text and can be used to display text, icons, and other information.

You can also use the `Chip()` component to display dynamic information. To do this, you can use the `modifier` property to specify a function that will be called to update the information displayed on the chip. You can look at the `Chip()` component to see what it accepts as its parameters.

The `ToggleChip()` composable function takes in several parameters; here are a few significant ones:

- `checked`: A Boolean value that represents whether the toggle chip is currently checked
- `onCheckedChange`: A lambda function that will be called when the checked state of the toggle chip changes
- `modifier`: An optional modifier that can be used to customize the appearance or behavior of the toggle chip
- `colors`: An optional `ToggleChipColors` object that can be used to customize the colors of the toggle chip

We use `TextOverflow` to handle overflowing text since we are dealing with small screens. Check out *Figure 10.15* for more details on what `ToggleChip` takes in as parameters:

```
@Composable
public fun ToggleChip(
    checked: Boolean,
    onCheckedChange: (Boolean) -> Unit,
    label: @Composable () -> Unit,
    modifier: Modifier = Modifier,
    toggleControl: @Composable () -> Unit = { ToggleChipDefaults.CheckboxIcon(checked = che
    appIcon: @Composable (() -> Unit)? = null,
    secondaryLabel: @Composable (() -> Unit)? = null,
    colors: ToggleChipColors = ToggleChipDefaults.toggleChipColors(),
    enabled: Boolean = true,
    interactionSource: MutableInteractionSource = remember { MutableInteractionSource() },
    contentPadding: PaddingValues = ToggleChipDefaults.ContentPadding,
    shape: Shape = MaterialTheme.shapes.small,
) {
```

Figure 10.16 – What the ToggleChip composable function accepts as parameters

Implementing ScalingLazyColumn to showcase your content

ScalingLazyColumn extends LazyColumn, which is very powerful in Jetpack Compose. You can think of ScalingLazyColumn as a component in Wear OS that is used to display a list of items that can be scrolled vertically. The items are scaled and positioned based on their position in the list, and the entire list can be scrolled by dragging the top or bottom of the list.

You can use it, for example, to display a list of components; in our example, we will use it to display all the elements we created in previous recipes. You will also notice we used it in the *Implementing a scrollable list* recipe, where we have a list and displayed the items.

Getting ready

You will need to have completed the previous recipes to continue with this recipe. In addition, in this recipe, instead of commenting on all the elements we created, we will display them as items in ScalingLazyColumn.

How to do it...

Follow these steps to build your first ScalingLazyColumn:

1. In MainActivity, you will notice a comment:

```
/* If you have enough items in your list, use
[ScalingLazyColumn] which is an optimized
* version of LazyColumn for wear devices with some added
features. For more information,
* see d.android.com/wear/compose.
*/
```

   The comment is a callout to developers to utilize ScalingLazyColumn, which is an optimized version of LazyColumn for Wear OS.

2. We need to start by creating a scalingListState value and initialize it to rememberScalingLazyListState():

```
val scalingListState = rememberScalingLazyListState()
```

   The rememberScalingLazyListState() function simply does as its definition implies, which is to remember the state.

3. We will now need to clean up our Composable function by removing the modifiers we added and using one for all the views. Let's create a contentModifier = Modifier, and one for our icons:

```
val contentModifier =  Modifier
    .fillMaxWidth()
```

```
    .padding(bottom = 8.dp)
val iconModifier =  Modifier
    .size(24.dp)
    .wrapContentSize(align = Alignment.Center)
```

4. We will also need to create a `Scaffold()`, which implements the Wear Material Design visual layout structure. `Scaffold()` uses `modifier`, `vignette`, `positionIndicator`, `pageIndicator`, `timeText`, and `content`.
5. Let's go ahead and build our screen. In `Scaffold`, we will use three parameters: `vignette` (which is a full-screen slot for applying a vignette over the content of the scaffold), `positionIndicator`, and `timeText`. Look at the *How it works...* section to learn more about the parameters:

```
Scaffold(timeText = {} , vignette = {}, positionIndicator = {})
{. . .}
```

6. For `TimeText`, we will call `Modifier.scrollAway` and pass in `scalingListState`:

```
TimeText(modifier = Modifier.scrollAway(scalingListState))
```

7. Since we only have one screen for our project sample, which is scrollable, we will try to show all items simultaneously and all the time. Hence, in `vignette`, we will say the position will be `TopAndBottom`:

```
Vignette(vignettePosition = VignettePosition.TopAndBottom)
```

8. Finally, on `positionIndicator`, we will just pass `scalingListState`:

```
PositionIndicator( scalingLazyListState = scalingListState)
```

9. Now, we can finally build our `ScalingLazyColumn()`. We will use `fillMaxSize` for the modifier, and `autoCentering` will be set to index zero; then for `state`, pass our already created `scalingListState`, and in the items, pass our components:

```
Scaffold(
    timeText = { TimeText(modifier =
        Modifier.scrollAway(scalingListState)) },
    vignette = { Vignette(vignettePosition =
        VignettePosition.TopAndBottom) },
    positionIndicator = {
        PositionIndicator(
            scalingLazyListState = scalingListState
        )
    }
) {
    ScalingLazyColumn(
```

```
            modifier = Modifier.fillMaxSize(),
            autoCentering = AutoCenteringParams(
                itemIndex = 0),
            state = scalingListState
        ){
            item { /*TODO*/ }
            item { /*TODO*/ }
            item { /*TODO*/ }
            item { /*TODO*/ }
        }
    }
```

10. You can get the entire code in the *Technical requirements* section. To clean up some of the code in `item{ }`, we have the following:

```
item { SampleButton(contentModifier) }
item { SampleButton2(contentModifier, iconModifier) }
item { MessageCard(contentModifier, iconModifier) }
item { ChipWearExample(contentModifier, iconModifier) }
item { ToggleChipWearExample(contentModifier) }
```

11. Finally, when you run the application, you should be able to see all the items displayed and be able to scroll smoothly.

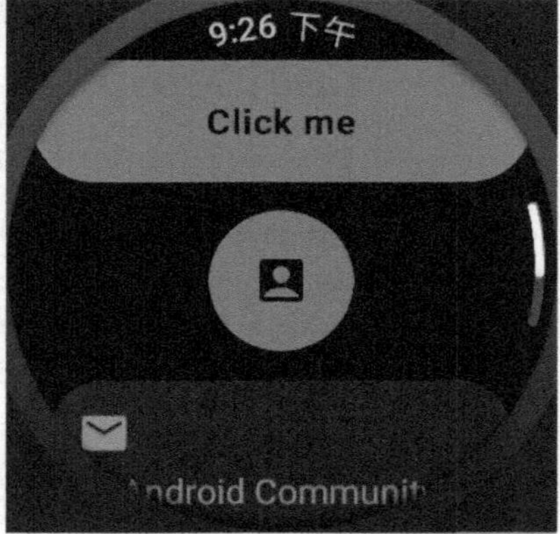

Figure 10.17 – Our composable elements on Wear OS

How it works...

Wear OS Jetpack Compose is a UI toolkit for building Wear OS apps using the Jetpack Compose framework. It is designed to make it easier and more efficient for developers to create wearable apps with a modern and responsive UI. As mentioned before, the `Composable` function called `Scaffold()` has several inputs. In *Figure 10.18*, you will see their meaning and why you might want to use them:

Params: `modifier` - optional Modifier for the root of the `Scaffold`
`vignette` - a full screen slot for applying a vignette over the contents of the scaffold. The vignette is used to blur the screen edges when the main content is scrollable content that extends beyond the screen edge.
`positionIndicator` - slot for optional position indicator used to display information about the position of the Scaffold's contents. Usually a `PositionIndicator`. Common use cases for the position indicator are scroll indication for a list or rsb/bezel indication such as volume.
`pageIndicator` - slot for optional page indicator used to display information about the selected page of the Scaffold's contents. Usually a `HorizontalPageIndicator`. Common use case for the page indicator is a pager with horizontally swipeable pages.
`timeText` - time and potential application status message to display at the top middle of the screen. Expected to be a TimeText component.
Samples: `androidx.wear.compose.material.samples.SimpleScaffoldWithScrollIndicator`

Figure 10.18 – Scaffold function parameters

Some of the significant advantages of Wear OS in Jetpack Compose is that it provides a set of pre-built UI components that are optimized for the unique features of Wear OS devices. And one of the critical benefits is that it simplifies the development process by reducing the amount of boilerplate code that is required to create a UI.

It also provides a consistent and flexible UI design language that can be used across different apps. There is more to learn about Wear OS; also, since this is a new technology, many of the concepts here might change or advance due to API changes in the future, but for now, you can learn more by following this link: `https://developer.android.com/wear`.

Important note

There is more to build in Wear OS; for instance, you can build a tile and react when the tile items get clicked to perform an action. To learn more about how you can create your first tile, follow this link: `https://developer.android.com/codelabs/wear-tiles`.

11

GUI Alerts – What's New in Menus, Dialog, Toast, Snackbars, and More in Modern Android Development

Graphic User Interface (**GUI**) alerts are essential to users because they provide critical information about a program or application's status and can help users avoid errors and make informed decisions. Alerts can be triggered in various situations, such as when an error occurs, a program performs a critical operation, or when a user is about to perform an irreversible action.

One of the main benefits of GUI alerts is that they provide immediate feedback to users. For example, if a user enters incorrect information into a form, an alert can quickly inform them of the error, allowing them to correct it before proceeding. This can help to prevent mistakes and save time in the long run.

Another benefit of GUI alerts is that they can help to prevent accidental actions. For example, if a user is about to delete an important file, an alert can warn them of the potential consequences of this action, giving them a chance to reconsider before proceeding. This chapter will examine how a GUI is implemented in Modern Android Development.

In this chapter, we'll cover the following recipes:

- Creating and displaying a menu in Modern Android Development
- Implementing Toast/Snackbars to alert users
- Creating an alert dialog
- Creating a `BottomSheet` dialog

- Creating a radio button
- Creating **Floating Action Buttons (FABs)** and extended FABs

Technical requirements

The complete source code for this chapter can be found at `https://github.com/PacktPublishing/Modern-Android-13-Development-Cookbook/tree/main/chapter_eleven`.

Creating and displaying a menu in Modern Android Development

Creating a menu in an Android app can provide several benefits:

- Menus can help users quickly access different features and functionalities within an app. A well-designed menu can improve the user experience by making it easy to navigate and use the app.
- A consistent menu across different screens in an app can help users quickly find what they're looking for, making the app feel more polished and professional.
- A menu can be used to group related options and functions in one place, reducing the need for cluttered screens with many buttons and options.
- Menus can also be customized to fit an app's specific needs, including different types of menus, such as context menus, pop-up menus, and navigation drawers.
- Menus should be designed with accessibility in mind, making it easier for users with disabilities to navigate the app.

That is to say, creating a menu in an Android app can improve the user experience, provide consistency, save space, and increase accessibility.

Getting ready

For this chapter, we will create a new Material 3 project and call it `GUIAlerts`; this is where we will add all our UI components for this chapter, and you can take advantage of the project to modify the views to suit your needs.

How to do it...

Follow the following steps to build your first hamburger menu:

1. Inside our newly created project, `GUIAlerts`, let's create a package component, and inside the package, create a Kotlin file and call it `MenuComponent.kt`.

2. Let's create a composable function, `OurMenu`, in our Kotlin file:

```
@Composable
fun OurMenu(){ }
```

3. Now, let's go ahead and create our menu. For our purposes, we will just showcase some items, and when someone clicks, nothing will happen since we will not implement the `onClick` function. First, we need to ensure it does not start as `expanded`, which means users will click to expand the menu and it will change to `true` in response:

```
@Composable
fun OurMenu(){
var expanded by remember { mutableStateOf(false) }
val menuItems = listOf("Item 1", "Item 2", "Item 3",
"Item 4") }
```

For our menu items, we will just showcase four items.

4. Next, we must create a `Box()`, align it to the center, and react to the `expanded` state in the modifier. We will also need to add an icon, `ArrowDropDown`, to inform users they can click and that we have more items:

```
Box(
        contentAlignment = Alignment.Center,
        modifier = Modifier
            .clickable { expanded = true }
) {
        Text(stringResource(id = R.string.menu))
        Icon(
            imageVector = Icons.Default.ArrowDropDown,
            contentDescription = stringResource(
                id = R.string.menu_drop_down),
            modifier = Modifier.align(Alignment.CenterEnd)
        )
}
```

5. Finally, we will need to add `DropDownMenu`, which will expand when we click the icon, and we will set `onDismissRequest` to `false`; it is called when the user requests to dismiss the menu, for instance, when tapping.

6. Then, we will display our items on the `DropdownMenuItem` function so that when it is clicked, it performs an action. For our example, we don't do anything:

```
DropdownMenu(
    expanded = expanded,
    onDismissRequest = { expanded = false }
) {
```

```
        menuItems.forEachIndexed { index, item ->
            DropdownMenuItem(text = { Text(item)},
                onClick = { /*TODO*/ })
        }
    }
```

7. Finally, when you run the app, you should see a menu dropdown with items you can click.

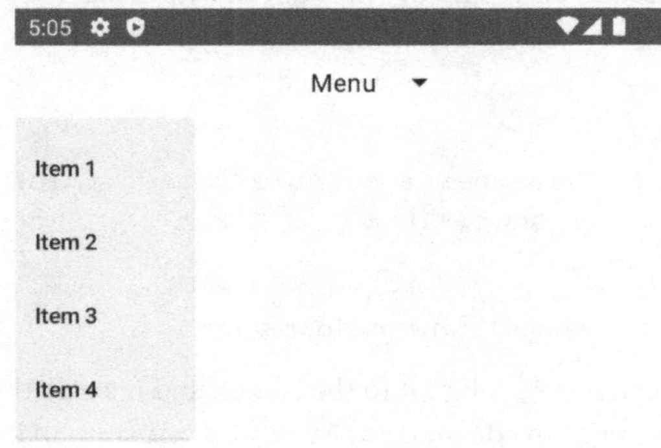

Figure 11.1 – The drop-down menu

> **Important note**
> You can customize the drop-down menu to fit your needs and style.

How it works...

In our example, we first declare a mutable state variable, `expanded`, to keep track of whether the menu is expanded or not and another mutable state variable, `selectedMenuItem`, to keep track of the currently selected menu item.

We also define a list of `menuItems` which helps us know the menu list.

Inside our `Box`, we define a `Column(){}`, which contains the menu title, a clickable `Box`, which displays the selected menu item, and a `DropdownMenu`, which displays the menu items when expanded. We use the `Box` and `DropdownMenu` components to position the menu items relative to the clickable `Box`.

`DropDownMenu` takes in a couple of inputs, as you can see in *Figure 11.2*, and this helps you customize your drop-down menu based on your needs.

```
@Composable
fun DropdownMenuItem(
    text: @Composable () -> Unit,
    onClick: () -> Unit,
    modifier: Modifier = Modifier,
    leadingIcon: @Composable (() -> Unit)? = null,
    trailingIcon: @Composable (() -> Unit)? = null,
    enabled: Boolean = true,
    colors: MenuItemColors = MenuDefaults.itemColors(),
    contentPadding: PaddingValues = MenuDefaults.DropdownMenuItemContentPadding,
    interactionSource: MutableInteractionSource = remember { MutableInteractionSource() },
) {
    DropdownMenuItemContent(
        text = text,
        onClick = onClick,
        modifier = modifier,
        leadingIcon = leadingIcon,
        trailingIcon = trailingIcon,
        enabled = enabled,
        colors = colors,
        contentPadding = contentPadding,
        interactionSource = interactionSource,
    )
}
```

Figure 11.2 – The DropDownMenuItem input parameters

Finally, we use the `DropdownMenuItem` component to display each menu item and update the `selectedMenuItem` and `expanded` variables when a menu item is clicked.

Implementing a Toast/Snackbar to alert users

In Android development, a Toast/Snackbar is a small pop-up message that appears on the screen, usually at the bottom. It's used to provide brief information or feedback to the user. It is a simple way to display short messages to the user without interrupting the user's workflow.

Getting ready

In this section, we will react to the items we created in our `DropMenuItem`, so you must have followed the previous recipe to continue with this one.

How to do it...

Execute the following steps to add a message when the items are clicked to tell the users they've picked a particular item:

1. Creating a Toast is very straightforward in Android; you can simply do that using the `Toast` class the Android SDK provides. You can create a new `Toast` object by calling the static `makeText()` method of the `Toast` class and passing it the context, message, and duration of the Toast.
2. Once you have created the `Toast` object, you can call the `show()` method to display it on the screen:

```
Toast.makeText(context, "Hello, Android!", Toast.LENGTH_SHORT).
show();
```

3. In Jetpack Compose, however, to display a `Toast`, we will need to use `coroutineScope`, but note you do not need a coroutine to display a Toast in all instances, in our example however, we will use the `launch` function to launch a coroutine that displays the Toast message:

```
val coroutineScope = rememberCoroutine()
coroutineScope.launch {
    Toast.makeText(
        context,
        "Selected item: $item",
        Toast.LENGTH_SHORT
    ).show()
}
```

4. To hook up `onClick()`, please see the code in the *Technical requirements* section to get the entire code. Finally, when you run the app, you should see a `Toast` message with the item selected as the message.

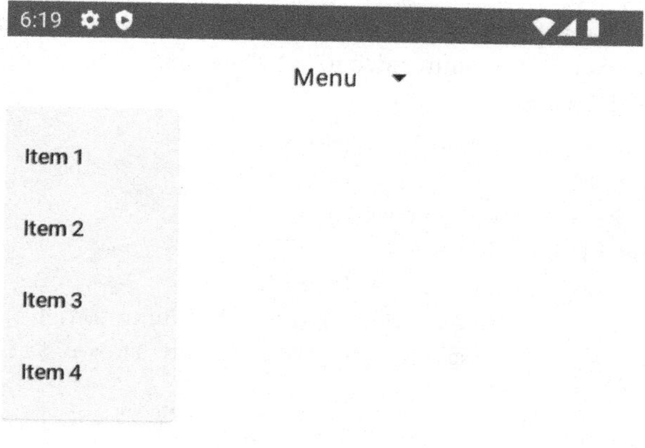

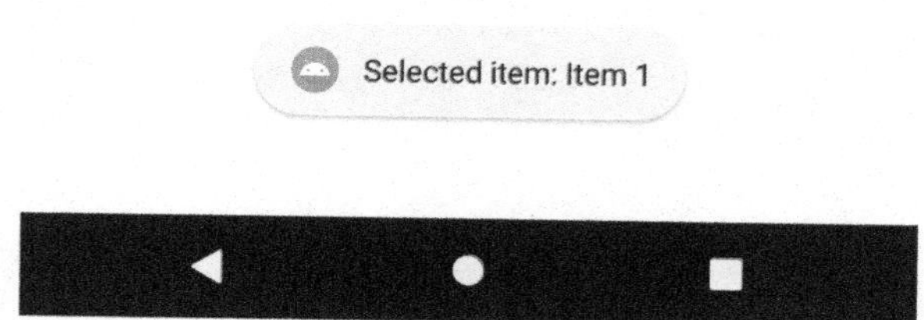

Figure 11.3 – The Toast message displayed

5. In the following example, we will use a Snackbar now instead of a Toast:

```
coroutineScope.launch {
    Toast.makeText(
        context,
        "Selected item: $item",
        Toast.LENGTH_SHORT
    ).show()
}
```

There are different ways of using a Snackbar in Jetpack Compose; you can use it with a `Scaffold` or without it. However, it is recommended to use a Snackbar with a `Scaffold`. In our example, we will use a `Scaffold`:

```
menuItems.forEachIndexed { index, item ->
    DropdownMenuItem(
        text = { Text(item) },
        onClick = {
            coroutineScope.launch {
                snackbarHostState.showSnackbar(
                    message = "Selected Item: $item"
                )
            }
        }
    )
}
```

6. Finally, when you run the app, you will see a Snackbar with the selected item text and item selected. Both `Toast` and `Snackbar` serve the same purpose.

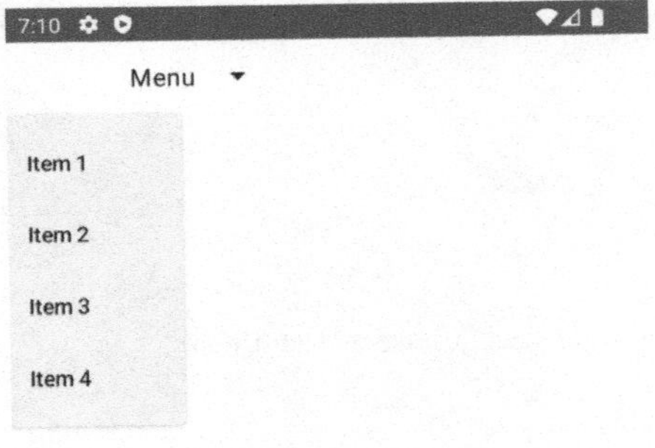

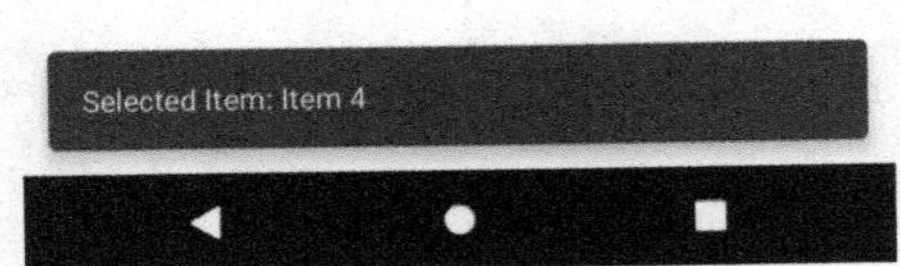

Figure 11.4 – The Snackbar message displayed

How it works...

Toasts and Snackbars are two types of notification messages that can be used in Android applications to display short messages to the user.

The main differences between Toasts and Snackbars are as follows:

- Toast messages are typically displayed in the center of the screen, while Snackbar messages are usually displayed at the bottom of the screen.
- Toast messages typically last for a short period of time, usually around 2-3 seconds, and then disappear automatically. Snackbar messages are usually displayed for a more extended period of time and can be dismissed by the user by swiping them away or by tapping on a button.
- Toast messages are not interactive and cannot be dismissed by the user. Snackbar messages, on the other hand, can contain action buttons that allow the user to take specific actions in response to the message.
- Toast messages are typically plain text messages that appear in a small pop-up window. Snackbar messages, on the other hand, can be styled to include icons, colors, and other visual elements to make them more visually appealing and informative.

We modify the `onClick` callback of the `DropdownMenuItem` component to launch a coroutine that displays the `Toast` message using the `Toast.makeText` function. We pass in the current context using `LocalContext.current`, which gets the current context function and the text to display in the `Toast` message as a string. You should also specify the duration of your `Toast`, either `Short` or `Long`.

When using `Snackbar`, we create a `SnackbarHostState`, which we pass in our `Scaffold`. Our composable includes a `snackbarHost` parameter specifying a function to display the Snackbar when shown. The `SnackbarHost` function takes two parameters: `snackbarData`, which contains the message and action button of the Snackbar, and a lambda that specifies how to create the `Snackbar` composable.

In Android, `Scaffold` is a pre-built UI component or layout that provides an essential structure for building screens and UI components. The term **Scaffold** is often used interchangeably with the term template or boilerplate.

Scaffolds are commonly used in Android app development frameworks such as Flutter or Jetpack Compose to provide a starting point for creating new screens or UI components.

For example, the Material Design library in Android provides several pre-built scaffolds for common screen types, such as a login screen, a settings screen, or a list screen. These scaffolds provide a consistent look and feel and help ensure the app follows the Material Design guidelines.

Using scaffolds can save time and effort in app development by providing a starting point for building screens and UI components. However, developers can also customize and extend scaffolds to meet the specific requirements of their app.

Creating an alert dialog

Pop-up alert dialogs are an essential component of the UI in Android applications. They are used to display important messages, notifications, and warnings to the user. Some reasons why using a pop-up alert dialog is essential in Android are as follows:

- They can help highlight important information the user needs to know. For example, if the user is about to perform an action resulting in data loss or damage, the app can display a warning message in a pop-up alert dialog to ensure the user knows the consequences.
- They can be used to obtain user confirmation for necessary actions, such as deleting a file or purchasing something. By displaying a message that asks the user to confirm the action, the app can help prevent accidental or unwanted actions.
- They can be used to provide feedback to the user, such as letting them know that an action was successful or unsuccessful. For example, if the user tries to save a file that already exists, the app can display a pop-up alert dialog that informs the user of the issue and provides suggestions on how to proceed.
- They can help improve the overall user experience of an app by providing precise and concise messages that help users understand what is happening within the app.

Alert dialogs are an essential component of Android app design. They can be used to highlight important information, obtain user confirmation, provide feedback, and improve the overall user experience.

Getting ready

We will continue using the same project, so ensure you have completed previous recipes. To follow along, please also ensure you get the code in the *Technical requirements* section.

How to do it...

Follow these steps to create an alert dialog:

1. Let's start by creating a Kotlin file and calling it `AlertDialogDemo.kt`.
2. Inside `AlertDialogDemo`, create a composable function and call it `AlertDialogExample()`:

```
@Composable
fun AlertDialogExample() {...}
```

   There are different ways to implement `AlertDialog()`; in our example, we will create a button that will be clicked to start `dialog()`.

3. Then, we must add the title and text properties to `AlertDialog`. We use the `Text` component to define the title and message text and set the `fontWeight` and `color` properties as needed:

```
AlertDialog(
    onDismissRequest = { dialog.value = false },
    title = {
        Text(
            text = stringResource(
                id = R.string.title_message),
            fontWeight = FontWeight.Bold,
            color = Color.Black
        )
    },
    text = {
        Text(
            text = stringResource(id = R.string.body),
            color = Color.Gray
        )
    },
    . . .
```

4. Then, we will add the `confirmButton` and `dismissButton` properties to `AlertDialog`. We use the `Button` component to define the buttons and set the `onClick` property to a lambda that will perform the appropriate action when the button is clicked:

```
    confirmButton = {
        Button(
            onClick = {/*TODO*/ }
        ) {
            Text(text = stringResource(
                id = R.string.ok))
        }
    },
    dismissButton = {
        Button(
            onClick = { dialog.value = false }
        ) {
            Text(text = stringResource(
                id = R.string.cancel))
        }
    },
)
}
    . . .
```

5. Finally, when you run the application, you will see a dialog with a title, message, and two calls to action, **Confirm** or **Cancel**.

Figure 11.5 – The alert dialog

How it works...

In our example, we first create a `mutableStateOf` variable called `openDialog` with a Boolean value indicating whether the dialog should be displayed. We then use this variable to render the `AlertDialog` component using an `if` statement conditionally.

The `AlertDialog` component has several properties that we can set, including the title, text, `confirmButton`, and `dismissButton`. We can also set the background and content colors using the `backgroundColor` and `contentColor` properties.

Finally, we add a `Button` component that toggles the `openDialog` variable when clicked, causing the dialog to be displayed or hidden.

Creating a bottom sheet dialog

Bottom sheet dialogs are a popular design pattern in Android because they provide a simple and efficient way to display contextual information or actions without taking up too much space on the screen. When developing Android apps, here are some of the reasons why bottom sheet dialogs are considered a good choice:

- They are designed to slide up from the bottom of the screen, taking up minimal screen space. This makes them an excellent option for displaying supplementary information or actions without overwhelming the user.
- They are often used to provide additional information relevant to the current context, such as options or settings specific to the current view.
- Because bottom sheet dialogs are designed to slide up from the bottom of the screen, they give users a sense of control over the interaction. Users can easily dismiss the dialog by swiping it down or tapping outside of the dialog.

Overall, bottom sheet dialogs are an excellent choice because they provide a space-saving, contextual, and user-friendly way to display additional information or actions to the user.

Getting ready

We will continue using the same project, so ensure you have completed previous recipes.

How to do it...

Using the same project, follow these steps to build your first `BottomSheet` dialog:

1. Let's start by creating a Kotlin file and calling it `BottomSheetDemo.kt`.
2. Inside `BottomSheetDemo`, create a composable function and call it `BottomSheetExample()`:

```
@Composable
fun BottomSheetExample() {...}
```

3. Since we are using Material 3, we will acknowledge that most of the APIs are still experimental, meaning a lot might change. Let's create our state for our bottom sheet dialog:

```
val bottomSheetState =
rememberModalBottomSheetState(skipPartiallyExpanded = true)
```

The `skipPartiallyExpanded` Boolean checks whether the partially expanded state should be skipped if the sheet is tall enough.

4. Now we need to go ahead and create our `ModalBottomSheet ()`, which takes in several parameters; we will just use `onDismiss` and `sheetState`:

```
ModalBottomSheet(
    onDismissRequest = { openBottomSheet = false },
    sheetState = bottomSheetState,
) {
    Column(Modifier.fillMaxWidth(),
        horizontalAlignment =
            Alignment.CenterHorizontally) {
        Button(
            onClick = {
                coroutineScope.launch {
                    bottomSheetState.hide() }
                    .invokeOnCompletion {
                    if (
                        !bottomSheetState.isVisible
                    ) {
                        openBottomSheet = false
                    }
                }
            }
        ) {
            Text(text = stringResource(
                id = R.string.content))
    }
. . .
```

5. Following the *Technical requirements* section, now let's go ahead and implement the two buttons and get the entire code.
6. Finally, run the app, and you will have implemented your bottom sheet dialog. Note you might want to add more logic based on your needs.

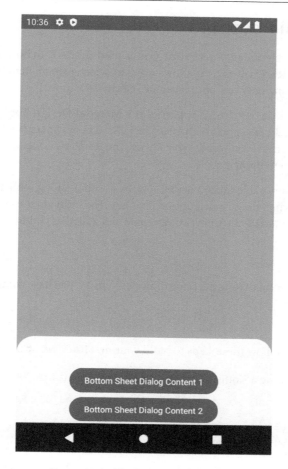

Figure 11.6 – The bottom sheet dialog

How it works...

In our example, `ModalBottomSheet` is used as an alternative to inline menus or simple dialogs on mobile, especially when offering a long list of action items or when items require longer descriptions and icons.

Like any other dialog in Android, modal bottom sheets appear before app content.

There is more...

Read more about bottom sheet dialogs and the available experimental features by going to the following link: `https://m3.material.io/components/bottom-sheets/overview`.

Creating a radio button

In Modern Android Development, `RadioButton` is used similarly to how it is used in traditional Android development. `RadioButton` allows users to select a single item from a list of mutually exclusive options, meaning only one option can be selected at a time.

In Jetpack Compose, `RadioButton` is part of the Material Design library and can be used by importing the `Androidx.compose.Material.RadioButton` package. To create a group of `RadioButton` instances, you would typically use the `RadioGroup` composable, which is also part of the Material Design library.

The `RadioGroup` composable takes a list of options as input, along with a selected option and a callback that is called when the selected option changes. The individual `RadioButton` instances can be created using the `RadioButton` composable and added as children of `RadioGroup`.

Getting ready

In this recipe, we will continue using the same project, so ensure you have completed previous recipes.

How to do it...

Using the same project, follow these steps to build your first `RadioButton`:

1. Let's start by creating a Kotlin file and calling it `RadioButtonDemo.kt`.
2. Inside RadioButtonDemo, create a composable function and call it `RadioButtonExample()`:

```
@Composable
fun RadioButtonExample() {...}
```

3. We will start creating a list of choices, and in our example, we can use fruit, then keep track of selected choices:

```
val choices = listOf("Mangoes", "Avocado", "Oranges")
var selectedOption by remember {
    mutableStateOf(choices[0]) }
```

4. Since we are using the `RadioButton` composable provided by Google, based on your needs, you can customize your `RadioButton` however you like:

```
Row(
    Modifier.fillMaxWidth(),
    verticalAlignment = Alignment.CenterVertically
) {
    RadioButton(
        selected = selectedOption == option,
```

```
        onClick = { selectedOption = option }
    )
    Text(
        text = option,
        style = MaterialTheme.typography.body1,
        modifier = Modifier.padding(start = 6.dp)
    )
}
```

5. Finally, when we run the app, you should see something similar to *Figure 11.7*.

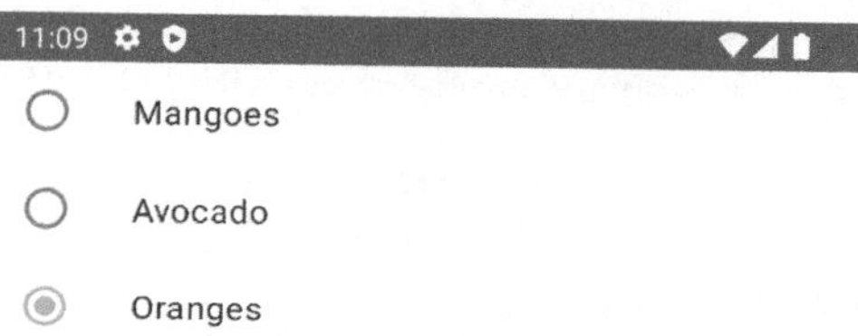

Figure 11.7 – The radio button

How it works...

In our example, we create a `RadioButtonExample()` composable that displays a group of `RadioButton` instances with the following choices– `Mangoes`, `Avocado`, and `Oranges`.

The selected option is stored in a `selectedOption` variable using the `remember` composable to maintain the state across recomposition. Each `RadioButton` is wrapped in a `Row(){...}` that includes the choice text, and the selected property of the `RadioButton` is set based on whether the current option matches the selected option.

When the user clicks on `RadioButton`, the `selectedOption` variable is updated with the newly selected option.

Creating a FAB/extended FAB

A **FAB** is a circular button that appears to *float* above the UI of an Android application. It is often used to represent a primary action in the app and is placed in a visible location for easy access.

An extended FAB is a variation of a FAB in Android that provides users with more options and functionality. The extended FAB is a rectangular button that can display text and an icon and expands into a menu of related actions when pressed.

Getting ready

In this recipe, we will continue using the same project, so ensure you have completed previous recipes.

How to do it...

Using the same project, follow these steps to build a FAB and extended FAB:

1. Let's start by creating a Kotlin file and calling it `ActionComponentsDemo.kt`.
2. Inside `ActionComponentsDemo`, create a composable function and call it `ActionComponentsExample()`:

```
@Composable
fun RadioButtonExample() {...}
```

3. Inside `ActionComponentsDemo`, create a composable function and call it `ActionComponentsExample()`.
4. We will start by creating a FAB. `FloatingActionButton` is a circular button that floats above the UI and is typically used to trigger the primary action in an app. You can use `FloatingActionButton` in Jetpack Compose to create a `FloatingActionButton` composable:

```
FloatingActionButton(onClick = { /* do something */ }) {
    Icon(Icons.Default.Add, contentDescription =
        stringResource(id = R.string.add))
}
```

`ExtendedFloatingActionButton` is a `FloatingActionButton` instance with additional text or iconography. It's often used for secondary actions in an app.

5. To create `ExtendedFloatingActionButton` in Jetpack Compose, you can use the `ExtendedFloatingActionButton` composable. This code creates it with a text label of `"Add item"` and an plus icon. The `onClick` parameter specifies the action to perform when the button is clicked:

```
ExtendedFloatingActionButton(
    text = { Text("Add item") },
    onClick = { /* do something */ },
    icon = {
        Icon(
            Icons.Default.Add,
            contentDescription = stringResource(
                id = R.string.add)
        )
    }
)
```

6. When you run the app, you should see two buttons, a floating button and an extended button:

Figure 11.8 – The FAB and extended FAB

How it works...

An extended FAB is similar to a FAB but provides additional space for text and/or an icon. It is typically used to provide more context or information about the action that will be performed when the button is tapped. For example, an **Extended Floating Action Button** (**EFAB**) might display the text **Create new budget** along with a pen icon.

Both FABs and EFABs are part of the Material Design guidelines and are available as a component in Jetpack Compose.

There more ...

To learn more about Material 3 Components and guidelines, see the following links: `https://m3.Material.io/` and `https://developer.android.com/reference/kotlin/androidx/compose/material3/package-summary`.

12

Android Studio Tips and Tricks to Help You during Development

As an Android developer, writing code should not just be the end goal; rather, understanding how to find issues in your applications, using formatting tips to navigate the code base faster, and other skills come in handy.

The programming process includes a lot of collaboration. This can be in peer code review, pair programming, or debugging issues. In these situations, it is handy if you can move fast, for instance, when debugging or formatting code before you submit your pull request. In this chapter, you will learn great Git and Android Studio tips and tricks to help in your day-to-day development.

In this chapter, we'll be covering the following recipes:

- The importance of profiling your Android applications
- Quick Android shortcuts to make your development faster
- JetBrains Toolbox and essential plugins to know
- Debugging your code
- How to extract methods and method parameters
- Understanding Git essentials

Technical requirements

The complete source code for this chapter can be found at `https://github.com/PacktPublishing/Modern-Android-13-Development-Cookbook`.

The importance of profiling your Android applications

In Android, **profiling** is the process of analyzing an application's performance to identify its strengths and weaknesses. Profiling your Android applications is crucial for the following reasons:

- It helps you identify performance bottlenecks such as slow code, memory leaks, and excessive CPU usage. This knowledge can help you optimize your code and make your application run more efficiently.
- It improves the user experience. A poorly performing application can lead to user frustration and negative reviews. By profiling your application and optimizing its performance, you can provide a better user experience, leading to increased user engagement and positive reviews.
- It helps save time and money. It is much easier and less expensive to fix performance issues early on than to try to fix them later when they have become more complex.

Hence, in this recipe, we will explore why profiling your Android applications is essential and look at best practices and tips.

Getting ready

For this recipe, we will be looking at how to use the Profiler to profile our Android application. You do not need to create a new project; you can simply use a pre-existing project to follow along.

How to do it...

Follow these steps to get started with using a Profiler in Android:

1. For this chapter, we are using Android Studio Flamingo 2022.2.1 Patch 1. In your Android Studio, go to **View | Tool Windows | Profiler** and click the Profiler, which will launch it.

> **Note**
>
> To be able to see any activity, you need to start your emulator.

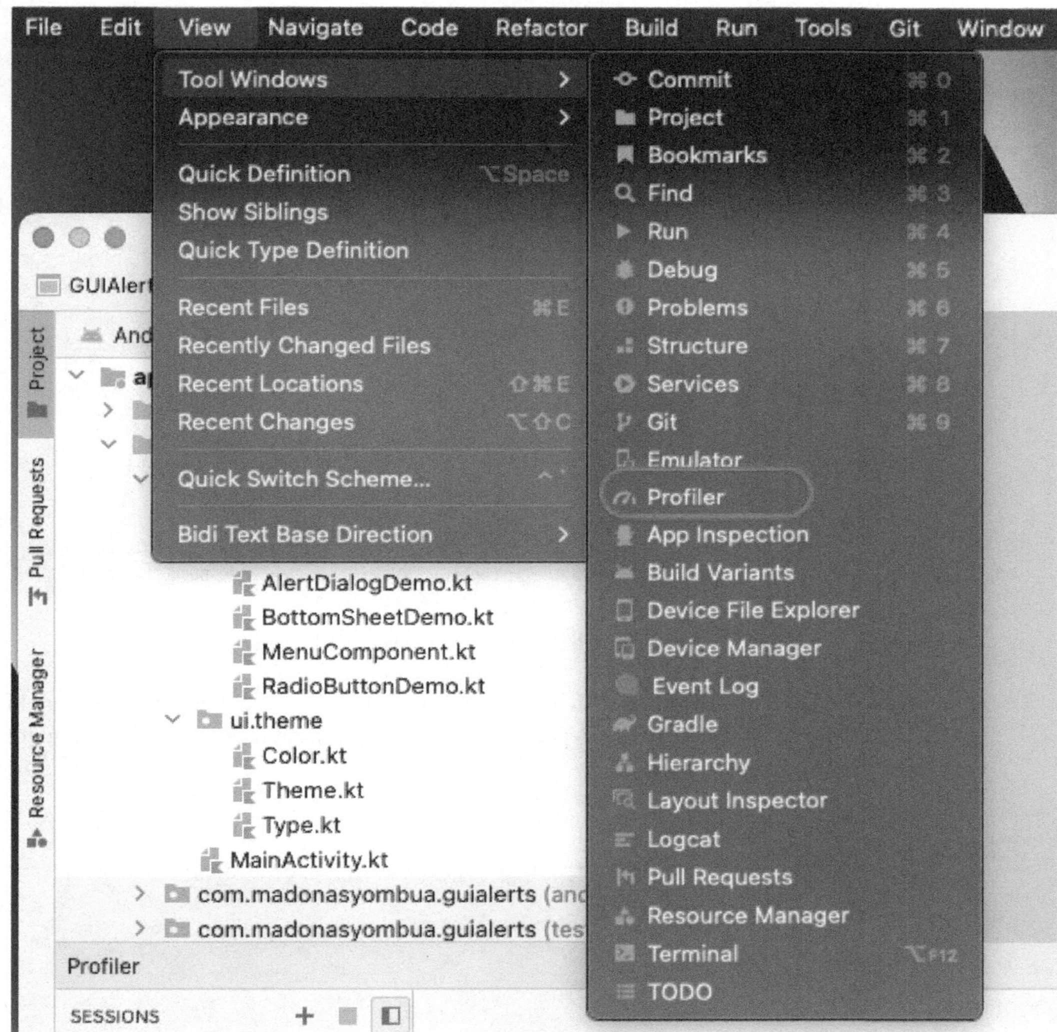

Figure 12.1 – The Profiler in Android Studio

2. You can also navigate to the bottom menu option, near to **App Inspection**; see the green arrow in *Figure 12.2*, which indicates another place you can start a Profiler from. The read arrow indicates the emulator that is attached to visualize the profile.

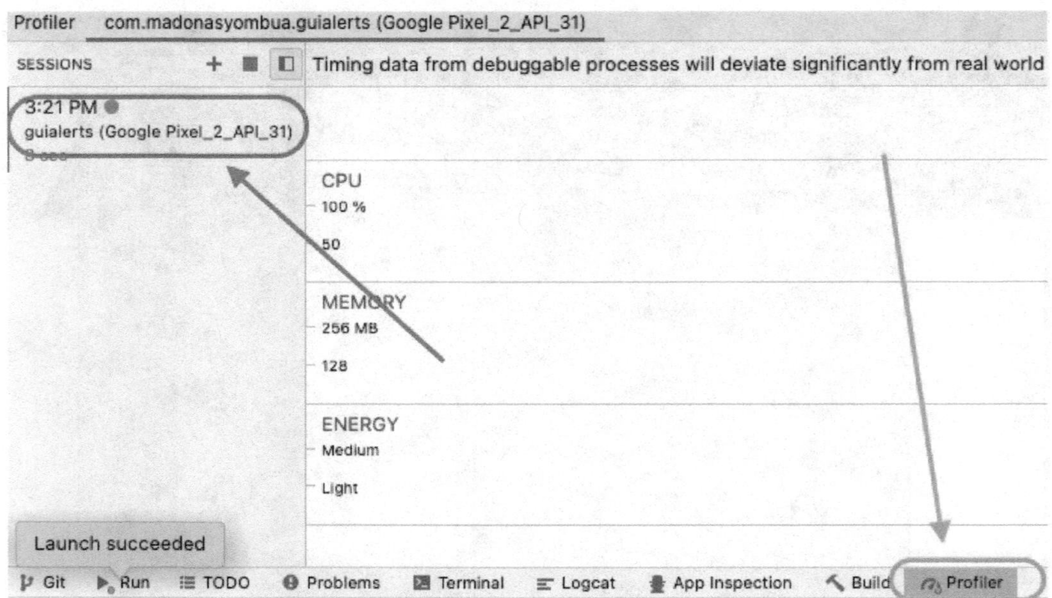

Figure 12.2 – The Profiler started in Android Studio

3. When your Profiler starts running, which means it is attached to your application, you should see **CPU**, **MEMORY**, and **ENERGY**. Depending on your application resources, the data might vary from what you see in *Figure 12.3*.

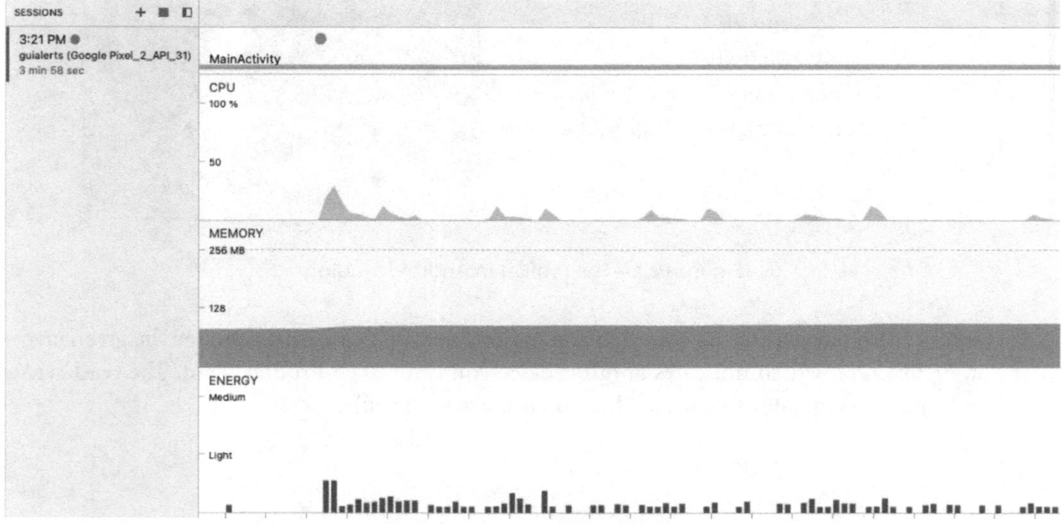

Figure 12.3 – The Profiler running

4. You can do a lot, such as simply recording all your method traces, looking at how your resources are utilized, and analyzing the flame chart.

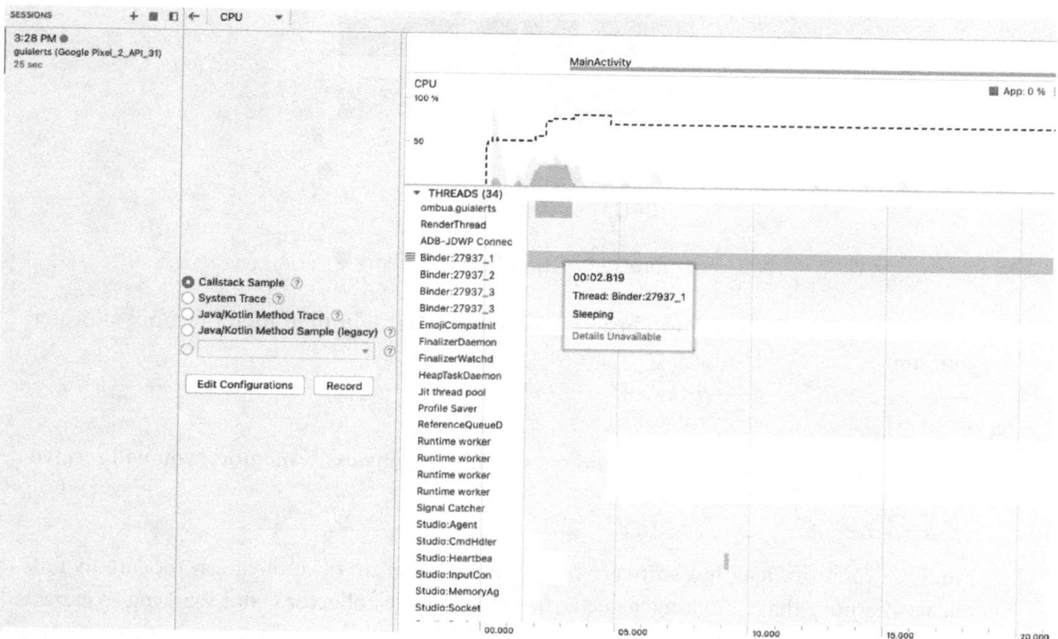

Figure 12.4 – Different ways to utilize the Profiler

5. A CPU flame chart is a type of performance visualization that shows the hierarchical structure of a program's execution over time. It typically includes a timeline at the top of the chart, with function calls represented as rectangles stacked vertically.

   Depending on the color, the width of each rectangle represents the duration of the function call, and the rectangle's color represents the CPU usage of that function. The chart allows Android developers to identify which functions take up the most CPU time quickly and can help inform them where to debug and optimize performance, as shown in *Figure 12.5*.

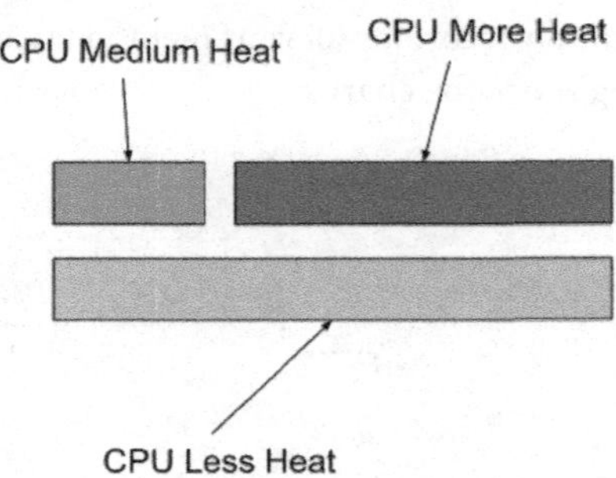

Figure 12.5 – The CPU flame chart

In other words, the application heap is a dedicated, hard, limited memory pool allocated to your app.

> **Note**
>
> If your app reaches the heap capacity and tries to allocate any extra memory, you will receive an `OutOfMemoryError` message.

6. Finally, a memory leak is a software bug where a program or application repeatedly fails to release memory that it no longer needs, or your garbage collector is not working as expected. This can cause the program to gradually consume more and more memory over time, eventually leading to poor performance or the crashing of your application.

How it works...

An app performs poorly if it responds slowly, has choppy animations, freezes a lot, or consumes a lot of power. Fixing performance problems involves identifying areas where your application does not optimize the use of resources, such as the CPU, memory, graphics, network, or device battery.

Android Studio offers several tools to help developers spot and visualize potential problems:

- The CPU Profiler, which helps track runtime performance issues
- The Memory Profiler, which helps track any memory allocations
- The Network Profiler, which monitors network traffic usage
- The Energy Profiler, which tracks energy usage, which can contribute to battery drain

You can think of profiling in Android through a lens of inspecting, improving, and monitoring your code base. See *Figure 12.6*.

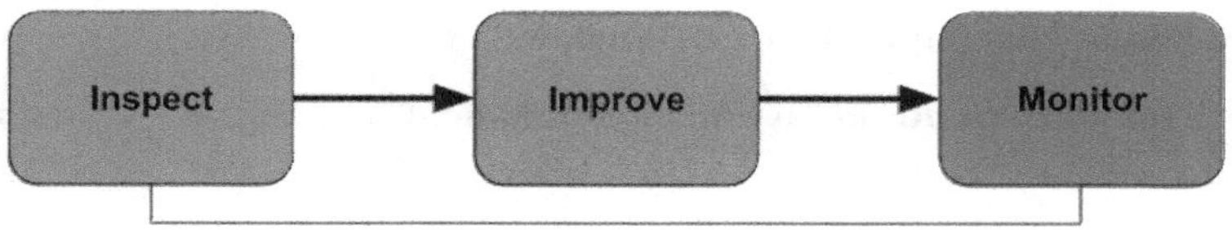

Figure 12.6 – The model for performance source (android.developer.com)

See more...

Learn more about `OutOfMemoryError` by following this link: `https://developer.Android.com/reference/java/lang/OutOfMemoryError`. You can also learn more about profiling by simply using this link: `https://developer.android.com/studio/profile`.

Quick Android shortcuts to make your development faster

Shortcuts can be helpful to developers by making their work quicker and more efficient, allowing them to focus on writing code and solving problems rather than navigating menus and toolbars. Shortcuts can help automate repetitive tasks such as formatting code, renaming variables, or navigating between files, freeing developers' time and mental energy for more meaningful work.

In addition, when developers use the same shortcuts across different tools and applications, it can help maintain consistency in their workflows and reduce the risk of errors caused by accidentally using the wrong command or tool. Also, for developers with disabilities or physical limitations, using shortcuts can be a more accessible way to interact with software than using a mouse or trackpad.

Getting ready

This isn't really a recipe but a list of useful shortcuts, we will look at widely used shortcuts in Windows and Mac, which are the most popular operating systems used on laptops.

How to do it...

Here are some Android Studio shortcuts in both Mac and Windows operating systems that can help you speed up your workflow:

- Here are some basic navigation shortcuts:
    - **Open class or file**: *Ctrl* + *N* (Windows) or *Cmd* + *O* (Mac)
    - **Find text across project**: *Ctrl* + *Shift* + *F* (Windows) or *Cmd* + *Shift* + *F* (Mac)

    - **Open Recent Files popup**: *Ctrl* + *E* (Windows) or *Cmd* + *E* (Mac)
    - **Search for and execute any action or command**: *Ctrl* + *Shift* + *A* (Windows) or *Cmd* + *Shift* + *A* (Mac)

- Code editing shortcuts:
    - **Code completion suggestions**: *Ctrl* + spacebar (Windows and Mac)
    - **Complete current statement**: *Ctrl* + *Shift* + *Enter* (Windows) or *Cmd* + *Shift* + *Enter* (Mac)
    - **Duplicate current line**: *Ctrl* + *D* (Windows) and (Mac) *Cmd* + *D*
    - **Cut current line**: *Ctrl* + *X* (Windows) and (Mac) *Cmd* + *X*
    - **Move current line up or down**: *Ctrl* + *Shift* + up/down (Windows) or *Cmd* + *Shift* + up/down (Mac)
- Refactoring shortcuts:
    - **Extract method from current code block**: *Ctrl* + *Alt* + *M* (Windows) and *Cmd* + *Option* + *M* (Mac)
    - **Extract variable from current code block**: *Ctrl* + *Alt* + *V* (Windows) and *Cmd* + *Option* + *V* (Mac)
    - **Extract field from current code block**: *Ctrl* + *Alt* + *F* (Windows) and *Cmd* + *Option* + *F* (Mac)
    - **Rename class, method, or variable**: *Shift* + *F6* (Windows) and *Fn* + *Shift* +*F6* (Mac)
- Debugging shortcuts:
    - **Step over to the next line of code**: *F8* (Windows and Mac)
    - **Step into the current line of code**: *F7* (Windows and Mac)
    - **Step out of the current method**: *Shift* + *F8* (Windows and Mac)
    - **Toggle breakpoint on the current line of code**: *Ctrl* + *F8* (Windows) or *Cmd* + *F8* (Mac)
- Miscellaneous shortcuts:
    - **Run app**: *Ctrl* + *Shift* + *F10* (Windows) or *Cmd* + *Shift* + *F10* (Mac)
    - **Debug app**: *Ctrl* + *Shift* + *F9* (Windows) or *Cmd* + *Shift* + *F9* (Mac)

Important note

Please note that some shortcuts may differ depending on your specific keyboard layout or operating system preferences. Also, remember that many more Android Studio shortcuts are available, so be sure to explore the Keymap settings to find additional shortcuts that can make your development workflow more efficient.

How it works...

Shortcuts can be a powerful tool for developers looking to streamline their workflows, improve their productivity, and reduce the risk of errors and repetitive strain injuries when developing.

JetBrains Toolbox and essential plugins to know

JetBrains Toolbox is a software management tool that allows developers to manage and install JetBrains IDEs and related tools on their computers. JetBrains is a software company that provides powerful IDEs (namely IntelliJ) for various programming languages, such as Java, Kotlin, Python, Ruby, and JavaScript. In other words, a plugin is simply any class that implements the plugin interface.

Here are some JetBrains Toolbox features and reasons why you should try using it:

- You can easily download and install any JetBrains IDE from Toolbox. It also ensures that you have the latest version of the IDE installed on your computer.
- Toolbox automatically checks for updates and keeps all the installed JetBrains IDEs and plugins up to date, which means if your current Android Studio is not stable, you can revert to a more stable version.
- You can manage your JetBrains licenses and activate/deactivate them from Toolbox.
- Toolbox provides a way to share projects with your team members by creating a shareable link.
- Toolbox integrates with JetBrains services such as JetBrains Account and JetBrains Space.

Getting ready

This isn't really a recipe but a list of useful plugins, we will look at some useful plugins for developers.

How to do it...

Let' go ahead and look at how we can utilize Gradle for our day to day Android Development.

- Gradle is a build automation tool used to build and deploy Android apps. It can help you to manage dependencies, generate APKs, and run tests.
- The ADB plugin provides a graphical user interface for **Android Debug Bridge** (**ADB**), a command-line tool that can interact with an Android device or emulator.
- Live Templates allows you to insert commonly used code snippets quickly. For example, you can create a live template for a toast message and then simply type in the shortcut and hit the Tab to insert the code. To create a live template, go to **Android Studio | Settings | Editor | Live Templates**.

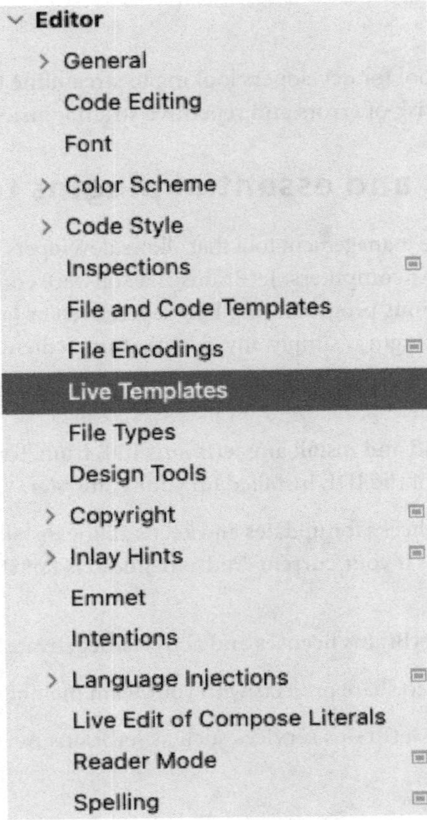

Figure 12.7 – How to access Live Templates

- Android Studio's code completion feature can save you a lot of time. As you type, Android Studio will suggest possible completions for your code. Use the *Tab* key to accept the suggestion.
- A debugger is a powerful tool for finding and fixing bugs in your code. You will learn how to use the debugger to step through your code and see what's happening at each step in the *Debugging your code* recipe.
- Android Studio's layout editor lets you easily create and modify your app's user interface. You can use the layout editor to drag and drop user interface components onto your layout and easily modify their properties.
- The resource manager allows you to easily manage your app's resources, such as images, strings, and colors. You can use the resource manager to add and modify resources and easily reference them in your code.
- Android Studio supports a variety of plugins that can extend its functionality. You can also easily search for plugins to help you with tasks such as generating code or managing dependencies.

- LeakCanary is a memory leak detection library that can help you identify and fix your app's memory leaks. This helps developers when finding leaks.
- Firebase is a suite of mobile development tools that can be used to add features such as authentication, analytics, and cloud messaging to your app. You can take advantage of this when building your first project as an indie developer.

How it works...

You can easily find Keymap by simply going to **AndroidStudio | Setting | Keymap** and using the drop-down menu to see what keymaps are available, as shown in *Figure 12.8*.

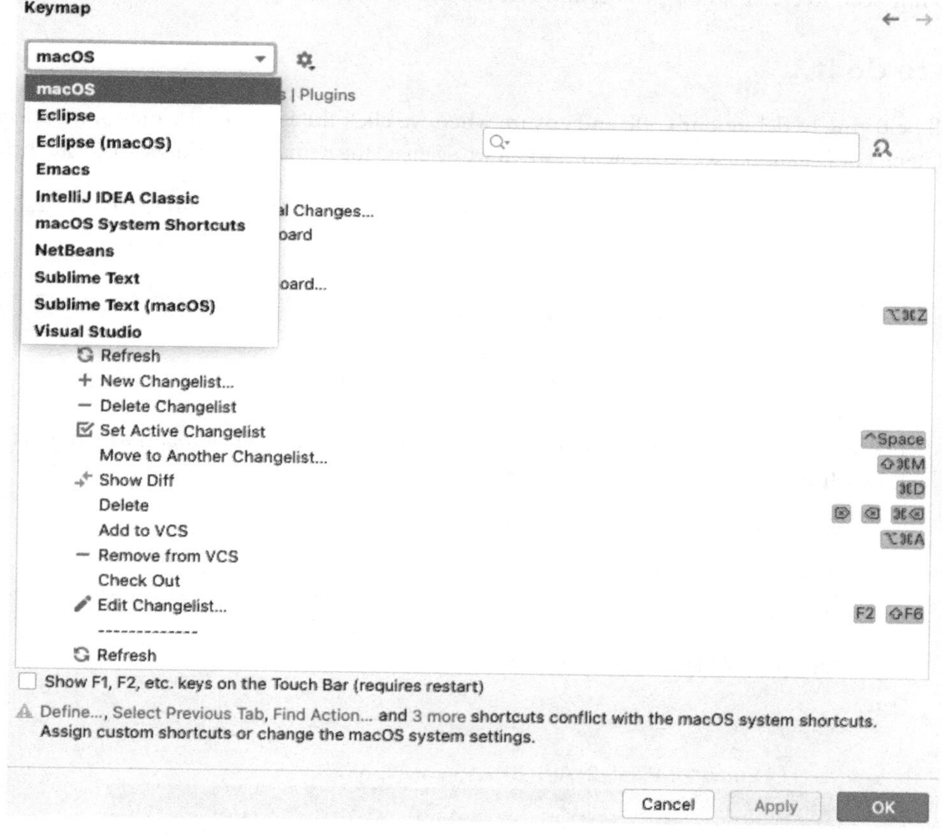

Figure 12.8 – Keymap

> **Important note**
>
> Find out what Android Studio's latest release is and what features are offered by following this link: `https://developer.android.com/studio/releases`.

Debugging your code

As an Android developer, debugging is an essential part of the software development process because it helps identify and fix errors in your code. When debugging, you can quickly identify and fix errors or bugs in your code that can cause your application to crash, behave unexpectedly, or produce incorrect results.

In this recipe, we will explore how you can easily add a breakpoint and debug your code.

Getting ready

To get started with this recipe, you need to have a project open and run the project on your emulator. You do not need to create a new project and can use the `GUIAlert` project.

How to do it...

We will be trying to debug our code and ensure when we click the items in the menu, we select the correct item. For instance, if we select item 2, when we evaluate the item, we should see the result being 2:

1. First, you need to ensure your app is running; then, click the icon shown in *Figure 12.9*.

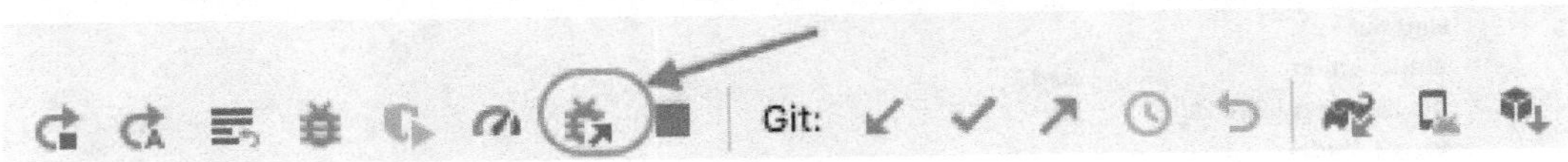

Figure 12.9 – The debugger icon

2. When you click the icon shown in *Figure 12.9*, a pop-up screen will appear, which means you will attach your running application to the debugger.

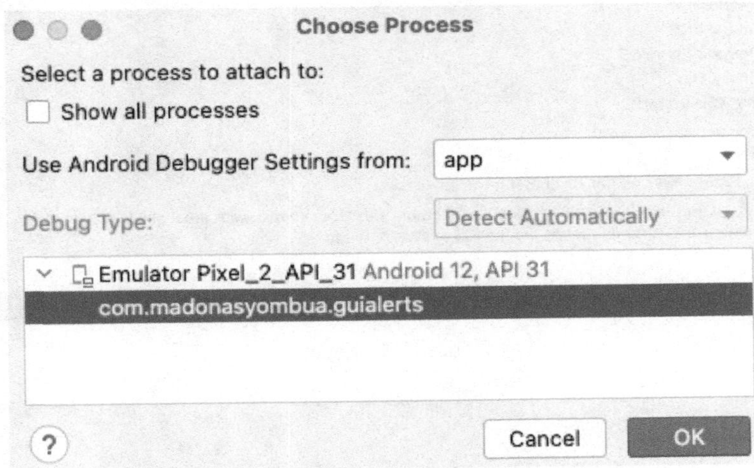

Figure 12.10 – The options on the package to attach the debugger

3. Now, go back to the code base and add breakpoints. You add breakpoints by clicking on the sidebar on the line number where you wish to test your logic.

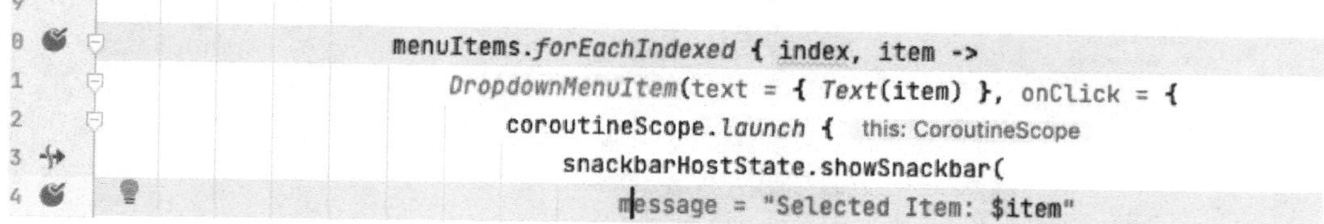

Figure 12.11 – Breakpoints

4. If your app is running when you click on the item, say option 1, the debugger will show an active state, which means the lines we put the breakpoints on were hit. Then, a pop-up window will appear with controls.

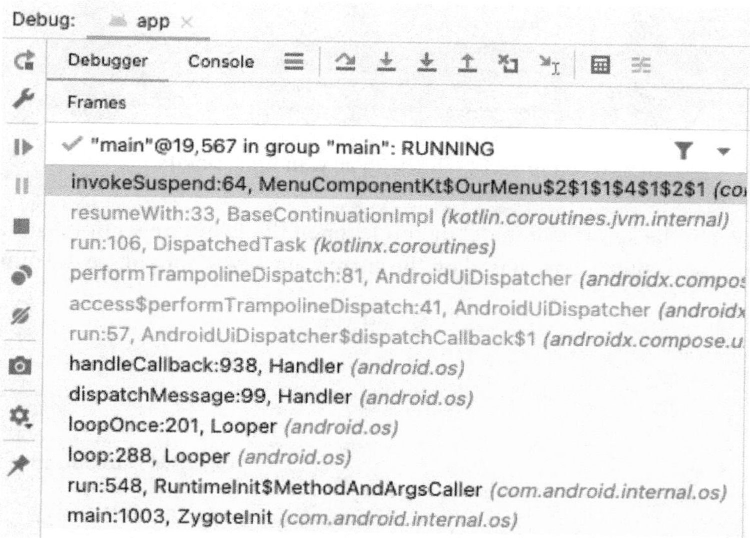

Figure 12.12 – Debug being active

5. You can use the green button on the left to run and the red square button to stop. You can also use **Step Over**, **Step Into**, **Force Step Into**, **Step Out**, **Drop Frame**, **Run to Cursor**, and **Evaluate Expression…**. We will use **Evaluate Expression…** in our example.

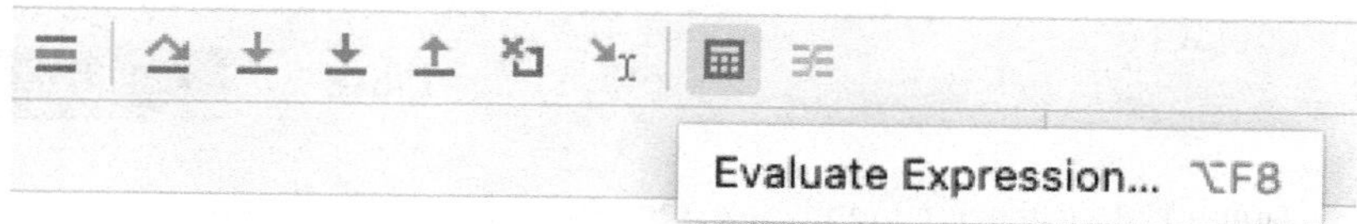

Figure 12.13 – Debug button steps

6. Sometimes, you might have extra breakpoints that might slow down the process. In this case, you can use the option pointed out by the red arrow in *Figure 12.14* to see all your breakpoints.

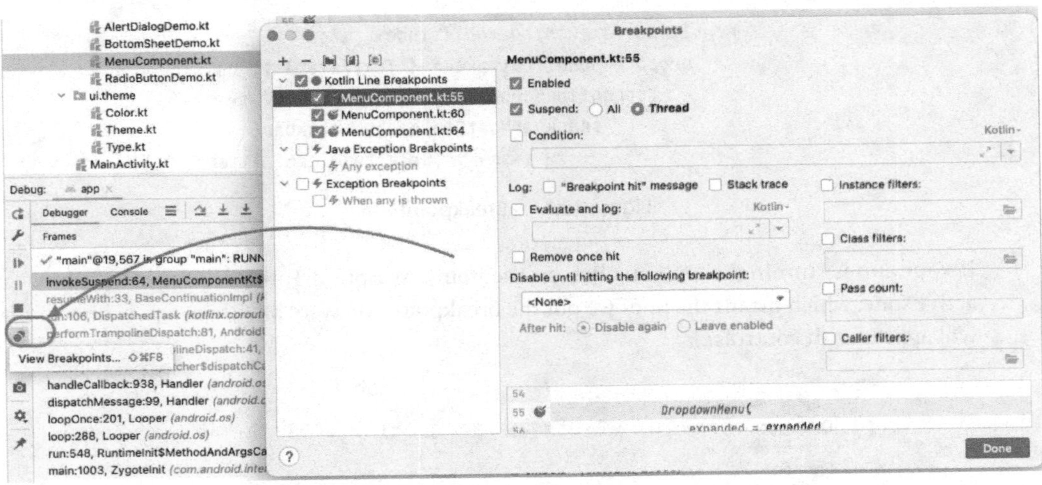

Figure 12.14 – Tracking all your breakpoints

7. Finally, when the app is still in debug mode, open the **Evaluate** section, go back to step 5 of this recipe, and enter `Item`. Based on the current item, you should see the number displayed.

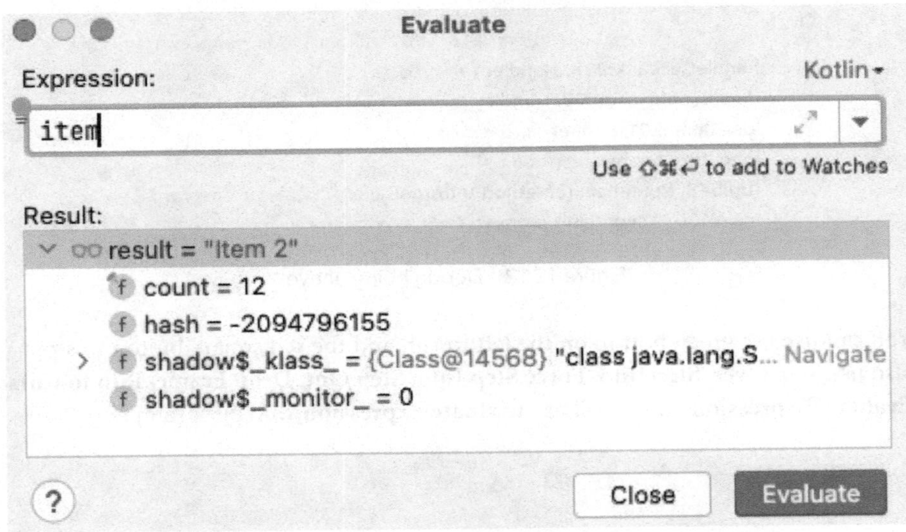

Figure 12.15 – Item is currently selected when we evaluate the breakpoint

How it works...

Android Studio includes a powerful debugger for us developers to use. To debug an application using Android Studio, you need to first build and deploy the app on the device or emulator, then attach the debugger to the running process. This is also a skill that needs to be learned and practiced becoming good at it. Hence, knowing how you can debug your application, either using logs or breakpoints, comes in handy.

> **Important note**
>
> There is more to learn about debugging, and more than one recipe is needed to cover this topic. Follow this link to learn more: `https://developer.android.com/studio/debug`.

How to extract methods and method parameters

Extracting methods and method parameters can add additional imports to your code. This happens because when you extract a method or a parameter, the code that used to be inside the method or parameter is moved to a separate method. If this code relies on other classes or methods that are not already imported into your code, the extraction process may automatically add the necessary import statements to your file.

For example, suppose you have a Kotlin class that contains a method that performs some calculations and returns a result. This method relies on a helper class defined in another package, and you still need to import this class into your code. If you decide to extract the method to a particular method in the same or a different class, the extraction process may add an `import` statement for the helper class so that the code inside the extracted method can reference the helper class.

Similarly, when you extract a method parameter, the extraction process may need to include adding import statements to ensure that any classes or interfaces that are used in the parameter type are correctly resolved.

Getting ready

You do not need to create any project to follow this recipe.

How to do it...

To extract methods and method parameters in Android, you can follow these steps:

1. Open the Kotlin file where you want to extract the methods and parameters.
2. Identify the class containing the methods and parameters you want to extract.
3. Place your cursor inside the class declaration, and right-click to open the context menu.

4. Select the **Refactor** option from the context menu, and then select **Extract** from the submenu.
5. In the **Extract** submenu, you will see options to extract a method or parameter. Select the option that matches the element you want to extract.
6. Follow the prompts in the **Extract** wizard to configure the extraction process. You may need to provide a name for the extracted element, specify the element's scope, or configure other settings depending on the element you are extracting.
7. Once configured in the extraction process, click **Finish** to extract the element from your code.

How it works...

Adding imports during method or parameter extraction is a normal part of the refactoring process and helps ensure that your code remains well organized and easy to maintain.

Understanding Git essentials

This recipe is meant to help any new developers that might have stumbled upon this book. **Git** is a popular version control system that allows developers to manage and track changes to their code base.

Here are some essential concepts to understand:

- A **repository** is a collection of files and folders that Git is tracking. It's also known as a **repo**. This is the most common term.
- A **commit** is a snapshot of the changes made to a repository. Each commit has a unique identifier containing information about the changes made, such as the author, the date, and a message describing the changes.
- A **branch** is a separate line of development that allows developers to work on different features or versions of a project simultaneously. It's like a parallel universe of the repository.
- When developing, **merging** your work refers to combining changes from one branch into another. It's typically used when a feature is complete and ready to be integrated into the main branch.
- A **pull request** is a GitHub feature that allows developers to propose changes to a repository and request that they be merged into the main branch. It includes a description of the changes and any supporting documentation or tests.
- **Cloning** is creating a copy of a repository on your local machine.
- **Pushing** is the process of sending changes from your local machine to a remote repository, such as GitHub or GitLab.
- **Pulling** is the process of downloading changes from a remote repository to your local machine.

By understanding these essential concepts, you can effectively use Git to manage your code base and collaborate with other developers.

Getting ready

We will not follow a recipe here but look at what Git commands you can utilize to make collaboration easier.

How to do it...

Here are some of the most commonly used Git commands:

- To initialize a new Git repository in the current directory. You can simply do the following:

```
$ git init
```

- When you want to add changes to the staging area, you can simply use `git add`:

```
$ git add file.txt
```

- When committing changes to the repository, simply use the following:

```
$ git commit -m "message"
```

- Most important, when you start collaborating, is being able to clone the project; you can simply run the following:

```
$ git clone git@github.com:PacktPublishing/Modern-Android-13-
Development-Cookbook.git
```

- When you want to pull changes from a remote repository to the local repository, simply use the following:

```
$ git pull origin main
```

- You can also push changes from the local repository to a remote repository by using the following:

```
$ git push origin main
```

- List all the local branches by using `git branch`:

```
$ git branch
```

- The following command switches to a different branch:

```
$ git checkout branch_name
```

- Check out a new branch with the following:

```
$ git checkout -b branch_name
```

- Merge changes from one branch into another with the following. Note you can also use `rebase`; this is based on the organization's preference:

```
$ git merge branch_name
```

These are just a few of the most commonly used Git commands. Many more Git commands and options are available, so it's worth exploring the Git documentation to learn more.

How it works...

Git is a distributed version control system allowing users to track code changes over time. Here's a high-level overview of how Git works.

Git doesn't just store the changes you make to your code; it actually stores snapshots of your entire project at different times. Each snapshot represents the state of the project at a specific moment. It stores your code in a tree-like structure, with each project snapshot represented by a commit object.

Each commit object points to the snapshot of the project that it represents and the commit objects that came before it. It also uses a unique pointer called `HEAD` to keep track of the current branch and the most recent commit on that branch.

When you make a new commit, Git updates the HEAD pointer to point to the new commit. In addition, each commit in Git is identified by a unique hash value, which is a 40-character string of letters and numbers. This hash value is generated based on the contents of the commit and the hash values of any previous commits that it points to.

Because Git stores snapshots of your project locally on your computer, you can work offline and still make commits to your project. When you're ready to share your changes, you can push them to a remote repository.

These are just a few of the key concepts behind how Git works. Git is a powerful and flexible tool with many advanced features, so it's worth learning more about how it works.

Index

A

B

G

H

I

J

K

L

M

N

O

P

www.packtpub.com

Subscribe to our online digital library for full access to over 7,000 books and videos, as well as industry leading tools to help you plan your personal development and advance your career. For more information, please visit our website.

Why subscribe?

- Spend less time learning and more time coding with practical eBooks and Videos from over 4,000 industry professionals
- Improve your learning with Skill Plans built especially for you
- Get a free eBook or video every month
- Fully searchable for easy access to vital information
- Copy and paste, print, and bookmark content

Did you know that Packt offers eBook versions of every book published, with PDF and ePub files available? You can upgrade to the eBook version at packtpub.com and as a print book customer, you are entitled to a discount on the eBook copy. Get in touch with us at customercare@packtpub.com for more details.

At www.packtpub.com, you can also read a collection of free technical articles, sign up for a range of free newsletters, and receive exclusive discounts and offers on Packt books and eBooks.

Other Books You May Enjoy

If you enjoyed this book, you may be interested in these other books by Packt:

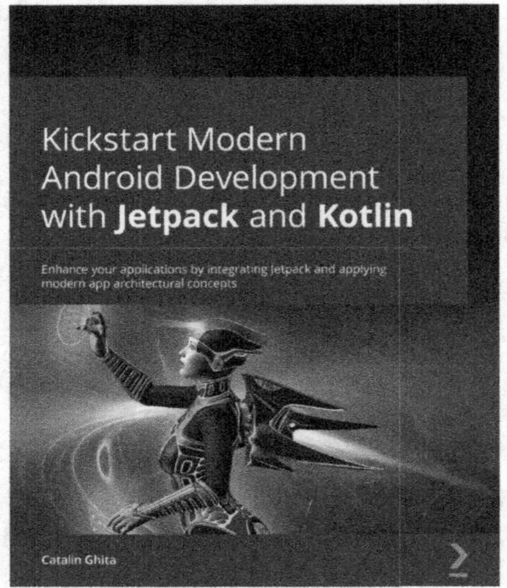

Kickstart Modern Android Development with Jetpack and Kotlin

Catalin Ghita

ISBN: 978-1-80181-107-1

- Integrate popular Jetpack libraries such as Compose, ViewModel, Hilt, and Navigation into real Android apps with Kotlin
- Apply modern app architecture concepts such as MVVM, dependency injection, and clean architecture
- Explore Android libraries such as Retrofit, Coroutines, and Flow
- Integrate Compose with the rest of the Jetpack libraries or other popular Android libraries
- Work with other Jetpack libraries such as Paging and Room while integrating a real REST API that supports pagination
- Test Compose UI and the application logic through unit tests

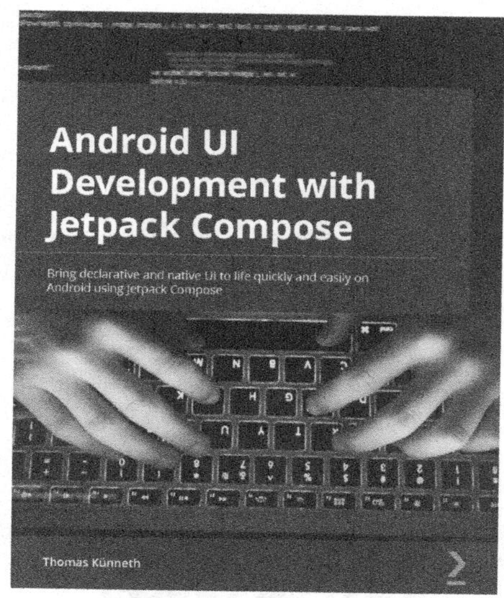

Android UI Development with Jetpack Compose

Thomas Künneth

ISBN: 978-1-80181-216-0

- Gain a solid understanding of the core concepts of Jetpack Compose
- Develop beautiful, neat, and immersive UI elements that are user friendly, reliable, and performant
- Build a complete app using Jetpack Compose
- Add Jetpack Compose to your existing Android applications
- Test and debug apps that use Jetpack Compose
- Find out how Jetpack Compose can be used on other platforms

Packt is searching for authors like you

If you're interested in becoming an author for Packt, please visit `authors.packtpub.com` and apply today. We have worked with thousands of developers and tech professionals, just like you, to help them share their insight with the global tech community. You can make a general application, apply for a specific hot topic that we are recruiting an author for, or submit your own idea.

Share Your Thoughts

Now you've finished *Modern Android 13 Development Cookbook*, we'd love to hear your thoughts! Scan the QR code below to go straight to the Amazon review page for this book and share your feedback or leave a review on the site that you purchased it from.

`https://www.amazon.in/review/create-review/?asin=1803235578`

Your review is important to us and the tech community and will help us make sure we're delivering excellent quality content.

Download a free PDF copy of this book

Thanks for purchasing this book!

Do you like to read on the go but are unable to carry your print books everywhere? Is your eBook purchase not compatible with the device of your choice?

Don't worry, now with every Packt book you get a DRM-free PDF version of that book at no cost.

Read anywhere, any place, on any device. Search, copy, and paste code from your favorite technical books directly into your application.

The perks don't stop there, you can get exclusive access to discounts, newsletters, and great free content in your inbox daily

Follow these simple steps to get the benefits:

1. Scan the QR code or visit the link below

`https://packt.link/free-ebook/9781803235578`

2. Submit your proof of purchase
3. That's it! We'll send your free PDF and other benefits to your email directly